ON WHAT THE CONSTITUTION MEANS

On
What the
Constitution
Means.

SOTIRIOS A. BARBER

THE JOHNS HOPKINS UNIVERSITY PRESS
Baltimore and London

KF
4550
.B26
1984

This book has been brought to publication with the generous
assistance of the National Endowment for the Humanities.

The Johns Hopkins University Press, Baltimore, Maryland 21218
The Johns Hopkins Press Ltd., London

Library of Congress Cataloging in Publication Data

Barber, Sotirios A.
On what the Constitution means.
Includes bibliographical references and index.
1. United States—Constitutional law—Interpretation
and construction. I. Title.
KF4550.B26 1984   342.73′029   83–48049
    ISBN 0–8018–3020–6   347.30229

Contents

Preface

AMERICANS PRE-
pare to celebrate the bicentennial of the Constitution of 1789 at a
time of renewed controversy over the constitutional duties of officials
and the responsibilities of a constitutional government for the way
people live. In order to aid in determining how we should understand
and address such problems, I submit here a general theory of what
the Constitution is and what it means. My principal thesis is that if
we are to make sense of what the Constitution says, we shall have
to interpret and apply its provisions in light of our best understanding
of an ideal state of affairs adumbrated by those provisions. At the
center of this constitutionally ideal state of affairs is a typical citizen,
who is governed by an attitude that places the highest social or political value on the activity of reasoning about how one ought to live.
I consider this attitude a kind of liberalism because it tolerates, even
as it works through government to weaken, such unconstitutional
attitudes as racism, sexism, self-righteousness, zealotry, willfulness,
acquisitiveness, and moral skepticism. Some readers may suspect that
I have constructed an illiberal and therefore self-contradictory liberalism that arbitrarily favors the elitist values of what some writers
are now calling "the reasoning class." Readers may also question
whether a concentration on constitutional ideals offers much of significance to a field of commentary and practice dominated by what
judges declare the law to be as they try to settle concrete disputes.

I hope to show, however, that the ideal I outline here constitutes the political aspirations not of a special class but of all who really accept the Constitution's authority, assuming without asserting that some can be found who really do. I argue further that constitutional meaning is accessible to the typical citizen without need of the special assistance of judges, lawyers, or any other authorities. As for the usefulness of this work for constitutional law as a field of political practice, I hope to persuade the reader that whatever the specifics, a normative constitutional ideal of some description is presupposed and therefore present as a real dimension of what lawyers, historians, and other case-oriented or litigation-minded observers call "constitutional law." At least some of the time, therefore, authentically realistic observers will look beyond the cases, as I try to do here.

Not unmindful of what I say in chapter 4 about the constitutional powers and ends of the national government, I acknowledge with gratitude the support of the National Endowment for the Humanities; this book would not have been possible without the philosophy of governmental responsibility that the Endowment represents so well. I am grateful also for the supplementary support I received from my department and college at the University of South Florida, especially the word processing of Mike Copeland and his staff, and from the University's Research Council and President's Council. I am grateful to Regis Factor, Theodore Lowi, Gordon Schloming, Paul Sigmund, and Sharon Swarze for helpful criticisms of early drafts. I am especially grateful to Will Harris and Don Mason for comments on a later draft. My greatest debt is to Jim Fleming and Karen Flax. Conversations with Fleming brought important changes in my understanding of this subject, though not always with his agreement. Flax shared her own research and assisted throughout the later drafts with footnotes, style, and matters of substance in the case-law background of the issues I discuss; her help was indispensable.

ON WHAT THE CONSTITUTION MEANS

1

Introduction

I N MAY 1979, JUSTICE
Thurgood Marshall delivered what was to be a widely reported address to a group of federal judges meeting in Buck Hill Falls, Penn-
sylvania. These lower federal judges were members of the Second
Circuit Judicial Conference, and Justice Marshall was addressing this
annual meeting of the conference in his capacity as the associate
justice of the Supreme Court assigned certain supervisory responsibilities over the circuit. As was his practice in these talks, Justice
Marshall gave his impression of "how well the Second Circuit has
done in the Supreme Court" during the preceding year. He observed
that with a month remaining in the high court's annual term, it had
reversed six of the nine decisions it had accepted for review from the
prestigious Court of Appeals for the Second Circuit. This was not
too commendable a record, as percentages go. Justice Marshall had
more than the authority of numbers and judicial hierarchy in mind
on this occasion, however, for there was also a question of whether
the Supreme Court had been right in all of its reversals of the lower
court. Justice Marshall thought not, and he began by telling the
conference judges that in "two of the most important" cases of the
term, "your performance was far better than that of my Brethren."[1]

In the first of these cases, *Herbert* v. *Lando*,[2] a retired military
officer sued a television journalist for an allegedly defamatory broad-

1

cast. The retired officer had asked the journalist to answer pretrial questions about his state of mind in preparing the broadcast. Through these questions the retired officer was seeking to discover the journalist's beliefs about the truth of the broadcast, his intentions in editing the film, and his editorial conversations with other journalists. The journalist refused to answer the questions because he regarded them as intrusions into an area protected by the First Amendment's guarantee of freedom of the press. The journalist lost at trial and appealed. The appeals court agreed with the journalist and reversed the district court, but the Supreme Court held for the retired officer. A majority of the Justices pointed out that prior cases had held that even though the First Amendment protected journalists from being sued for inadvertently false statements about public figures, it did not protect the press when damaging falsehoods were made recklessly or maliciously. Therefore, said the Court, the retired officer could try to discover whether the journalist had acted with recklessness or malice by asking the journalist what had been on his mind in preparing the broadcast. Justice Marshall dissented, and he repeated the gist of that dissent for the assembled judges of the Second Circuit. Editorial autonomy deserved "the utmost protection" as a necessary means to "the widest possible range of information and insights," he said, and plaintiffs had better ways of showing whether broadcasters and publishers had bad motives, ways that would not defeat "a climate of free interchange among journalists."

Justice Marshall had much harsher words for the Supreme Court's decision in *Bell* v. *Wolfish*,[3] a case whose primary focus was the rights of criminal defendants while in jail awaiting trial. The defendants were in jail either without bond or because they could not make bond. Two lower courts had reasoned that since these pretrial detainees had not been convicted, they should not be subject to punishment, and therefore that the restrictions on them and the severity of the conditions under which they were being held should not exceed those essential for holding them for trial and maintaining jail security. Applying this test, the lower courts said that certain conditions and practices of a federal institution in New York were unconstitutional, including overcrowding and routine body cavity searches after all visits, even from attorneys. The Supreme Court had reversed the Court of Appeals, arguing that the "judgment calls" of prison management were matters for administrators, not judges, and that practices and conditions reasonably related to detention and institutional needs did not constitute " 'punishment' in the constitutional sense." This case was an occasion for bitter words among the Justices. Justice William H. Rehnquist's opinion for the majority evinced contempt for liberal sensibilities and past constitutional decisions. He belittled concern about prison conditions with the remark that a "detainee's desire to be free from discomfort . . . does not arise to the level of . . . fundamental" constitutional rights. He disapprovingly alluded to one of the great decisions of the Warren Court as he mocked the concern for prison overcrowding with the quip that there was no " 'one man, one cell' principle lurking in the Due Process Clause."[4]

Dissenting in *Wolfish*, Justice Marshall labeled the majority's approach blind deference to prison administrators and an abdication of judicial responsibility. In light of the strict security precautions under which prison visiting took place, Justice Marshall called the routine body-cavity search "so unnecessarily degrading that it 'shocks the conscience.' "[5] Continuing this attack in his address before the judges of the Second Circuit, Justice Marshall emphasized the disproportionate impact of detention practices on the poor, most detainees being held because they could not afford bond. He called *Wolfish* "one of the most troubling opinions to come from the Supreme Court in quite some time," adding, "I can only hope that district and appellate judges will read the decision narrowly," lest detainees be left with "virtually no constitutional protection." "This Circuit has done well and must continue to do so," said Justice Marshall at the conclusion of his address. "Ill conceived reversals should be considered as no more than temporary interruptions. We must stand fast for the fullest protection of individual rights."

Justice Marshall's remarks attracted an unusual amount of public attention, for this was not the kind of talk one usually hears from members of the Supreme Court. According to the front page of the *New York Times* of May 28, 1979, some of the judges in Justice Marshall's audience "gasped" at his concluding admonition. Surely, a measure of shock was understandable; here was a top judicial official appearing to exhort the judges of his circuit to take advantage of whatever opportunities they might have to undermine the will of the Supreme Court. Justice Marshall knew that his advice could have an effect on the course of decision in the lower courts. Although the Supreme Court can use its contempt power to punish outright defiance of its judgments, uncooperative lower court judges need not resort to outright defiance, for the high court cannot write its opinions in ways that eliminate opportunities for blunting or deflecting its policies.[6] This the nation learned well in the decade after 1954 when many federal district judges in the southern states rationalized local attempts to evade or delay implementation of the School Desegregation Decision. Such uncooperative activity by the lower courts clearly threatens the prestige and power of the federal judiciary as a whole, and for that reason few in Justice Marshall's audience of federal judges could have been completely happy with his speech.

More so than elected officials, who enjoy the "powers of purse and sword," judges depend on the willingness of others in and out of government to accept their decisions in a spirit of respect for the law, even when convinced that the judges are wrong. Because the judges of the Second Circuit know this, they might have found a great deal to applaud in something Justice Rehnquist said in trying to justify his deference to the prison administrators in *Wolfish*: "[U]nder the Constitution, the first question to be answered is not whose plan is best, but in what branch of the Government is lodged the authority to initially devise the plan."[7] More bluntly, and in light of the outcome in *Wolfish*, Justice Rehnquist might have put his point in the following terms: "What is important under the Constitution is not what is right or best, but who is in charge of what." By the same reasoning it might be said that the decisions of the Supreme Court—right or wrong—should govern the lower courts. This seems implicit in the very notion of a supreme court. An emphasis on who is in charge often has a certain toughness that may make one uncomfortable. Nevertheless, this emphasis is a natural response to the regrettable but all too familiar fact that it seems easier to recognize who is in charge than to agree on what is right or best. Most people would excuse an emphasis on who is in charge by a need for tranquility and order, a need that would be satisfied not only at the expense of what is best but perhaps even at some expense to what is fair and decent.

On the other hand, one can say in behalf of Justice Marshall that, the need for order notwithstanding, it is still not absolutely clear that higher courts should govern lower courts in every case, for the lower court is obligated to follow both the law (especially the law of the Constitution) as well as the decisions of the higher court, and there is no denying that sometimes these two different obligations can conflict. One cannot accept an absolute requirement that the lower courts should always give full cooperation to the Supreme Court unless one is prepared to affirm at least one of the following two propositions: (1) It is impossible for the Supreme Court to err about the law; (2) the Supreme Court has the final say about the law, even when it errs. I shall argue more extensively later that neither of these propositions is consistent with the Constitution. For now, it suffices to point out that the Supreme Court itself sometimes admits it has erred about the law. Individual Justices charge the Court with error every time they write dissenting opinions; the Court as a whole admits error and, in a way (i.e., in changing its mind), rejects its own authority as absolute when it overrules its prior decisions. By what is in effect its own admission, therefore, the Court can be wrong about the Constitution.

If the Court can be wrong, however, why should it have the final say? Should the judges of the lower courts cooperate even when they are fully convinced that the Supreme Court's decisions are unconstitutional? Those who answer yes believe either that the word of the Court is superior to the Constitution or that it is better for the lower courts to avoid conflict with the Supreme Court than to decide cases in a manner that the Constitution requires—i.e., a manner consistent with the Constitution itself. A judge acting on either of these beliefs, however, would act contrary to the supremacy clause of Article VI, for this provision amounts to a declaration that the *Constitution* is supreme law, not the word of the Court or anyone's opinion on the requisites for harmony within the government. Judges who really took the Constitution seriously would take its claim to supremacy seriously. They would concede that it is possible for the Court to be wrong about the Consititution, and they would do what they could to defeat the will of the Court when they were convinced the Court was wrong. They would willingly give the Court the final word only when they believed the Court was right about the Constitution or when they believed reasonable persons could disagree about the Court's understanding of the meaning of the Constitution. When reasonable doubt does exist, the lower judges have at least one constitutional reason for following the Supreme Court: the Constitution establishes that court as a supreme court. In the presence of doubt about the Court's decisions, one has no firm reason to feel the Supreme Court is not acting as the particular supreme court established by the Constitution—i.e., the supreme court that follows the Constitution as supreme law. In sum, lower judges can reconcile the Constitution's supremacy with the Supreme Court's supremacy only when they believe the Supreme Court is either right or arguably right about the Constitution. The authority of the Supreme Court, therefore, is not strictly independent of its conformity with the Constitution. Moreover, everyone can imagine decisions so outrageous as to be beyond the pale of anyone's obligation to obey in the Constitution's name.

Judging from the tone of his address to the Second Circuit, Justice Marshall believed rather strongly that the high court was wrong in *Lando* and *Wolfish*. So one cannot say he intentionally rejected the authority of the Constitution in urging evasion of the will of the Supreme Court. Nor is it beyond dispute that he rejected the authority of the Supreme Court (as an institution, rather than a mere collection of nine individuals) in light of what seems to be the unavoidable dependence of the Court's authority on being right or arguably right about the Constitution. Indeed, if one assumes that the *Lando* and *Wolfish* majorities wanted to be right about the Constitution more than they wanted to hurt journalists and criminal defendants in conflicts with retired military officers and prison administrators—and the majority would certainly want and expect this to be the assumption— Justice Marshall's speech may even appear as an attempt to serve the will of the Court—the *real* will, that is, of justices who seem to be falling short of what it is assumed they really want to do: construe the Constitution correctly.

One can say, therefore, that those who were shocked by Justice Marshall's address either forgot, failed to appreciate, or did not really believe the Supreme Court's traditional claim about the nature of its authority. But Justice Marshall believed, or spoke as if he believed, that the authority of judges depends on their fidelity to the Constitution as supreme law, not on their fidelity to their personal convictions, to each other as institutional brothers and sisters, or to the judicial institution itself as a set of practices beyond the influence of the Constitution. Justice Marshall's position presupposes that though judges personally may want what they believe the Constitution requires, what the Constitution does require has a status that is independent of what the judges want. Thus, while Justice Marshall doubtlessly wanted to stop the routine body-cavity searches in *Wolfish*, he spoke as if he believed that the practice was unconstitutional regardless of his personal preferences or those of anyone else. One can state Justice Marshall's position, or the position embodied in his address to the Second Circuit, as follows: (1) The Constitution has a meaning independent of what the members of the Supreme Court, or anyone else, might want it to mean; (2) that meaning can be known;

(3) the authority of the Supreme Court depends on its being right or arguably right about the Constitution's meaning; (4) lower judges (and, perhaps, others) who truly accept the Constitution's supremacy will not cooperate with the Supreme Court when it is clearly wrong but instead will try to perform their duties (as officials and as citizens) in ways that make the government's departure from the Constitution no more than temporary. Anyone who truly accepts the Constitution's authority must eventually accept these propositions.

If we assume for a moment that we cannot successfully deny the proposition that the meaning of the Constitution is independent of what the Supreme Court or any other interpreter might want it to mean, it would seem that at least one of the important aims of constitutional thought and scholarship would be a general theory of what the Constitution actually means. The possibility of such a theory is presupposed by anyone who criticizes courts or others for interpreting the Constitution incorrectly, and there is no waning of the frequency and intensity of such criticism among lawyers, academics, judges, office holders, community leaders, editorial writers, and others. However, despite so many people criticizing the Court from time to time, some academicians believe that a general theory of what the Constitution means is something that we cannot achieve. I think that a theory of what the Constitution means is possible, that we should pursue it, and that pursuing it in the right way is a good in itself despite continuing doubts about answers to the concrete questions of constitutional meaning. I offer such a theory in this book, as well as a theory of how to read the Constitution. Taken together, these theories can aid in deciding which answers, or at least which attitudes, to adopt when problems of the kind presented by *Lando* and *Wolfish* appear. Like most other essays in constitutional law, I shall discuss past and future problems before the courts. Generally, though not always, my proposals and positions will be closer to Justice Marshall's than to Justice Rehnquist's.

Unlike most constitutional commentaries, however, the focus of this book does not concern, nor is its way of looking for constitutional meaning confined to, the methods and decisions of judges. Having elected to find the meaning of the Constitution itself, I am interested in what the Constitution means, not primarily in what judges and others say it means. Since judicial methods and limitations are themselves matters of controversy rooted in different understandings of what the Constitution means, I cannot regard matters peculiarly judicial as fundamental. Nor am I particularly interested in the doctrinal history of the Supreme Court (i.e., the story of how one judicial version of the law follows another), and it will become evident to the reader why I consider the confounding of that history with constitutional law a denial, albeit inadvertent, of constitutional supremacy and the value of constitutionalism itself. I shall comment on selected cases throughout the book, but when I do comment on cases I do so only to illustrate what I consider correct or incorrect decisions. At no point do I assume that case commentary is the only proper idiom of constitutional law. On the contrary, I shall show why it is a mistake to assume that constitutional theory can be developed from the perspective of judges, lawyers, litigants, and others whose needs lead them to the false assumption that it would be beneficial to eliminate disagreement about general ideas like due process, equal protection, and free speech. In excluding the authority of anyone or anything other than the Constitution itself, I exclude not only the authority of courts but also the authority of political philosophers and the constitutional commentaries of others. As with judicial decisions, when I mention the commentaries of scholars and historical figures in a favorable way, I will do so not to cite authorities but rather to illustrate what I believe to be interpretations of the Constitution that can be supported by the best theory of what the Constitution means. Finally, I do not assume that the test of my interpretations is some version of what is politically feasible in America today, for my aim is to discover what the Constitution means, not whether it is workable. Thus, segregated schools, what present-day conservatives praise as "judicial self-restraint," and congressional buckpassing could be (and are) contrary to the Constitution even if real integration, a sustained judicial activism, and a courageous, responsible Congress lie beyond reasonable hopes. Believing a particular interpretation "unworkable" is not enough to dismiss it as inaccurate because, as I shall show, the logic of the Constitution compels the conclusion that the Constitution can fail as law and that we can fail as a people capable of constituting the self-restraining sovereign that the Constitution depicts us to be. Those who assume that they can find interpretations of the Constitution that make it workable in all circumstances inadvertently reject the Constitution's authority.

Academic readers of this book may seek to relate it to the current debate among teachers of constitutional law and others over the kinds of inquiry judges should conduct (into the intentions of the framers, for example, or the consensus of today's public opinion or the probable consensus of tomorrow's public opinion) in trying to resolve such difficult constitutional problems as those involving abortion and racial quotas.[8] Though much of what I shall say here is relevant to this academic debate, I am going to comment on the debate as such only to the extent that I have to in order to submit my theory of what the Constitution means. As I have already said, the focus here will be on the Constitution itself, not on what different scholars say about the problems of interpreting the Constitution, except when and to the extent that the latter is necessary to the former.

I am leaving most of the current academic debate in the background of this work because the assumptions and categories of that debate appear artificial from the perspective I have chosen: that of the ordinary citizen who tries to take the Constitution's authority seriously. Participants in the current debate usually distinguish and defend one of several approaches, including a *textual* approach, approaches oriented to the *intentions of the framers*, a present or emerging *consensus* of the American people, ideas of social *progress*, what is simply or *naturally right*, and so on. But these notions and their common-sense counterparts are not separable in our ordinary thinking about constitutional matters. No approach to constitutional meaning can dispense altogether with the idea of a document or text. And the text itself suggests the objects upon which the other approaches focus. Thus, the text suggests what is naturally right, at least in the way the Constitution's Preamble refers to "Justice" and the "general Welfare." The text also suggests an original authority like the framers or the founding generation in the Preamble and the ratification provisions of Article VII. When the Preamble speaks of a "We the People of the United States" adopting the Constitution as a means to ends presumably desirable both to "ourselves" and to "our Posterity," it lends at least some constitutional status to values like consensus and progress. Instead of separating and opposing the several aspects or dimensions of constitutional meaning, therefore, I shall argue that the only way to make complete sense of the Constitution is to understand it in light of what our best thinking shows Americans do and ought to stand for as a people—past, present, and future. In more technical terms, I shall defend an *aspirational* approach to constitutional meaning, an approach that combines elements of textual, intentionalist, consensual, and other approaches.

Not only does the current academic debate artificially separate the several dimensions of constitutional meaning, it begs crucial questions in identifying the conflict between judicial review and democracy as the central problem of constitutional theory. The current debate is a debate about whether and how one can reconcile judicial review with democracy.[9] Now, people of all sorts do complain regularly about the decisions of electorally unaccountable judges; a rare few may even disapprove the very existence of electorally unaccountable judges. This is enough to indicate conflicts between some versions of democracy and judicial review. Of course, the tension does not stop there, for some versions of democracy can conflict with any known form of government and certainly with any of the usual understandings of the Constitution. Surely, if the Constitution expresses merely the raw will of its drafters or ratifiers or any other numerically minor part of the whole people to which it now applies and will continue to apply, the Constitution offends a particular, perhaps widely held conception of democracy.[10]

We cannot simply assume, however, that the conceptions of democracy and judicial review in conflict are the right conceptions—by which I mean here the conceptions we shall have to have if we are to see the Constitution for what it says it is: the supreme law *and* an instrument of justice as well as the other ends of the Preamble. In chapter 3 I shall argue that if we are to make sense of the Constitution we must understand its provisions in light of an ideal way of life to which those provisions, as a whole, and in a sense, point. I shall argue in chapters 4 and 5 that at the center of this constitutionally ideal state of affairs one finds citizens who exhibit what I shall call a constitutional attitude or frame of mind. I shall argue in chapter 6 that these citizens would not be able to accept the monopoly we know today as judicial review—that, in other words, today's judicial review is not the institution envisioned by the Constitution. The same, however, seems to be true of the attitude of today's officialdom and citizenry. The Constitution cannot envision this attitude, either, because those who have this attitude cannot fully comprehend the Constitution. If a genuinely constitutional attitude did prevail, a widespread personal and collective effort to maintain a constitutionally ideal state of affairs would eliminate the conditions that support to-day's judicial monopoly.

If these arguments prove persuasive, judicial review does not really conflict with democracy, as the relevant terms would be understood from a genuinely constitutional point of view. The problem addressed by today's mainstream constitutional scholars would not be a problem of constitutional law as much as a problem for a people that erroneously believes itself to be living under a constitution it does not fully understand. Whether there is a conflict between the right conceptions of judicial review and democracy can be determined only through an inquiry into what the Constitution is and what it requires of our conceptions of judicial review and democracy. For this reason an inquiry into what the Constitution means logically precedes the current debate about democracy and judicial review.

Although I believe the theory presented in this book results from the most defensible reading of the Constitution itself and not from an attempt to make the Constitution fit the mold of some external political or academic teaching, much of what I have discovered supports the general, though internally diverse, view that difficult constitutional questions should be resolved in ways that contribute to some picture or notion of the just and good society, or the moral aspirations of the American people, or moral growth simply.[11] I shall also discuss what it means to be a "framer" of what the Constitution says it is, and in accordance with that understanding I can agree that constitutional commentary should seek the intentions of the framers. I disagree, however, with those who confuse the intentions of the framers of the Constitution with the mere likes and dislikes of those who drafted and voted for the constitutional document and its several amendments.[12] My arguments also lend some support to those who would consult a past, present, or anticipated consensus of the American people, as long as they are talking about a constitutionally authoritative consensus. One cannot discover such a consensus in the results of opinion polls, election returns, and other signs of what one or another group or population seems to like or dislike. Nor is a constitutionally authoritative consensus closed to ideas of independent content and worth, like simple justice; it cannot be grasped through an "ethical approach" in an anthropological sense of that term, which might be closed to anything beyond an "American ethic."[13]

On the other hand, I reject as a *constitutional* teaching the view that difficult constitutional questions should be resolved solely with an eye to what seems necessary to achieve the good society.[14] I shall argue that the Constitution is and must be partially open to higher political values and that it should be construed accordingly where possible. But I shall also show why there must be a limit to construction, why the Constitution itself requires us to concede that it can fail to be what it says it is, and why, therefore, citizens and lawyers must eventually stand aside for lawgivers.

2

Toward a Theory
of What the
Constitution Means

ALTHOUGH I AM
much more interested in developing and defending a theory of what
the Constitution means than in discussing what jurists and academicians have written about such enterprises, I must say something
about the most important of those arguments that have attempted to
deny my leading assumption: that the Constitution has a meaning
independent of what anyone in particular might want it to mean. If
I can show that no one can successfully deny this assumption, I can
proceed to the discussion of the Constitution itself. Readers whose
thinking about these matters is governed more by reliable common
sense than by academic doctrine or professional habit will agree immediately that in fact we do and must presuppose an independent
constitutional meaning and that the more interesting and difficult
questions concern what the Constitution means and how it should
influence the decisions of those who want to follow it. As untenable
as they are, however, arguments against the possibility of an independent constitutional meaning continue to be influential among academics, and, with regrets for having to digress from what counts
most, I will deal with these arguments as briefly as I can.

Earlier in this century a diverse group of American jurists and
legal philosophers, loosely called the "American legal realists," at-

tacked the common-sense view that judges are supposed to follow the law in deciding between the contending parties in lawsuits. The legal realists argued, in relevant part, that in all but the simplest cases judges could not follow the law because, for one reason or another, how the law applied to the facts of such cases was a matter of controversy. Sometimes, they pointed out, different legal rules or principles could apply to the same facts with different results, as when a newspaper reporter's First Amendment claim to freedom of the press conflicts with a defendant's due process claim to a trial free of prejudicial publicity. Sometimes an obviously applicable rule is ambiguous or too vague to settle a case in an uncontroversial way, they said, as when we ask whether "commerce among the several states" means commerce *between* states or *intermingled within* the states, or whether "commerce" refers to all or just some forms of economic activity. Reflection on these and other problems (including the political problem of how to answer a pre–New Deal federal judicial establishment whose members disclaimed personal responsibility for reactionary decisions) moved the legal realists toward an untenable extreme often condensed in the aphorism: "The Constitution means what the Supreme Court says it means."[1]

To those lawyers, judges, and others who needed persuading— and one wonders who these gullible people might have been—the legal realists proved what should have been obvious: Attitudes do make a difference in how judges and others read the law. So the legal realists may have done the world a service by deflating the machine-like indifference that some judges affected toward contending versions of the common good. But the legal realists, or some of them, went too far in contending that degrees of uncertainty about the meaning and application of some parts of the law in some circumstances showed that laws can have no binding influence whatever on judges.[2] H.L.A. Hart commented that these extreme legal realists were reacting to the uncertainties in the law in the manner of "disappointed absolutist[s]."[3] It was as if they believed that if the laws could not settle all questions mechanically, the meaning of the laws was completely up for grabs. The legal realists could show that the Constitution could not settle concrete judicial questions in a mechanical way. They could not show, however, that the Constitution could provide no guidance whatever, or that there was no difference between the meaning of the Constitution and whatever a particular majority of the Supreme Court might say about the meaning of the Constitution.

American legal realism was part of a broader intellectual persuasion that sought to deny the reality of general ideas, as opposed to what were called "empirical facts," and ends or purposes, as opposed to ultimately subconscious "behavioral determinants" of events most people call "actions." Legal realism came to dominate legal thought in America and continues by inertia to be the dominant influence on the academic study of law despite realism's great loss of influence among philosophers of law. Most academics continue to think about the Constitution and the Court as if persuaded by the legal realists, whether having actually examined their arguments or not. So, the exaggerated emphasis of the legal realists on the uncertainties of litigation has distracted many from reflecting on the fact that much of the time large areas of what the Constitution says are clear.

From the perspective of current political problems we may think we know less about the meaning of, say, the First Amendment than we would like to. In an earlier time Americans were more troubled by the meaning of the commerce clause and the Tenth Amendment. Judicial problems typically arise when some person, corporation, or institution suffers harm at the hands of another, and we tend to concern ourselves with constitutional questions from the actual or hypothetical perspective of parties in lawsuits. Therefore, we have more questions about the meaning of constitutional provisions concerning what government can and cannot legally do than we do about those constitutional provisions concerned with the identity of governmental officials, the manner by which they come to occupy their offices, their tenure of office, and the basic kinds of things they are supposed to do relative to each other. In other words (and without trying to propose an adequate scheme for classifying different kinds of constitutional provision), fewer questions arise about the identity of constitutional officials and their fundamental duties than about their specific activities—fewer questions about who or what our *officials* and *institutions* are and more questions about their *powers* and our individual *rights*. If we forget about *powers* and *rights* for a moment and think about the knowledge we have about the identity of our officials and institutions, we can see one respect in which a great deal of knowledge about the government comes straight from the Constitution, without benefit of any special interpretation of the Constitution.

How is it, for example, that we know what the Supreme Court is and who its members are? Who in particular has had to tell us how to distinguish the Court from, say, the Joint Economic Committee of the Congress? Even when it comes to governmental powers and individual rights, we know some things without benefit of special interpretations of the Constitution. We know, for example, at least the kinds of questions appropriately raised under the First Amendment, which knowledge may or may not be much (we shall have to see) but surely is something. So it seems the legal realists contradicted themselves when they said the Constitution means what the Supreme Court says it means. For in making that statement they presupposed knowledge of who and what to count as the Supreme Court and as relevant statements of the Court, and since that knowledge would have to be available before we could recognize any of the Supreme Court's revelations as such, that knowledge cannot depend on the Court's revelations. This is why Hart said that if one states the position of extreme legal realism "in an unqualified general form . . . , it is indeed quite incoherent."[4]

As common sense might have suggested at the outset, therefore, some parts of the Constitution are immediately clear, while others may not be. Perhaps a better understanding of what is immediately clear could help us discover the meaning of what is obscure, but that is a larger question for the reader. At this point one can say that the indeterminacies of constitutional meaning are no barrier to inquiry into the meaning of the Constitution. For, so far, the legal realist has proved incapable of escaping the assumption everyone makes when talking about the Constitution and related phenomena, the assumption that we can in some respects distinguish what the Constitution means from what the Supreme Court says it means.

The realists might come back, however, with a related but different argument against the possiblity of independent constitutional meaning. They might say that there is no necessary connection between words and things in the world and that the meanings of words change with the changing purposes of those who use them. Accordingly, so their argument would go, one cannot say that an interpretation of the Constitution which serves the purposes of any given majority of the Supreme Court is any less constitutional than an interpretation that serves other purposes, even those purposes that originally motivated the framers and the founding generation to draft and ratify the words in question. This is the argument supporting Charles P. Curtis's influential thesis that constitutional interpretation is a "handicraft" for shaping the words of the document to suit our political and social purposes and that the words of the document should not be taken as bearers of meaning but as actual *warrants* for determining their meaning.[5]

A little reflection suffices to show that Curtis could not have intended his theory to apply to all instances of interpretation without licensing his own readers to construe the words in which he couched his theory in accordance with the readers' purposes, whatever those purposes might be, including that of refuting or denying Curtis's theory. We could have no talk of "law" under this theory of meaning to the extent that talk of *law* is appropriate only where we assume some inclinations on the part of those subject to laws to act in ways contrary to the laws.[6] If laws mean whatever those to whom they are addressed might want them to mean (assuming arguendo that we could identify the addressees of such laws) then laws cannot prescribe contrary to the inclinations of their addressees. But something that cannot prescribe contrary to our wants is not a law. This observation warrants the conclusion that Curtis could not have intended his theory of meaning to apply to any and all communications, especially communications among individuals of the same group or generation. In fact, his expressed purpose was rather to free one generation from laws imposed by another generation; he wanted to free the Supreme Court as an agency of his generation from having to "chase the meaning of our Constitution through the basement door of our ancestors' intentions."[7] If Curtis's theory is ever to figure in an actual choice between alternative interpretations of the Constitution, however, it would contradict itself because it would have to presuppose that the Constitution can mean something other than what we want it to mean.

To see this, accept for the moment Curtis's view that the meanings of words change with our purposes, which also change. In any situation that would call for an act of interpretation the interpreter either would or would not be aware that his meaning differed from the meaning of the speaker or writer of the communication to be interpreted. If the interpreter is aware of no relevant difference between his meaning and the meaning of the writer or speaker, no problem is presented, for we need not be troubled by meanings of which we are unaware. It is a fact, however, that we do perceive differences between our purposes and the purposes of others, including the purposes of those who wrote the laws. *Disagreement* is one way appropriately to describe differences of purpose. If we do not have the same purposes as the founding generation, we simply disagree with the founding generation to that extent. Since Curtis's theory would be pointless in any context other than that of known or anticipated disagreement between them and us, it can influence our decisions only when we are preparing to invoke our purposes to disregard what we believe to be the meaning of the laws they sought to impose on themselves and on us. Curtis's theory, therefore, is not really a theory of constitutional interpretation—it is not a theory for finding out what the law means. It is actually a theory of political right that would leave us free to disregard what we believe to be the meaning of those who ratified the Constitution. As such, Curtis's theory undermines any attempt by any generation—our own as well as the founding— to lay down "supreme Law" for "ourselves and our Posterity." Unlike some who would assert a higher right of revolution against the Constitution, Curtis looked upon this right to disregard the original purpose of the framers as a *constitutional* right. He contended that the Constitution is the voice of a "we the present generation," and that it was Chief Justice John Marshall who, in the famous case of *McCulloch* v. *Maryland* (1819),[8] "offer[ed] us, the people of the United States, in whose name the Constitution was written, the opportunity to sign it, adding our names to those of the convention."[9] In this way, Curtis turned Marshall's opinion in *McCulloch* into a mystery, for by Curtis's account Marshall would have knowingly authorized all possible future purposes, including those destructive of his own objectives. In *McCulloch*, as I shall show in chapter 4, Marshall did say that the national government could pursue its authorized ends as it thought necessary, but he cautioned against pursuing both unauthorized ends and authorized ends in violation of protected rights. *McCulloch*, therefore, was a far cry from telling the government to do whatever it thought necessary, and throughout his judicial career Marshall himself held fast to what he viewed as the most authoritative vision of the Constitution in the face of powerful popular and official impulses to the contrary.[10]

In sum, Curtis did not succeed in his attempt to deny that the Constitution has meaning independent of our wants and its judicial gloss. Indeed, his attempt to justify an orientation to current needs presupposed the perception of clashes between those needs and what the Constitution permits. He contradicted himself when he claimed a basis for his theory in the very founding intentions whose limitations on current demands he initially set out to remove. In effect, he argued either that the framers intended the disregard of their intentions or that they had no intentions relative to our conduct. His theory is untenable because one cannot imagine lawgivers qua lawgivers deliberately creating warrants to defeat the purposes that motivated their actions in the first place.

The most widely discussed recent argument against the possibility of an independent constitutional meaning was published in 1978 by John Hart Ely.[11] Ely's argument is reminiscent of Curtis's in important respects, even though Curtis emphasized a theory of how words mean, whereas Ely claimed support in the general intentions or aspirations of the framers and assumed the stability of the meanings of words over lengthy spans of time. Ely felt that the words of the Constitution signify general ideas, concepts, and long-range purposes to be pursued or general evils to be avoided, as distinguished from the particular historical practices and narrow demands of the framers, and that from the perspective of those general ideas, there was no reason to believe the words of the Constitution had changed their meaning over time. Ely treated the words of the constitutional document as the best evidence both for the general intentions of the framers and for what the Constitution means. Even with these generous concessions to the traditional theory of constitutional interpretation, however, Ely arrived at the dramatic conclusion that the traditional theory was "impossible"—that, as Curtis had concluded from different premises, we have to understand the Constitution as delegating power to judges to look beyond the Constitution itself for the major premises of decision in constitutional cases.[12] Ely recognized a threat to democratic values in any suggestion that judges could look beyond the law. But, having argued that the Constitution compels judges to look beyond its provisions, Ely promised a theory of judicial review that would reconcile democracy with a judicial practice of consulting values beyond the Constitution.[13]

Ely's argument that the Constitution cannot guide judicial decision was untenable from the beginning, and he actually abandoned it in a book published two years later.[14] Ely now follows a particular version of the traditional view that the Constitution does have meaning independent of what the judges want it to mean and that it can guide judges in constitutional cases.[15] But Ely has chosen to obscure his return to a version of the traditional approach to constitutional meaning. He has not told his considerable readership why he was unable to follow through on his initial proposal for an extraconstitutional theory of interpretation or that he has abandoned it. This has left some confusion about whether Ely still stands by his dramatic conclusion that it is impossible for the Constitution to guide judicial decision.[16] Ely is a figure of central importance in current constitutional discussion, and his initial attempt to prove that the Constitution cannot guide the judges can be influential even among those who reject his affirmative theory of judicial review. Ely deserves this influence despite the defects of his argument, for some parts of his argument against the traditional approach are sound and must find a place in any successful theory of constitutional interpretation. For these reasons I shall discuss Ely's initial argument as if it were still before us.

Ely's 1978 paper sets out to show the "impossibility" of "interpretivism," which he defines as the normative position that judges deciding constitutional questions should take their "starting points" from premises "fairly discoverable" in the language of the Constitution. Opposed is "noninterpretivism," which holds that judges ought to go beyond constitutional language and enforce values that cannot be discovered in the document. At the beginning of his article Ely pointedly distinguishes interpretivism from a position with which he later confuses it, the position that judges should declare unconstitutional only specific practices of the kind thought to be opposed by the framers.[17] This position is that of Raoul Berger's recent attack on the Warren Court's use of the Fourteenth Amendment to achieve certain reforms in the areas of voting rights, criminal justice, and race relations. Berger's approach enables him to cite the "racism" of northern legislators and public opinion after the Civil War as proof that the Fourteenth Amendment should not be used to combat racial segregation.[18] Contrary to Berger, Ely believes the Constitution "[m]ore often proceeds by briefly indicating certain fundamental principles whose general purport is clear enough but whose specific implications for each age were meant to be determined in specific context."[19] Ely is thus willing to allow that as general as their terms might be, the due process clause of the Fourteenth Amendment, the provisions of the First Amendment, and even the cruel and unusual punishment

clause of the Eighth Amendment are all significant guides to judicial
decision because they successfully communicate the general sorts of
evil the framers intended to proscribe, notwithstanding the inevitable
debates over how best to understand the specific implications of those
general ideas from case to case.[20] Nevertheless, toward the end of
his article, Ely identifies three clauses he says must be understood as
"delegations to future constitution decision makers to define and
protect rights that the document neither lists, at least not exhaustively,
nor in any remotely specific way gives directions for finding." These
wide-open clauses are the Ninth Amendment and the equal protection
and privileges and immunities clauses of the Fourteenth Amendment—all of which he says invite judges to engage in "across-the-
board substantive review" of legislation.[21]

   With this, Ely concludes that "one cannot be an interpretivist."[22]
He insists that because it contains the three open-ended clauses, it is
the *Constitution* that compels us to look elsewhere for guidance in
constitutional issues. He criticizes Justice Hugo Black's insistence that
the open-ended clauses of the Constitution be closed by the specific
provisions of the first eight amendments in order to avoid a wide-
ranging judicial discretion that Black believed incompatible with democracy. Ely makes an important point when he says Black's understanding of the judicial function is inconsistent with Black's own
commitment to the Constitution because there is no relevant difference between rejecting the document's substantive implications (implications Black accepted when he insisted that judges respect the
absolute force of the First Amendment) and rejecting what Ely calls
its institutional implication: that judges are authorized to apply the
document's open-ended provisions. Had Black been the constitutionalist he thought he was he would have accepted the Constitution's
authorization to look beyond the document, its language, and its
history. According to Ely, this authorization to look beyond is implicit
in the very open-endedness of the provisions Black wanted to close.
Black's position was motivated by a desire to reconcile judicial review
with democracy. Ely shares this desire and infers, basically from the
Constitution's ratification provisions, that the Constitution itself mandates democracy. Black could not see how the Constitution could
mandate both democracy and the extraconstitutional decisions of
electorally irresponsible judges. Ely, however, can see a way out of
the problem and promises to show the way in a forthcoming book.
Ely thus presents himself as more of an interpretivist than Black, for

Ely undertakes an obligation Black failed to understand or accept: the obligation to find a democratic way to obey the Constitution's command to look beyond the Constitution itself for the major premises of judicial decision.[23]

Ely might well believe that this obligation to find a way to reconcile a constitutionally unbounded judicial review with democracy derives from a desire to accept the Constitution as law. The Constitution cannot function as law to the extent that we believe it prescribes contradictory things, since to that extent it cannot guide our conduct. That is why one who would be a loyal subject of the Constitution would look for a way to remove a contradiction within the Constitution. We can therefore describe Ely's enterprise as one of trying to save the Constitution as law by showing a way to obey what Black saw as the incoherent command simultaneously to proceed democratically and to look beyond the Constitution. By resolving what he calls "the critical question facing constitutional scholarship" we can say that Ely would become *the* interpretivist, even *the* constitutionalist, because he would make obedience to the Constitution a possibility at last.[24]

This examination of Ely's argument is enough to reveal a vacillating conception of "interpretivism," or being guided by the Constitution, and a paradoxical understanding of "noninterpretivism," or looking beyond the Constitution. In the early part of his article Ely defines interpretivism in terms of the constitutional document as a source of general ideas that provide general guidance. But by the end of the article he criticizes interpretivists for failing to show how the document can provide specific directions to—even the particular premises of—judicial decisions in changing circumstances. The referent of "interpretivism" thus quietly changes from a familiar approach to constitutional meaning to an approach fairly imputed to no contemporary writer.[25] As for Ely's criticism of Justice Black, the upshot seems to be that a thoroughgoing interpretivist is really a noninterpretivist because, Ely claims, the document itself points to sources beyond its boundaries. Ely makes it clear, moreover, that he does not really hold the moderate view that one must look beyond the Constitution only some of the time, for, as he says, virtually any claim can be couched in one or all of the three clauses that compel judges to look beyond the Constitution.[26] This is why he contends that these three clauses invite "across-the-board substantive review of legislation." Ely does promise principles for guiding this kind of review and for reconciling its exercise with democracy. But his 1978 article clearly indicates that these will be extraconstitutional principles, coming as they do from sources beyond what he calls "the four corners" of the document, and extraconstitutional principles will still leave us with the paradox of a law commanding that we take our bearings from norms other than itself, the same paradox we encountered in Curtis's theory.

As Ely sees it, his three "open-ended delegations to the future" bespeak what Alexander Bickel termed "an awareness on the part of the framers that it was a *constitution* they were writing, which led to a choice of language capable of growth."[27] In Ely's thinking a judicial practice of looking beyond the Constitution furthers the value of constitutional growth. Prior to this approving reference to Bickel, however, Ely mentions another kind of growth, a constitutionalist's or an interpretivist's understanding of growth. The latter kind of growth is made possible, says Ely, by the Constitution's "briefly indicating certain fundamental principles whose general purport is clear enough but whose specific implications for each age were meant to be determined in contemporary context."[28] Ely regards this as the kind of growth the framers intended in the "line[s] of growth" he perceives in the case law of the First and Eighth Amendments, the due process clause of the Fourteenth Amendment, and the democratization of the franchise achieved through both judicial decisions and constitutional amendments since ratification. Ely speaks of such lines of growth as interpretivist lines of growth because he sees them originating in the democratic commitments of the founding.[29] By contrast, noninterpretivist growth does not begin in general norms or values thought to have been embodied in the Constitution at the founding. Noninterpretivist growth takes place along different lines; it is extraconstitutional in substance. Ely nevertheless regards noninterpretivist growth as constitutional in form because he believes the framers intended *that* it occur. Ely does not contend that this extraconstitutional growth is *right* or *good*, or even *necessary* or *inevitable*—his point is that it is *constitutional*. He argues that the framers invited extraconstitutional growth because they delegated power to effect it. Positing that the language of the constitutional document is the best evidence of the framers' intentions, Ely finds the language of three clauses devoid of content, and he takes this as sufficient for him to conclude that the framers intentionally delegated power to import content from ideas other than those they sought to express in the Constitution.

If we keep in mind the distinction between interpretivist (constitutional) and noninterpretivist (extraconstitutional) growth, we can see that the framers could not have deliberately authorized the latter, for in doing so they would have authorized the defeat of the values that moved them to establish the Constitution in the first place. Ely and others attracted to the idea of noninterpretivist growth might reply that new constitutional principles and values do not have to be inconsistent with what is already there. But this contention may ignore that constitutional principles and values are found not only in individual rights and structural limitations of the kind enforced by courts, they lie also in the social benefits or ends for the sake of which the founding generation delegated the *powers* of government. The language of the Constitution and the nation's history since ratification show that satisfying needs like national defense and economic prosperity depends upon what the framers called an energetic exercise of the powers of government.[30] The Constitution limits the proper exercise of these powers to moves that are consistent with constitutional rights. Ely recognizes the potency of values embodied in constitutional rights when he says that "rights can cut across or 'trump' powers."[31] We begin to appreciate the real significance of rights upon realizing that the powers that rights can trump, or at least burden, were established for meeting some of our most urgent needs.

I shall argue in chapter 3 that the commerce clause and related powers, for example, are best understood as Marshall understood them in *McCulloch*: delegations of authority to Congress to enact its best judgment of what is requisite for the nation's economic health in changing circumstances. By allowing authorized congressional policies to defeat otherwise permissible exercises of the states' reserved powers over education, public morals, and the like, the supremacy clause insures that where they conflict Congress's conceptions of economic health can defeat a state legislature's version of, say, moral health, intellectual excellence, or cultural integrity—values Congress cannot pursue as ends in themselves, not by a strict reading of the Constitution, at any rate. So, although we may have hoped to avoid it, Americans seem prepared to pay a price for the ends entrusted to Congress, and a history of state-federal conflict since ratification shows how much the nation has been willing to pay. But if nationally authorized ends can overpower values reserved to the protection of the states, the pursuit of nationally authorized ends cannot constitutionally defeat all social values, for Congress must either abandon or severely restrict policies that conflict with the constitutional rights of individuals. The value of free speech, for example, can constitutionally burden our foreign policy while the value of autonomous local control over antisocial conduct, as in the case of unruly visiting diplomats, cannot. The potential price of constitutional rights is indicated well in Patrick Henry's famous exhortation to the Virginia ratifying convention "not to inquire how your trade may be increased, nor how you are to become a great and powerful people, but how your liberties can be secured; for liberty ought to be the end of your government."[32] If rights trump powers—and I shall show in chapter 4 that the logic of the Constitution requires it—then those of us who take the Constitution seriously have to be prepared to make real sacrifices for rights. Thus, we can derive from the Constitution's arrangement of rights and powers a general statement of constitutional priorities. If, for example, contingencies should force a choice between what we acknowledge to be fair trials and the nation's economic health, the language of the Constitution supports the claim that the value of a fair trial takes priority over the value of economic health. If the values embodied by the Bill of Rights can in fact trump the powers of government, then the Bill of Rights embodies our highest political values, or so one can claim on the basis of the constitutional document. The adoption by any generation of Americans of genuinely new constitutional rights imposes additional restraints on our power to achieve such social goals as economic, personal, and even national security. Because real rights require real sacrifices, authorizing the recognition of genuinely new rights is not something likely to have been done without requiring extraordinary care, as the stringent amending provisions of Article V indicate. Yet Ely would have us believe that the document evinces an intention of the framers to authorize the defeat of their own priorities through the comparatively ordinary processes established to administer those priorities. It is far more plausible to suppose that if the framers invited constitutional growth, they invited what Ely would call interpretivist growth, not noninterpretivist growth.

How then would a judge who wanted to be guided by the Constitution deal with the indeterminacies of the privileges and immunities clause, the due process clause, and the Ninth Amendment? I submit that he would do what Ely does with the indeterminate character of the due process clause, a provision whose power to guide decision Ely admits: Try to ascertain the general values the framers sought to serve either through specific clauses or the Constitution as a whole, and construe the rules accordingly in changing circumstances. This is the only approach to the open-ended clauses consistent with the notion of constitutional supremacy, for, as Ely says at one point during his argument, "something that was not ratified cannot be a part of our Constitution, and there are times when, in order to know what was ratified, we need to know what was intended."[33] He also says that the language of the document is itself the best evidence of the framers' intentions.[34] But this means for Ely what it has typically meant in constitutional interpretation: Language, whenever possible, must be construed in accordance with one's best theory of purposes that may not be evident on the surface of the language alone. A good example of this kind of old-fashioned interpretivism is Ely's argument that the privileges and immunities clause of the Fourteenth Amendment protects *persons* generally, not just *citizens*, despite language that reads "citizens." The language, says Ely, "seems out of accord with what we are quite sure was the purpose," and therefore, "we owe it to the framers and to ourselves" to construe the language to read that "there is a set of entitlements, 'the privileges and immunities of citizens of the United States,' which states are not to deny to anyone."[35] Ely's contention about this clause remains debatable, of course, but there is nothing "impossible" about this approach to the document in general or to the three clauses Ely employs to argue for noninterpretivism. Thus, it is not impossible (though it is wrong, I think) to look into the purposes of the framers and agree with Justice Rehnquist that the equal protection clause is most plausibly limited to racial and related forms of discrimination.[36] One could also agree that Justice Black had good arguments grounded in the nature of the judicial function for concluding that the privileges and immunities clause protects only the substantive guarantees of the Bill of Rights.[37] One could also invoke original expectations in support of the penumbral-rights theory of the Ninth Amendment defended by Justice Arthur Goldberg.[38] Each of these theories is and would remain controversial; but each purports to explicate what is already there in the Constitution. *As an imputation to the framers*, therefore, each is better than Ely's theory of open-ended delegations to the future, for, once again, we cannot imagine lawgivers who deliberately delegate power freely to disregard the values that move them to enact their laws. Ely may have had this problem in mind two years later when he quietly abandoned an extraconstitutional approach to the open-ended provisions. This later work construes these clauses in accordance with a particular understanding of what Ely calls the Constitution's "broader themes," something a more traditional scholar might have referred to as "the meaning of the Constitution as a whole."[39]

In evaluating Ely's work on constitutional interpretation it is important to keep in mind something that distinguishes him from many of his contemporaries: Ely writes for the most part as if he would deny that controversy over the meaning and concrete applications of constitutional provisions is enough to defeat those provisions as meaningful sources of guidance in judicial decision. This position is evident in the following statement about the meaning of the due process clause:

> Until recently [i.e., until the 1972 decisions of the Supreme Court in *Board of Regents* v. *Roth* and *Perry* v. *Sinderman*] the general outlines of the law of procedural due process were pretty clear and uncontroversial. The phrase "life, liberty or property" was essentially read as a unit and given an open-ended, functional interpretation, which meant that the government simply could not seriously hurt you without due process of law. What process was "due" varied, naturally enough, with context, in particular with how seriously you were being hurt and what procedures were feasible under the circumstances. But if you were seriously hurt by the state you were entitled to due process. Over the past few years, however, the Court has changed all that, holding that henceforth, before it can be determined that you are entitled to "due process" at all (and thus necessarily before it can be decided what process is "due,") you must show that what you have been deprived of amounts to a "liberty interest" or perhaps a "property interest." What has ensued has been a disaster, in both practical and theoretical terms.[40]

In the immediate sequel Ely says that "asking what process is due will get the Court into some questions to which the Constitution does not begin to provide answers." He calls the power to decide questions of what is due in concrete cases a "delegation." But he insists nevertheless that with all the doubt and ensuing controversy from case to case about what processes are due, "the delegation . . . is a limited and not very frightening one," essentially because the due process clause simply means that people are "entitled to fair procedures" and "what procedures are needed fairly to make what decisions are the sorts of questions lawyers and judges are good at."[41] Thus, Ely gives the due process clause to the interpretivists—that is, to those who believe the Constitution can provide at least the starting points for judicial decision.

Does Ely give away too much? Many would argue that he does. They might say a general idea of "fairness" is a mere abstraction too far removed from the fray of litigation to help, and that attempts to make the general idea of fairness less abstract result only in particular versions of fairness with which many people disagree. These critics would say an abstraction like "fairness" is therefore without relevance to constitutional disputes between different conceptions or versions of fairness. No simple or natural fairness hovers above these disputes over particular conceptions of fairness, Ely's critics would add, and all we ever have is a distinction between those particular conceptions (if any) that are widely shared by the members of a community and those conceptions held by this or that individual or minority. Well might these critics oppose the suggestion that lawyers and judges are better than the rest of us at figuring out what fairness requires us to do—or at least better than the elected and removable lawyers on the judiciary committees of our state and national legislatures. They might conclude that judges have no special competence to discern either a value of sufficient dignity or a value with sufficient public support to justify judicial reversals of what we the people, acting through our representatives, really want.

Ely may have difficulty answering this challenge to his theory of due process, for in later writings he himself directs a similar challenge to those who argue that courts should look to general ideas of what is right for the derivation of "fundamental rights" worthy of judicial protection against the demands of democratic majorities.[42] Yet an independent idea of fairness does help to explain what Ely says about the meaning of the due process clause and the legitimate power of courts to stop the agents of the majority from hurting people as they might wish. What good is it to pretend one has no idea what Ely is talking about? Who can deny that everyone who thinks about how to act toward others assumes there is something called fairness? Disagreement over what is fair does not make this assumption an illusion, for one cannot disagree about what is fair without assuming that one ought to be fair and that the other person, at least, is wrong about what fairness requires.[43] Ely's interpretation of the due process clause clearly depends on the belief that the language of the clause evinces an intention to serve a purpose he believes ought to be served. He makes this judgment from the perspective of a contemporary citizen to whom the language of the due process clause is addressed as law. He correctly says he has no reason to believe the language "meant something different a century ago from what it means now," and that in ascertaining its meaning "recourse must be to the obvious overall policy informing the language."[44] This overall policy answers no concrete questions automatically, but it does make up part of the answer to the question of what the concrete disputes are all about. Moreover, the idea of fairness expressed by the due process clause can and does motivate attempts to defend particular conceptions of fairness beyond their mere agreeableness to those who hold them. Through the debates that the general idea motivates and justifies, it aids in exposing implications that move us to prefer some answers to others. Thus, Ely makes an effective point against *Roth* and *Sinderman* in saying they imply that the government may sometimes injure persons seriously without affording them procedural fairness: this, he says, is hardly a proposition "that cries out for affirmation."[45] He is right *if* one accepts as a major premise the proposition that the due process clause requires that the government deal with people fairly. Before the decisions in *Roth* and *Sinderman* this pronouncement might have been regarded a truism; it is no longer. Ely is aware of this. He notes that the *Roth* and *Sinderman* doctrine has provoked widespread scholarly condemnation, and he says, sardonically, that in view of its negative reception we can expect the Court to abandon the *Roth* and *Sinderman* doctrine sometime in the next thirty years.[46] We may not have to wait as long as Ely suggests, however, for the Court has already weakened the *Roth* and *Sinderman* doctrine and may be moving toward reversing it.[47] There is no reason to doubt that the scholarly condemnation Ely refers to is at least partly responsible for this development. Debates over the meaning of general ideas can have consequences for actual decisions, and it is hard to see how, of all people, academic lawyers can suggest otherwise. Ely's own assessment of the *Roth* and *Sinderman* doctrine shows that, far from being useless, the most general ideas and principles can make important differences in the concrete controversies of those who take them seriously, as Ely does, despite occasional affectations of skepticism.[48]

A stubborn critic might nevertheless continue to object that Ely's glossing the due process clause with the more abstract notion of "procedural fairness" serves only to license rejecting the framers' conceptions of fairness in behalf of *current* conceptions—which is to say, *our* conceptions or, noticing that we have no set of consistent conceptions, *Ely's* or some other interpreter's *personal* conceptions. Our critic might then argue that if Ely were really interested in locating his major premises in what was ratified he would study the framers' actual attitudes and practices in an effort to discover their historical conceptions. Assuming, arguendo, that this effort could succeed, our critic might accept Raoul Berger's view that what the words mean—i.e., what they mean to us—does not indicate what was actually ratified as reliably as does the historical evidence of the framers' intentions and that, for an interpretivist, at least, the historical evidence of the framers' intentions should defeat the meaning of the document when there is a clash between them.[49]

I want to defend Ely from this kind of attack because I believe his way of interpreting the due process clause is close to the proper approach to constitutional interpretation in general. I would say Ely's method is the proper approach were it not for his lapses into what he virtually admits are inherited academic doctrines about the conventional and, perhaps, even emotive nature of moral principles and standards.[50] Ely's analysis of the meaning of the due process clause is close to common sense at its best. If we pursue the implications of that clause to the ordinary citizen, however, we shall eventually arrive at the belief that treating people fairly is simply right and treating them unfairly, simply wrong—not merely conventionally right or wrong, or right or wrong relative to this perspective or that, just right or wrong. Clearly, we do not act as if we believed fairness a mere concomitant of our raw likes and dislikes; if we did, we would not debate what is fair as seriously as we do. No one actually debates what is fair by saying, "I say this is fair because this is what I like." Someone saying this is more likely to be giving up on further debate by merely asserting a preference in a take-it-or-leave-it fashion. One who wants to continue debate would say, "I like this result, yes; but I like it *because* it's fair."

We also do not act as if fairness were merely conventional, for we would not try to persuade anyone to our view of fairness by saying, "This is fair because we Americans [or Texans, or females, or any particular group] say so." As before, this assertion of what "we say" is likely to occur when one wants done with further debate. Although it might stop a debate, it cannot settle one because the fact of the debate itself is enough to reveal that there is disagreement over what "we believe." Where there is such disagreement, to settle a debate by asserting "we say such and so," one would have to succeed in defending a test or formula of some sort for what ought to count as what "we say." In defending such a test, however, one would have to argue that it simply is the right test. One could not say it is right because we say so, since the test is supposed to be a test for what we say. One would believe, in other words, that it would be right to have a certain test (say, majority rule) for what would count as what "we say." Nor could Ely reply to all this that what is fair depends on what the law says is fair, because it is to the general idea of fairness that he appeals in trying to settle the meaning of the law, the law of the due process clause, in this case. This clause, moreover, with the rest of the Constitution, is the result of a series of actions officially beginning with a proposal in Congress and ending with ratification in the state legislatures, with much public debate along the way. All this deliberative activity indicates that there had to be what we would call "reasons" for adopting the due process clause. Because there had to be reasons for the clause prior to its having acquired the status of law, what is fair cannot be determined solely by what the law says is fair. If we really believed otherwise, we could never try to make laws fairer or change the laws in the name of fairness. So, one cannot, and in fact we do not, believe that fairness is merely what one says it is or what we say it is.

Surprisingly, the weakness of citing personal preference and social convention as the source of constitutional limitations is clear to Ely himself in another context, where he criticizes the personal preference of judges and what he calls "tradition" and "consensus" as sources of reasons for declaring legislation unconstitutional. Invoking the personal preference of judges is undemocratic, he says, assuming, quite naturally, that it should not count as "democratic," and adding that no one counts personal preference anyway. He says also that we cannot invoke tradition or consensus because we have conflicting traditions and the fact of disagreement belies the claim of an ascertainable consensus.[51] So if personal preferences and various sorts of convention cannot settle debates about what fairness requires, why not acknowledge that when we debate the issue in good faith we are trying to arrive at an understanding of what is simply fair? Ely will not admit this kind of talk; he assures his readers that he believes in "natural law" no more than he believes in "ghosts."[52] This would suggest that he does not believe constitutional rights are supported by what is simply right. But this leaves us wondering why he believes constitutional rights should trump the powers of government. Why should rights trump powers if they are ultimately any less real than or even equal in status to the needs served by those powers? One might have expected that if one or another version of what is naturally right is where the logic of our institutions leads us, a professed constitutionalist like Ely should have been willing to say so, whether comfortable in the company of ghosts or not. Because of these tensions in Ely's thought, one should not embrace his method of interpretation without reservation. But if that method can be separated from otherworldly teachings which arbitrarily deny the reality of our political practices as we ordinarily understand them, Ely's method of interpretation is well worth defending. Whether what I shall defend will still be *Ely's* method is a question that points to a more general problem of interpretation which we shall encounter again in several forms: Does a conscientious effort to understand a written work (like a treatise or a constitution) entitle us to say that the author or authors really want to say what we believe they would have to say in order to make sense?

How then might we defend Ely the constitutionalist against the charge of someone like Raoul Berger that Ely's method is a mere cover for his conceptions or ours at the expense of the framers' conceptions, *and* that this substitution of conceptions is contrary to the intentions of the framers? We note to begin with that Ely does claim to speak for the framers. His treatment of "citizens" in the privileges and immunities clause shows him prepared to look below the surface of language to historical context for the purpose that motivated adoption of a provision. He does not say the language of the document is always the only evidence of the framers' purposes; he says it is usually the best, and sometimes the only, evidence. He does not oppose *his* meaning or *our* meaning to *their* meaning, as Curtis does. He argues rather that where we have no evidence of a change in meaning we can rely, simply, on *the* meaning. In sum, Ely seems to believe his interpretivism is oriented to the intentions of the framers. Raoul Berger claims the same orientation, however, and comparison of the two writers reveals radically opposed pictures of the framers. Thus, where Berger sees what some would call the policies of racists and elitists,[53] Ely sees a commitment to "a *constitutional development . . . continuously, even relentlessly away from*" attitudes and institutions like racism and elitism.[54] Yet we may view Ely and Berger as describing the same group of framers if we acknowledge that the attitudes of the framers had different aspects. Ely proceeds as if he has in mind what might be called the political aspirations of the framers—that is, the models of citizen and polity whose realization we have reason to believe would have been a source of pride for them.[55] By contrast, when Berger speaks of the framers' intentions he seems to have in mind not their aspirations but their more immediate wants and fears, some of which could have been the very attitudes they aspired to rise above.

In comparing Ely's view of the framers with Berger's one is reminded of Abraham Lincoln's argument that Stephen Douglas and Chief Justice Roger Taney were wrong to exclude blacks from the statement of the Declaration of Independence that reaffirmed a belief in human equality.[56] Taney and Douglas had cited historical practices like slavery in support of their view that the framers had excluded blacks. But Lincoln argued as if he believed the issue could not be settled by pointing to historical practices, for he believed the Declaration of Independence stated an aspiration to rise above some of those practices. Lincoln thus called the statement about equality a "standard maxim for a free society, which should be familiar to all, and revered by all; constantly looked to, constantly labored for, and even though never perfectly attained, constantly approximated, and thereby constantly spreading and deepening its influence, and augmenting the happiness and value of life to all people of all colors everywhere." Lincoln went on to say that the maxim had no practical use "in effecting our separation from Great Britain," but was put there "for future use" as what he felt it had become in his time: "a stumbling block to those who in after times might seek to turn a free people back into the hateful paths of despotism." With this understanding of the statement, Lincoln had some justification for saying: "I think the authors intended to include *all* men . . . this they said, and this they meant."[57] Lincoln may have been right about the existence of an aspiration to rise above the practice of slavery. Whether he was right or not, however, one cannot refute his view by citing the historical facts of slavery and the attitudes that sustained it, for his argument presupposes these facts. Aspiring to a society free of slavery presupposes an existing state of slavery. One does not aspire to be what one has become or what one will become inevitably or without exertion.

Ely's reading of the Constitution thus seems similar to Lincoln's reading of the Declaration of Independence. Both emphasize the aspirational aspects of the framer's intentions. If Ely is right about an original constitutional commitment to democracy he is justified in emphasizing constitutional language at the expense of those historical attitudes and practices inimical to democracy, because aspirations typically involve gaps between prescriptive words and the empirical attitudes and patterns of conduct they would transform. Ely would also be justified in giving therapeutic constructions to words and phrases that do not fit the aspirations he discerns, as "citizens" does not fit what he believes to have been the overall objective of the privileges and immunities clause. And because aspirations presuppose the need for self-improvement, he would even be justified in viewing parts of the constitutional document as temporary expedients that the framers expected to be dismantled at some point along the way to a truly constitutional state of affairs; the clauses of the Constitution that were predicated on slavery could serve as obvious examples.[58] Ely can thus defend his approach to the document if he is right about the aspirational nature of the framers' intentions and if it is at least possible to be right about the content of those aspirations.

If we approach the Constitution in a manner mindful of the distinction between aspirations and immediate wants and aversions, much of what we see in constitutional language and history is clearly aspirational. A salient feature of the public psychology of the founding period was the attitude that Americans were "in a special category, uniquely placed by history to capitalize on, to complete and fulfill the promise of man's existence."[59] *The Federalist* opens with an appeal to this psychology and repeats it throughout its lengthy argument for ratification. Originating in the seventeenth-century "Pride in the liberty-preserving constitution of Britain," this desire to be admired by other nations seems intermittent in America. The aspirational tone of the Constitution is unmistakable in the Preamble. As in the Constitution's history and text, an aspirational dimension is present in the Constitution's logic. The remaining chapters of this book show that by viewing constitutional problems in light of a commitment to a constitutionally ideal state of affairs, constitutional theory acquires a coherence it cannot otherwise achieve. I argue, for instance, that only when persons generally would be willing to sacrifice for each other's rights could judges avoid "conflict-of-rights" litigation, which now forces them to violate their oath to respect all rights as trumps on the powers of government. Rights as real trumps on powers will prove to make little sense in the thinking of a people that does not desire to achieve the competence and courage that express themselves in the self-restraint and sacrifice involved in honoring rights. I argue also that one can account for the paradox of declaring "supreme Law" a document depicted by the Preamble as a set of means by translating those means (i.e., the provisions of the document) into a description of an ideal state of affairs which can be regarded as an end in itself—a state of affairs in which Congress, for example, would actually make no laws abridging speech, no matter what the provocation, and where the peculiar tension between legislative and executive government could be seen as the institutionalization of reasoned decision, a thing of intrinsic dignity.

Construing the document in terms of constitutional aspirations need not necessitate reading one's preferences into the document. Of course, our preferences may happen to coincide with constitutional aspirations; indeed, I shall show that some coincidence is essential if we are to accept the authority of the Constitution. No matter what we think it means, however, there is no necessity that we believe the Constitution rational and just or that we accept it as a worthy guide to our political aspirations. There is much in the Constitution that will remain hopelessly mistaken to many and potentially to all of us. One could mention here what some believe to be the constitutional commitment to the unlimited acquisition of private wealth and an ever-expanding gross national product, commitments that may yet dehumanize us and destroy the earth as we know it. The Constitution may express the best in us, and it may be best to read the Constitution as if it did. But that does not mean the best in us is good enough. I shall argue that a continuing awareness of the possibility of better constitutions is essential not only for the long-range prospects of constitutionalism but even for a continuing sense of obligation to pursue our present constitution.

A belief that it is possible for the Constitution to be a guide in constitutional decision does not require actual agreement about the meaning of constitutional language; it requires only a belief in the possibility of agreement. True, those who look to the Constitution for guidance treat the Constitution as a law, and a law cannot be a law if it prescribes contradictory courses of action. So we have to assume consistency of meaning in order to treat the Constitution as law. But those who take the Constitution seriously enough as law to debate its meaning act as if it is possible to distinguish better understandings of the Constitution from worse. The idea of right answers or better answers in constitutional decision has been opposed by observers who follow what appears to be an unwritten rule of constitutional commentary that the document be construed to accommodate change, at least that kind of change for which general approval is thought to exist. Although change in our understanding of the Constitution will prove to be an essential part of living by the Constitution, one cannot deny the difference between change that is and change that is not consistent with a foundational set of values. Those with an eye to constitutional flexibility who claim that the Constitution itself permits fundamentally conflicting courses of action—that a properly overruled doctrine (like the "separate but equal" doctrine) was really the law of the Constitution in its own time—are inadvertently criticizing the document as law or rejecting the idea of constitutions as real planning documents for the future. Far from a requisite for constitutional survival, this historicist view cannot comprehend a constitution that refers to itself as "supreme Law" both for one generation and for its "Posterity," for such a constitution presupposes that some values are both fundamental and transhistorical. The person who is prepared to criticize the present constitution for its shortcomings is therefore more of a constitutionalist than one who would render the document a delegation for whatever the future might invite. Constitutionalism need not die with this or that constitution. But our American constitutions do presuppose that constitutionalism makes sense. If our present constitution is open to anything and everything, it does not make sense as the law it claims to be, and constitutionalism itself serves only as a salutary myth. Again, looking for guidance in the Constitution requires only a belief in the possibility of ascertaining what the Constitution means; those who believe it can mean nothing in particular cannot take it seriously as law. Those who take it seriously as law must believe it means something, however much they may debate that meaning or oppose it politically.

Ely's analysis of the due process clause can serve as a model for approaching constitutional meaning because it is oriented to an understanding of the intentions of the framers without presupposing actual agreement on those intentions or on their concrete applications and because it reveals how the possibility of agreement can guide debate over what the Constitution should mean for concrete cases. Lawgivers seek to govern by rules of law, not personal command; sooner or later they must condition their expectations on what those who are subject to their laws understand their laws to mean. As subjects of the Constitution, therefore, we are entitled to take our understanding of its words and phrases as the best evidence of the framers' intentions, and by the intentions of the framers we are entitled to mean not their mere immediate wants and aversions but the general purposes that we believe make up what they believed would be a good and just society. We have no good reason to believe that our understanding of the words and phrases of the document differs from theirs, and we have good reasons for believing that their meanings lie more in their ideals than in their immediate interests. The least one can say is that their ideals constitute an aspect of the multidimensional phenomenon called "constitutional law," and that this aspect deserves explication in its own right as one of the several legitimate concerns of constitutional theory. Explication of the ideals embodied in constitutional language may or may not be governed by one's own political preferences, but we cannot prove that such undue influence has occurred in any given interpretation unless we can identify a difference between the framers' values and those of the interpreter— in which case we concede the possibility of correct assessments of the framers' purposes. The very decision to debate an interpretive judgment presupposes the possibility of, and justifies the quest for, the correct constitutional theory. Those who make a thorough attempt to deny the possibility of getting the meaning of the Constitution right will eventually have to explain their own reliance on the possibility of others correctly interpreting what they want to say.

3

Trying to Make Sense of the Supremacy Clause

WHAT IS THE CONSTI-
tution? What is it as a whole? Some might call the Constitution a
complex set of rules designed primarily to help us recognize the
institutions of our government and its officials. But the Constitution
also tells the government what it can and cannot legally do, thereby
telling the people what they can and cannot achieve through, or
demand from, the government. Some view the Constitution as an
imposition of the will of the framers on future generations. Others
see it as a set of procedures whereby people of today can minimize
the frequency and extent of unjust impositions on each other. Because
people with different attitudes and needs appeal to the Constitution
for different reasons, it would be difficult to classify the Constitution
as a whole in a way that is both politically meaningful to everyone
and logically simple. One can emphasize some of the Constitution's
attributes over others, however, and by emphasizing different attributes one favors different ways of reading the document. For example, those who see the Constitution, and perhaps law in general,
as an act of will whereby certain superiors, like the framers or the
founding generation, would control future generations as their subjects will understand constitutional interpretation as an attempt to
discover the expectations of the superiors without regard for the utility
or rightness of those expectations. Raoul Berger suggests this ap-

proach when he assumes that those who would be faithful to the Constitution would take the "Negrophobia" of the framers into account in ascertaining the scope of the Fourteenth Amendment.[1] John Hart Ely's emphasis is more forward looking or more *aspirational*. He views the Constitution as the result of an original commitment to a democracy that strives fairly to represent and benefit everyone— an imperfect commitment at the beginning, but a commitment nonetheless and therefore a sign of our aspirations as a people. To the extent that the language of the document permits, Ely construes the Constitution's provisions in ways that further his best understanding of those aspirations. He believes the Constitution marks out "lines of growth" toward the real values of the framers and away from those of their views and attitudes that were inconsistent with their aspirations.[2]

Disagreements over the nature of the Constitution and how to read it have always been a feature of constitutional discussion in America. Thomas Jefferson and his political allies called for a strict construction of the powers of the national government because, they said, the Constitution was a contract between the states as separate political entities who had agreed to give up just so much power to the central government and no more.[3] In opposition to the Jeffersonians, Alexander Hamilton and John Marshall emphasized the desiderata, or ends, to be achieved by the exercise of the powers of the national government, ends like national security and economic prosperity for the whole nation. By insisting on the supremacy of national policies over conflicting state policies Hamilton and Marshall assumed that the people of the nation as a whole wanted to achieve the ends entrusted to the national government more than they wanted the honor of membership in state and local communities with rights to pursue policies in conflict with nationally authorized ends. Thus, Hamilton and Marshall saw the Constitution not as a contract between sovereign states, but as an instrument for satisfying certain paramount wants of the people of the nation as a whole.[4]

At the bottom of debates over the nature of the Constitution lies a tension between what we might call the Constitution's *instrumental* and *obligational* aspects. The Constitution has an instrumental aspect because it was once a nonbinding political proposal presented to the electorate and defended as a way of achieving certain desirable states of affairs. True, the document seems to refer to itself as "the supreme Law of the Land" (Article VI, section 2), but we know that this clause was subject to the acceptance or rejection of the people of the founding generation as they felt it conducive to what the 1st *Federalist* called their "interest," and their "dignity . . . liberty . . . and . . . happiness."[5] As a logical and historical matter, the Constitution's authority cannot be understood to depend on our ignorance of its origin in a mere practical proposal, for provisions of the document itself remind us of this beginning. I refer, at least, to the Preamble, the ratification provisions of Article VII, and the amending provisions of Article V. These provisions serve as windows, so to speak, to an original state of affairs in which the Constitution was not yet established as supreme law. The Preamble records the purposive thrust of the Constitution as an abstract whole by asserting that "We the People . . . do ordain and establish this Constitution . . . in Order to" do and accomplish certain things—"form a more perfect Union, establish Justice, insure domestic Tranquility, provide for the common defence, promote the general Welfare, and secure the Blessings of Liberty to ourselves and our Posterity." Article VII records and thereby reminds us that the founding generation did not have to accept the Constitution, that its establishment depended on a deliberate act of acceptance called "Ratification," and that states whose constitutional conventions did not ratify the document were not to be bound by it. Most remarkably, Article V provides for amendments and thereby for further acts of ratification. This is an important sign that the document does not put its provisions altogether above the deliberative processes through which they were originally formed and established. Nor, as a historical matter, have Americans acted toward their constitutions in ways that deny the law's continuing dependence on the deliberative process in which it originates. Thus, James Madison himself appealed to the instrumental aspect of our constitutional understanding when he exhorted his generation to disregard the ratifying provisions of the Articles of Confederation in order to ratify our present constitution.[6] An instrumentalist understanding has moved scholars like Charles P. Curtis to treat the document less as a real restraint on public demands than as a set of empty symbols to be manipulated in ways that legitimize those demands.[7] We presuppose that the Constitution is an instrument of our immediate wants to the degree that we believe the Constitution requires judicial deference to the preferences of our elected representatives. Some scholars and jurists profess a belief in judicial deference for most of the really controversial constitutional questions that come before the courts.

Instrumentalism is thus a strong element of our constitutional history, the Constitution's language, constitutional commentary, and our constitutional psychology as a people. No successful theory of constitutional meaning can exclude it.

On the other hand, the Constitution must be understood as more than a mere instrument for satisfying immediate wants. Upon ratification the Constitution became the "supreme Law of the Land," and as the word is used in everyday political life, *law* presupposes both an obligation or duty to obey and at least some inclination to disobey. We do not enact laws for each other or for ourselves in order to promote conduct that would occur voluntarily in the absence of laws and supporting constraints.[8] We may not want, after some discussion, to go as far, but H.L.A. Hart has said, "The most prominent general feature of law at all times and places is that its existence means that certain kinds of human conduct are no longer optional, but in *some* sense obligatory."[9] The Constitution contains different kinds of provisions, of course, and a few of them (like the Preamble, the ratification provision, and even, some have said, the Tenth Amendment) are not appropriately referred to as laws. But all of the Constitution's provisions are somehow connected with the constraining of conduct. We shall see, for example, that even provisions, like the commerce clause, which affirmatively authorize the enactment of certain kinds of laws, can be taken negatively to imply a limited range of authorizations and therefore to limit the kinds of demands the national government can constitutionally satisfy. Such is the familiar states' rights argument about the negative or restrictive implication of the Constitution's enumeration of powers.[10] Certainly, the Constitution as a whole exhibits an obligational aspect. Thus, after it declares the Constitution "supreme Law," Article VI says that "the Judges in every State shall be bound thereby, any Thing in the Constitution or laws of any State to the Contrary notwithstanding." One can characterize the enterprise of constitution making with a famous remark from the 51st *Federalist*: "If men were angels, no government would be necessary. If angels were to govern men, neither external nor internal controuls on government would be necessary. In framing a government which is to be administered by men over men, the great difficulty lies in this: You must first enable the government to controul the governed; and in the next place oblige it to controul itself."[11]

Disputing what I have just said about the obligational aspect of the Constitution, someone might cite the amending provisions of

Article V and contend that the Constitution does not bind us in an ultimate way because it opens itself to whatever changes we might want to make. But this conclusion would be inconsistent with the language of Article V and with our ordinary understanding of what it means to change something that is considered to be part of a whole. Certainly, we would doubt that we were living under anything properly referred to as the same constitution if a very large faction in Congress and the electorate were to repeal, say, the First Amendment, the Civil War amendments, the provisions insuring the electoral accountability of officials, or the prohibition against titles of nobility. Of course, the amending provisions could be used to achieve results like these, but if such changes were made one could argue plausibly that the amending provisions had been misused because they would have produced not mere amendments but changes that were quite revolutionary. In our everyday discourse we distinguish amendments from fundamental changes because the word *amendment* ordinarily signifies incremental improvements or corrections of a larger whole. Article V seems to employ this usage when it says amendments "shall be valid to all Intents and Purposes, as Part of this Constitution." So if it makes sense to speak of the Constitution's larger commitments— like democracy and the public and private attitudes conducive thereto, or human dignity, or freedom from ideological or religious impositions—we can imagine some proposals that would be too revolutionary to count as "Part of this Constitution," even if they were processed through the provisions of Article V.[12] In addition to limits on what we could understand as "amendments" to "this Constitution," Article V says that "no State, without its consent, shall be deprived of its equal Suffrage in the Senate," a limitation that prompted Edward S. Corwin to say, "The amending, like all other powers organized in the Constitution, is in form a delegated, and hence a limited power."[13]

Someone continuing to resist the conclusion that the Constitution limits the demands we can pursue through government might argue that constitutional limits are essentially procedural, not substantive, and that as long as we follow constitutional procedures we can reach any results—any results that are consistent with a continuing adherence to the procedures themselves.[14] This familiar thesis often suggests itself to academicians when they imagine themselves in a judicial role trying to apply the Constitution to issues in which clear constitutional guidance is not available. It is easy for some observers to believe, for example, that the Constitution says nothing about abortion rights either way and, therefore, that the Constitution leaves the existence of those rights up to our elected representatives. Thus, relative to abortion rights, one could say that all that the Constitution guarantees is that the proabortion and antiabortion groups will have equal access to the legislative process, which process is to decide whether and what abortions to permit. One runs into trouble, however, when one tries to give a procedural gloss to the Constitution as a whole or when one tries to look at all or even most of what we now call substantive rights (of speech, for example, or religion) as essentially procedural in one sense or another.[15] The problem begins with the recognition that procedural commitments are not always clearly separated from substantive commitments in the thought of those who ratify and try to live by constitutions. Values like truth and human dignity and virtues like self-restraint and a sense of fair play seem integral to most of the Constitution's procedural values. What other kind of reason would those who felt they could remain in strategic positions of power have for honoring freedom from self-incrimination, the right to a fair trial, and the rights of others to vote and have their votes count? Procedures can also constitute practices or ways of life and government that seem to be valued as ends in themselves and treated as sources of pride when compared to the ways of other regimes. Thus, the right to speak out against the government, while procedural in some respects, makes up part of the image of a national character that many of us believe immeasurably more admirable than the images associated with communist Russia, fundamentalist Iran, or oligarchic El Salvador. The notion that procedure can be disassociated from the values that move people deliberately to adopt procedures in the first place—the notion of procedure detached from substance—is altogether removed from anything we do, or could, have a historical record of, for we could not understand someone to be proposing the adoption of a procedure if, from out of the blue, the procedure (so-called) aimed at no purpose at all. On those occasions, when we can clearly separate procedures from substantive values, we typically subordinate the procedures to those values. This is why substantive values often dominate procedural considerations in constitutional thought. Madison made the general point in the 40th *Federalist*: "There are two rules of construction dictated by plain reason as well as founded on legal axioms. The one is, that every part of the expression ought, if possible, to be allowed some meaning, and made to conspire to some common end. The other is, that where the several parts cannot be made to coincide, the less important should give way to the more important part; the means should be sacrificed to the end, rather than the end to the means."[16]

Whatever the content of the Constitution's limits on our demands, therefore, we do and must assume that those limits exist to be explicated, and this is enough to satisfy us that—instrumental though it be—the Constitution is simply not compatible with any and every conceivable state of affairs. Even if we could imagine or postulate the impossible—i.e., a set of governmental procedures neutral toward all conceivable wants—those who valued such procedures would value them precisely because of their neutrality, and the neutral procedures would be considered better than all nonneutral procedures. The Constitution would therefore exclude nonneutral procedures and bind us to its neutral procedures.[17] Thus, procedural rules bind, too, as long as they are legal rules in some sense, and as long as we can tell one set of procedures from another. Certainly, the amending provisions of Article V have proved restrictive of many demands in fact, whether open to all demands in principle or not. These considerations leave no escape from the conclusion that at some level of generality, inflexibility is an essential property of the Constitution as law—that, in other words, there are some results one cannot reach constitutionally.

Does this inflexibility make sense? Focusing on the Constitution's instrumental aspect we can always ask how one can transform a mere set of means—something of no intrinsic value—into a law that binds regardless of its success or in the face of patently better means. Assuming means to which substantive value did not attach, how could anyone disagree that "the means should be sacrificed to the end, rather than the end to the means"? The founding generation clearly did not pretend that we could not rightly reject constitutions simply because we had once accepted them. The Declaration of Independence asserts a right of revolution against all governments that become destructive of the ends of government; it does not exempt governments originally instituted by acts of popular acceptance. When the framers of our present constitution urged the American people to disregard the amending provisions of the Articles of Confederation, they emphasized the failure of the old government to achieve the end for which it was originally instituted, "the national happiness," and they rejected the idea of sacrificing that end to the mere preservation of the confederation.[18] So, although one can challenge the theory that an act of consent is always sufficient to transform a practical proposal into a law that remains a law beyond the period of its usefulness, I need not do so here because, as a matter of historical fact, the founding generation does not appear to have accepted an absolute principle of irreversible consent on the constitutional level. Without such a principle the transformation from practical proposal to supreme law is irrational if it is assumed that a set of means can fail, as must be assumed in the case of the Constitution.

Claiming supremacy for a set of mere means would not only be irrational, it would also be unjust. The Preamble and Article VII presuppose that a people has a right to a government that meets certain of its needs. The Declaration of Independence informed the world of the nation's belief in that right. But the Constitution would deny that right to generations after the founding. The Preamble refers to these later generations as the "Posterity" of the founding generation, a paternalism later generations may have wished to reject. Clearly, there is an apparent inequality of treatment here, and one must ask how it might be justified. What makes the founding generation so special? To what kind of authority can one appeal in its behalf? One cannot contend that the founding generation is this people's first or oldest generation, as the word *founding* might suggest, for America had acquired a national identity long before the ratification period, and as *The Federalist* acknowledges in several places, an advanced, if imperfect, constitutional philosophy had become part of that identity.[19] And so, despite the paternalistic language of the Preamble, the founding generation did not claim to be the first or the oldest generation. A different claim for the founding generation did appear in the 49th *Federalist*, where Madison suggested that largely because of its historical circumstances, the founding generation could claim to be less divided by special interests and a spirit of domestic partisanship than was likely for future generations. Madison claimed that the pressures of the revolution had inspired the American people to repress special interests and partisanship in favor of a confidence in their "patriotic leaders" and from a desire to show that they were capable of instituting new and better forms of government than those of the Old World.[20] Madison's words recall Hamilton's appeal in the 1st *Federalist* to the "inducements" of the virtues of "philanthropy" and "patriotism."[21]

The founding generation, then, had special virtues on which to base its claim to supremacy, or so it might be argued. Even if this argument were beyond challenge, however, it would not be sufficient to remove the injustice or potential injustice of the founding generation's claim to supremacy. We need not pause to ask whether the facts of history would move us to agree that the founding generation was especially philanthropic and patriotic, for no issue of concern to us here depends on such judgments. The point is that we could not assess the virtues of the founding generation without what we believed to be reliable criteria of the virtues in question; and since we would be applying these criteria to the founding generation (it might be asked, for example, Was the founding generation really patriotic?) we would concede the possibility that the founding generation could fall short of perfection and, therefore, that some future generation could come closer. Given this possibility, the claim of the founding generation remains at least potentially unjust. Surely, to the degree that the alleged virtues of the framers were in some way caused by the external dangers they faced, we may find ourselves an even more virtuous people in the future because the dangers of the future are or could be much greater than the dangers of the founding period.

The potential injustice of one generation's binding another has always been a matter of concern among constitutional scholars and statesmen. Jefferson once suggested that we could meet this problem by adopting new constitutions every nineteen years.[22] And, especially during the tenure of Chief Justice Earl Warren, many scholars had this injustice in mind when they approvingly described the Supreme Court as an engine of constitutional change made possible by the Court's power to give new meaning to the document's indeterminate words and phrases. I am not suggesting that commentators always have a good understanding of why it is unjust for one generation to bind another. In fact, this belief is often based on a number of problematic assumptions, like the assumption that when the people of today express wants contrary to the Constitution they reject both the authority of the Constitution and the justice of having an institution like the Supreme Court follow the Constitution in spite of the public's wants. This is not altogether unlike saying that everyone who smokes tobacco must reject the proposition that one ought not to smoke and that smokers must oppose the practice of discouraging smoking. One who believes this sort of thing ignores the familiar fact that our wants usually conflict. This position also ignores the conflict between wants and aspirations. Logically, one cannot aspire to be what one already has become. If one does aspire, one has not yet achieved that to which one aspires. As long as the Constitution embodies our aspirations, therefore, we can expect conflicts between our wants and the Constitution. It is no more impossible to have aspirations that conflict with wants than it is to have aspirations in the first place. Nor is it impossible to institutionalize the tension between our wants and the things to which we aspire. Indeed, one can argue that the members of the founding generation did just that when they ratified the Constitution as a set of limitations on their government—for since the government was to be their agent, by limiting the government they limited themselves.

Scholars usually overlook the necessary distance between wants and aspirations when they use public opinion polls and other indices of what the public wants as evidence of disagreement between current attitudes and the values embodied in the Bill of Rights. Asking respondents to opinion polls how they feel, say, about the death penalty is not the same as asking them whether they believe the death penalty is cruel or whether it is consistent with their best understanding of the ideal of humane treatment embodied in the Eighth Amendment. Those who respond to public opinion polls could want the death penalty precisely because they consider it cruel and therefore fitting payment for the cruelty visited upon the victims of brutal crimes. Nevertheless, the respondents in these polls might strongly oppose repealing the Eighth Amendment because, as a general proposition, they might continue to believe cruelty is wrong. They may or may not have regrets about wanting something they really believe wrong, depending on how well developed their sense of shame and their capacity to apply their standards to themselves. In any event, they probably would not admit their true feelings about the cruelty of the death penalty. For to do so in light of the Eighth Amendment might contribute to abolishing the death penalty, and that is something our hypothetical respondents would oppose. We need not have good evidence that most supporters of capital punishment actually feel this way in order to believe it plausible that they could feel this way. For this reason, it would probably take a lengthy dialogue with a trusted and friendly critic to bring out their real views about what the Constitution means and ought to mean. Opinion polls would not do. Nor would election returns, reports of conventional opinions, or descriptions of established practices.

The results of this hypothetical poll on the death penalty would show that the respondents were driven more by a desire for an avenging justice than by a constitutional principle opposed to acting on that desire. We could add this unflattering finding to those of scholarly studies that remind us of such other departures from constitutional principle as the persecution of British loyalists during the revolutionary period, the Alien and Sedition Acts, slavery, the Japanese-American "relocations" of World War II, McCarthyism, and the attempts to suppress protest against the Vietnam War. Episodes like these should be cause for national shame. Recalling them is enough to prove the weakness of our principles, and recognizing this weakness should alert us to the immorality of self-righteousness. We may even come to recognize the inadequacy of a constitutional system that has failed to educate a people to the importance of its principles. But shameful memories are not enough to prove that we do not have the principles by which the attitudes and practices in question are criticized and condemned. The Constitution itself evinces in several ways an expectation that most of us will want to act contrary to our principles. Consider the amending provisions of Article V, provisions whose stringency makes sense if we realize that what is morally and intellectually best in us is typically weaker than our immediate demands, that nations have better and worse moments just as individuals do, and that the best moments, though rarer, are the most authoritative. Because we have an awareness of all these things we try to fortify the best in us with constitutions that restrain the worst in us. Historians and other writers who produce sad reminders of past failures must acknowledge that our aspirations have survived our hypocrisies in some measure, for stories about past departures from principle would be uninteresting and pointless had the principles disappeared altogether.[23]

Having noted these difficulties in the usual complaints about one generation's binding others, however, I leave further criticism aside, for one cannot avoid concluding that adherence to the Constitution may prove to be irrational and unjust. Insofar as the Constitution is a set of mere means, we cannot hold it intrinsically worthy or deny the possibility of its failure. Neither the founding generation, the framers, nor the historical period of the founding possess attributes of authority that would be strictly impossible to find elsewhere. So the potential for irrationality and injustice is there; indeed, the framers were powerless to avoid it. This is so because it is impossible for us even to imagine a perfect government, much less establish one in practice. A government could not be perfect if it were in any way incompetent with respect to the purposes for which it was established. Thus, a perfect government would have to confront changing circumstances by remaining free to adopt whatever measures were best for realizing its ends. Anything preventing a free choice of measures would diminish the government's competence. A perfect government, therefore, would be confined only by the very general directive to seek its proper ends as best it could. The constitution of this government could contain nothing more than this very general directive because anything else would limit its power to adapt to change. The problem is, a constitution not only directs government to its proper ends, it also provides criteria through which the public recognizes who governs. A perfect government would still presuppose the need for government—the need, that is, for governing people whose imperfections put them in need of government. Being imperfect, either in wisdom or character, those needing government could not recognize government simply in accordance with the criterion "that which best serves the ends of government." Because government, like law, is appropriately spoken of only where human inclinations, to some degree, run contrary to authority, those persons needing government would have to have perfect wisdom and perfect self-control to recognize and follow a government by a criterion as general as "that which best serves the ends of government." But if they did have perfect wisdom and self-control they would not need government, and subjecting them to government would be unjust. A government over such people would not be a good government because it would not be a just government. Those who did need government, therefore, could not recognize and follow a perfect government. They would need relatively noncontroversial rules as at least a partial basis for recognizing authority in the presence of their inability to grasp and act upon what was simply beneficial and right.[24] A government even partially recognizable by relatively noncontroversial rules would have a more or less stable structure of offices. Sooner or later, this structure, itself a set of means to the ends of government, would limit the flexibility of this government to select the right measures in changing circumstances. Unless it could completely control historical change (and I will not pause to discuss that possibility or its implications), this government eventually would become incompetent to its purposes. A perfect government, therefore, is inconceivable.

What, then, are we to make of the declaration of Article VI that "[t]his Constitution, and the laws of the United States which shall be made in Pursuance thereof . . . shall be the supreme Law of the Land"? Clearly, this claim to supremacy is unavoidable, for, as Hamilton observed in the 33rd *Federalist*, the Constitution's supremacy would have been understood whether or not explicitly declared.[25] Nevertheless, the more one thinks about it, the less sense this declaration may make. Admittedly, few persons think about it very much, and the Constitution could not survive as a practical matter if many did. Thus, though the 1st *Federalist* says that this was to be a government established "from reflection and choice," the 49th *Federalist* concedes that even the "wisest and freest governments would not possess the requisite stability" without "the prejudices of the community on its side."[26] On the other hand, the 49th *Federalist* also says that, aside from the prejudices of the community at large, among the thoughtful "[a] reverence for the laws, would be sufficiently inculcated by the voice of an enlightened reason."[27] Surely, the prejudiced themselves presuppose, as part of their prejudice, that the laws make sense or would make sense to the very thoughtful. That is why it is a point of some practical, everyday significance to observe that, as a logical matter, there can be no constitutional reason for accepting the authority of a constitution that no longer serves the ends for which it was established. When circumstances make living under such a constitution the command of the supremacy clause, that command is contradicted by the Preamble, which says that the document whose supremacy is declared is an instrument of justice, the general welfare, and other ends. To put the point differently: One cannot have what one believes to be an unequivocally constitutional justification for accepting the Constitution's supremacy where one is convinced that doing so either would defeat or is not the best available way to serve one's best understanding of the ends for whose sake the Constitution was instituted. Of course, other considerations might lead one to accept the authority of a government or a scheme of governing that departs from what the Constitution says was established at ratification. For example, believing that an unconstitutional scheme or practice is beneficial, one may attempt to derive obligations of obedience or cooperation from the alleged benefit. One may also decide to obey the government from the belief that disobedience would make matters worse. There are other reasons for obeying unconstitutional authority, but there is no *constitutional* reason (i.e., a reason consistent with

the Constitution) for accepting the supremacy of a scheme of governing that has ceased to be what the Constitution expressly says it is: an instrument of justice and the other ends of government.

This conclusion does not ignore the juristic convention against treating preambles as rules of law or as provisions that guide in a direct way to the legal disposition of cases in the courts. Granting that preambles are not applied to facts in ways that directly help settle lawsuits, preambles still help to set the stage for interpreting laws by indicating something of their purposes, their sources, and the proper relationships between lawgivers and those subject to the laws. These matters form a large part of our understanding of the meaning of those laws that figure directly in the resolution of lawsuits, and there is no question of their influence on approaches to the meaning of the Constitution. We have already seen how different theories of the Constitution's source, purposes, and nature entered into the disagreement between Marshall and Jefferson on whether to construe the Constitution narrowly or liberally. We also saw why the Preamble was more helpful to Marshall's position than to Jefferson's.

If the Preamble is excluded from a theory of constitutional meaning on grounds that preambles are not laws, other norms that do not directly apply to facts in lawsuits will have to be excluded. This would cause considerable embarrassment because we should then be unable to account for a particular understanding that attaches to all of those parts of the law that would remove options from the sphere of things we are free to do: the understanding that laws are meant to be obeyed. That laws are meant to be obeyed is an essential part of what is usually meant by law. In recognizing this, however, we are acknowledging a social understanding or expectation about laws—i.e., that they are meant to be obeyed. We are not interpreting laws in accordance with a more general *law* that commands obedience to laws. If we cannot be sure laws are meant to be obeyed unless we have a more general law to that effect, we cannot be sure the more general law itself is meant to be obeyed without an even more general law, and so on, ad infinitum. Thus, our understanding that laws are meant to be obeyed is not itself a law.[28] Even if we were to formulate and enact it as a rule of law, its force would depend on the understanding we possessed prior to and independently of the enactment. Hamilton recognized this in the 33rd *Federalist* when he said of the supremacy clause that it "only declares a truth, which flows immediately and necessarily from the institution of a Federal government," and that the "operation of the intended government would be precisely the same" if the supremacy clause "were entirely obliterated" from the document as if it were "repeated in every article."[29] Hamilton said this because he looked on the supremacy clause as a general declaration addressed to all within the Constitution's jurisdiction, states and individuals alike, that the constitution of the "larger political society" of the United States was to be obeyed as such.[30] Thus, the supremacy clause simply makes explicit an understanding or expectation that attached to the original act of establishing the Constitution.

If the supremacy clause merely expresses one of the expectations implicit in the act of establishing a constitution, the Preamble and the ratification provisions show that we attach other expectations to the act of establishing constitutions. Madison invoked some of these expectations when he defended the Philadelphia Convention from those who criticized it for violating its charge. Congress had asked the Convention to propose limited revisions of the Articles of Confederation for subsequent submission to the legislatures of all the states, in the manner required by Article XIII for amendments. Instead of doing that, the Convention proposed a wholly new plan of government for submission to popularly elected ratifying conventions in the states, to be established among as few as nine states. Despite the nation's not having formally disestablished the Articles, Madison dismissed the charge of illegality against the Convention as an "absurdity" that would have given a veto to as little as "1/60th of the people of America." It was here that he stated as a rule of construction, "dictated by plain reason as well as founded on legal axioms," that "where several parts [of the charge to the Convention] cannot be made to coincide, the less important should give way to the more important part; the means should be sacrificed to the end rather than the end to the means."[31] The end, Madison contended, was given by those parts of the charge that called for "a firm national government," one that was "adequate to the exigencies of government and the preservation of the Union." This proved inconsistent with language in the charge that suggested mere amendments or alterations within the general framework of the Articles.[32]

When all these considerations are taken into account, I see no way to avoid the conclusion that circumstances can exist in which honoring the supremacy clause would be irrational and unjust by norms implicit in the Constitution itself. Indeed—given the Constitution's original status as a mere practical proposal as well as the need to justify the imposition of one generation on others—we might wonder whether the supremacy clause can ever amount to more than an incoherent legalism, notwithstanding the fact that it may be "honored" from unreflective habit or as a result of inertia, coercion, fear, prejudice, or extraconstitutional benefits. At bottom, the problem is one of elevating admitted means over ends; without some additional reason, this cannot be done sensibly by those who adopted the means for the sake of the ends in the first place. If the supremacy clause is to make sense, therefore, or more sense if not perfect sense, a way must be found to look upon the Constitution as a norm that combines the attributes of means and ends. I shall show how this might be done, and in a way that reflects the complexities of our understanding of the Constitution.

To begin with, we can easily see, in a general way, how we might understand the rules of the Constitution as envisioning desirable states of affairs. For example, by authorizing Congress to regulate commerce among the several states, the commerce clause can be seen as envisioning a state of affairs in which Congress is actually regulating commerce or, better (I shall show why it is better in chapter 4), a state of affairs in which Congress is doing its part to maintain the nation's economic health. Further, by construing the Fifth and Eighth amendments with the commerce clause, the Constitution would envision a successful pursuit of the nation's economic health that would not deprive people of their property unfairly or subject them to cruel and unusual punishment. Or consider the various clauses having to do with the military and the conduct of foreign affairs: collectively, these clauses envision the successful maintenance of national security. Adding the First Amendment to the foreign affairs powers, the Constitution envisions maintaining national security, or trying to, while honoring rights to criticize the way in which national security is being maintained, which includes the right publicly to deny that national security is being maintained. These exercises of constitutional power might be valued as both means and ends. Obviously, the activities of regulating commerce and conducting foreign affairs can be valued as means to national defense and the general welfare. Aside from the results they might yield, however, these and other exercises of constitutional power possess an aspect that makes them valuable as ends in themselves. The same can be said about honoring the First Amendment and other constitutional rights. Ideally, the powers of government are exercised through processes that are both representative and deliberative. The individuals and groups represented in these processes are to be the subjects of the laws enacted. By pursuing our needs through the system of representative self-government, we engage in exercises of deliberative autonomy, a practice or state that we admire and value as an end in itself. Representative self-government, again ideally, is an exercise also in the virtue of moderation because the number of votes necessary for legislative majorities in a large, diverse society compels each group represented to take the kind of moderate position others can support. Where constitutional rights are involved, representative self-government is an exercise also in self-restraint because when we, through our government, honor constitutional rights we restrain demands that would abridge constitutional rights. Exercising the powers of government and honoring constitutional rights can be valued as ends in themselves for the same reason that self-restraint, moderation, and autonomy are looked upon as virtues and objects of praise independently of their success as means to other desiderata.

Just as we can combine and understand the commerce clause and the First Amendment in terms of a desirable state of affairs, we may be able to understand the whole Constitution as envisioning a more complex state of affairs. I submit a general description of that more complex state of affairs in the remaining chapters. Before I begin that effort, however, we will need a better idea of the attitude we must have toward this constitutional state of affairs and toward the Constitution as law. I shall proceed by formulating an abstract practical inference that fits the act of ratifying the Constitution. If we can find a practical syllogism that describes ratification in a general way, we can discover the most general logical properties of the Constitution. This knowledge will be a valuable aid to resolving the problem of how to understand the Constitution in a way that will make sense of the supremacy clause. I will go through two unsuccessful attempts first because an awareness of what does not work will sharpen an appreciation of the syllogism that does work.

We can begin to outline a practical inference from which the Constitution could have resulted by considering the following:

Major premise: We the people want justice, the general welfare, domestic tranquility, the common defense—in brief, the ingredients of the good society.

Minor premise: Following this Constitution is the best way to achieve the good society.

Conclusion: We therefore accept this Constitution— that is, we accept it as supreme law.

My argument up to this point prevents us from accepting this syllogism because its minor premise conceives the Constitution as a mere instrument or means to the good society. If we understand the Constitution as mere means, we know in advance that it is possible for it to become inadequate to the ends for which it was instituted, and for that reason it makes no sense to accept it as something we cannot abandon later. Another version, then, of the minor premise might read as follows:

The ways envisioned by this Constitution constitute the good society, or the best society of which we are capable—a society that is either exactly what we want or as close as we can possibly get to what we want.

This second version of the minor premise is more attractive than the first because it may enable us to overcome the anomaly of elevating means to a position of superiority over ends. We could be wrong about the Constitution, of course, but if we were certain that the ways of the Constitution constituted the best society, accepting the Constitution's supremacy would at least make sense because we would believe that the Constitution's ways would constitute the best we could achieve for ourselves as a community. We might even believe that the problem of the Constitution's unfairness to subsequent generations had been solved. For if we were convinced beyond possible doubt that the ways of the Constitution were in fact the best, we would believe that no one who was in a position to give the matter adequate thought could disagree. In the same way that criminal law is not usually considered as an imposition of our ways on burglars, murderers, embezzlers, and the like, the Constitution would not be considered as an imposition on those who might disagree with our convictions. In each case we would be saying: "We are not imposing our values on you. These values are not good simply because they are ours; they would be your values too, if you were in a position to think about them aright. For this reason, these values are your real values, whether you agree at the moment or not."

As attractive as the second version of the minor premise might be to some, however, it cannot be the right version because the Constitution is open to criticism and change by virtue at least of the First Amendment and the amending provisions of Article V. If the Constitution were exactly what we wanted or the best we believed could ever be, the amending provisions would be pointless. Nevertheless, the first version of the minor premise cannot serve, because if it were to remain, the decision to accept the Constitution would make no sense. What we need, therefore, is a middle way. We have to move away from characterizing the Constitution as mere means without moving all the way to regarding the practices it prescribes as constitutive of the good society, pure and simple. The right reading of the minor premise is, therefore:

> The ways of the Constitution constitute our best current conception of the good society—our best understanding for now.

This third version of the minor premise gives the Constitution a tentativeness that is appropriate for a set of means and for a set of laws open to criticism and change. It also acknowledges, however, that the Constitution is more authoritative than mere means could be. By this version, the Constitution shares or borrows the brilliance of the good society. Thus conceived, the Constitution would be authoritative as a conception of an intrinsically authoritative idea, the good society. Since we would value the Constitution's ways only as a conception of the end we seek, we would remain open to the possibility of improved conceptions, and the Constitution would remain open to continuing criticism and improvement. Nevertheless, the Constitution would be the best conception of the good society known to us for the time being, without our knowing for certain that a better conception would ever come to light, and as long as it remained our best conception it would make sense to accept its claim to supremacy. By contrast, any attempt to transform mere means into supreme law would give more authority to the means than to the end, which would be anomalous even in the case of the best means, for the authority of means as means is always derivative, not intrinsic.

By adopting the third version of the minor premise leading to the Constitution's establishment as supreme law, one need not deny that the Constitution has an instrumental aspect. Instrumentalism, or proceduralism, is well represented in the notion that the Constitution envisions certain ways or practices. One denies only that these ways or practices are merely instrumental and therefore lacking in the value intrinsic to substantive goals. Pure instrumentalism is an approach that appeals to scholars who accept an academic value skepticism, which holds that values are either conventional or emotive, never simply valuable, and that reason can tell us only something of the costs of what we want and how to get it, not whether what we want is worth having. As we have seen, however, one cannot account for constitutional supremacy in purely instrumental terms. This leaves thoroughgoing value skeptics with no real reason for accepting the Constitution's authority or advising others on what the Constitution should mean. They cannot take seriously either the Constitution's claims or the claims of constitutional theory to discern good reasons for reading the Constitution one way rather than another. They cannot understand the Constitution because no constitutional provisions are separated altogether from substantive values they say they cannot perceive. Scholars who do take constitutions and constitutional theory seriously while simply assuming they should remain faithful to academic value skepticism have unsuccessfully tried to subordinate the substantive dimension of the Constitution to the procedural dimension so that they could appear to avoid what they call value judgments. They feel that choices between conflicting procedures are not really value choices because procedures lack intrinsic value. Reason, they feel, can distinguish between effective and ineffective procedures, and judges and scholars who can reduce constitutional substance to procedure can make choices without making value judgments. They might believe, for example, that a judge or scholar can rationally find that, as a matter of historical fact, the Constitution is committed to democracy; that, logically, a rule of "one person, one vote" is more democratic than schemes overrepresenting individual members of minority groups or regions; that the Constitution therefore requires a rule of one person, one vote; and that they can determine all this without necessarily deciding whether democracy is worth having or which version of democracy is worth holding. Even if procedures were separable from substantive values, however, the observable qualities of social and political conflict over competing procedures (different ways of counting votes or representing constituents, for example) would make it apparent that procedural values are values, too, and that pure proceduralism is an unnecessarily impoverished form of constitutionalism that cannot even account for the value it seems to attach to procedures themselves.[33] There can be no doubt that as a factual matter we as a people praise, take pride in, and attach intrinsic value to some constitutional procedures, practices, institutions, or—more generally—*ways*. I have respected that fact without denying either that a distinction between means and ends is useful in some contexts or that the Constitution has a procedural dimension.

To see why it is important not to deny the Constitution's procedural or instrumental dimension, let me elaborate a previous point. I have argued that constitutional supremacy makes sense only if we believe that the ways of the Constitution constitute our best conception of the good society. But since we are aware of the Constitution as a conception of the good society, we cannot know that it is our best conception of the good society unless we (1) continually try to improve our existing conception of the good society, and (2) continually measure our understanding of the Constitution against our best conception of the good society. This process will involve (3) altering our understanding of constitutional provisions within the arguable limits of the Constitution's language and tradition to see if our conception of the Constitution can be made to conform to our improved conception of the good society.[34] This last step is justified because it is necessary if we are to make sense of constitutional supremacy and because we have no good reason to believe either that earlier interpretations always make the Constitution's claims understandable or that it is wrong to seek the best interpretation.[35] The aim of this complex process is reaffirmation of the Constitution—because we want to be able to follow the Constitution, to accept it for what it says it is, we want successfully to test our belief as loyal subjects that the Constitution's ways constitute our best conception of the good society.[36] Even if we succeed in reaffirming that belief, however, a logical gap will remain between what we are conscious of as a conception of the good society and the good society itself or perfect, final knowledge of it. This gap will remain because one can always ask, "Is my best understanding simply best?" Our awareness that we may be able to improve our understanding makes tentative any judgment that a given understanding is really the best. Thus, the Constitution presupposes that our quest for knowledge of the good society is a continuing quest and, therefore, that the process of testing the Constitution's supremacy is a continuing process. This became apparent when the First Amendment and the amending procedures forced us to reject a version of the minor premise of ratification that flatly declared the ways of the Constitution constitutive of the good society. In this continuing process of reaffirmation one finds the original activity of which the pure proceduralism of academic value skeptics is but a poor imitation. Unlike the latter, the constitutional process is a continually self-critical quest to sharpen our vision of an ideal state of affairs and, to the extent that constitutional language and tradition permit, improve our conceptions of constitutional provisions accordingly. It is not a process whose end is simply posited as some impenetrable act of will or conceived as one or another kind of existential fact beyond our power to criticize and therefore to justify or to know as simply good.[37] As naive as it may be, and for what it is worth, those who follow the constitutional process take seriously the notion of what the 1st *Federalist* calls a "good government" established "from reflection and choice," promising freedom from a dependence on "accident and force," and capable of adding the "inducements of philanthropy to those of patriotism" for those who would support constitutional supremacy. We know that thoroughgoing value skeptics would find this kind of talk, and therewith the assumptions of constitutional supremacy, quite meaningless.

I am contending that because the Constitution's ways must constitute our best conception of the good society in order for us to make sense of the Constitution as supreme law, a practice of continuing reaffirmation is essential to a constitutional state of affairs. Because reaffirmation is a continuing need, however, it can only be achieved provisionally; it cannot be achieved in a final way. That makes constitutional supremacy an object of aspiration for those who accept the Constitution's claim to supremacy. Because they accept that claim, they accept its logical condition, reaffirmation, and therefore they commit themselves to testing the Constitution against their best conception of the good society in the hope that the Constitution will continue to meet that test. It is at moments of reaffirmation, and only then, that we get a glimpse of the Constitution as supreme law. Given the reflective self-criticism of those who quest for reaffirmation, and as we might have concluded from the words of the Preamble, constitutionalism for us is more a form of self-disciplined striving than a matter of willful self-assertion. Here the sovereign people appears to find virtue in self-restraint. Here the sovereign—being sovereign or "supreme"—aspires not to something it can believe is altogether higher than itself, but rather to its own best form. It does this by trying to defeat or reform the propensities that combat its progress toward its own best form. Such is the attitude of those who see themselves as members of this self-realizing sovereign. We shall see some of the manifestations of this attitude later, especially when we turn to the scope of constitutional rights and the responsibilities of officials and citizens.

In concluding this chapter, I want to distinguish what I call the process of reaffirming the Constitution's supremacy from a practice of using the Constitution's provisions as mere delegations of power or warrants for determining their meaning. The immediate difference is that between (1) reaffirming ideas and provisions thought to have been recognized or established by those who framed and ratified the Constitution and its amendments, and (2) altering constitutional norms to conform to changing political demands. I am arguing that those who fully accept the Constitution's authority strive continually to reaffirm the Constitution's ways as their best conception of the good society. But this does not license us to bestow constitutional status on all that we would regard good. Constitutionalism is a commitment to means as well as ends, and, as I have argued, legal inflexibility will prove characteristic of the means at some point. For better or worse, the American Constitution of 1789, as amended, suggests a particular hierarchy of social values and political institutions, and we cannot assume that this hierarchy will survive our best thought. Here, as I shall argue, we may well find that the most authoritative version of the nation's economic health (Congress's, under the commerce clause) would defeat via the supremacy clause and the necessary and proper clause conflicting versions of cultural integrity, community morality, and educational excellence as pursued by the states under their reserved powers. The public psychology of this society could be described as a kind of liberalism in that it would combine such emphasis on private economic gain and pleasure as is compatible with serious commitments to an equally protective state of affairs, free expression, due process, freedom from religious impositions, and other constitutional rights. One would believe oneself in a constitutional state of affairs if one believed it reasonable to describe the existing state of affairs in terms derived from the body of the Constitution, and that the existing state of affairs conformed to what would be one's best conception of the good society. But the Constitution cannot and ought not accommodate all states of affairs, though some that it cannot accommodate may prove better than the best it can accommodate. This is why I reject the notion of open-ended warrants and delegations at the service of changing political demands.

I must add that though it is an ideal to be achieved, a constitutional state of affairs could not be utopian, since it is one in which the Constitution is reaffirmed as law. As we have seen, where there is recognition of law there are inclinations running contrary to law; hence, the need for reasoned reaffirmations of the law. A general pattern of conduct would exist in a constitutional state of affairs such that unlawful inclinations would successfully be restrained by most of the citizenry most of the time. But unlawful inclinations would continue to exist, and where the self-restraint of individuals failed, coercion would be justified in the minds of those successfully exercising self-restraint, on grounds that coercion would be in the best interest of everyone.[38] Here, then, would be a state where conflicting demands would be pursued through institutions whose results, though often disappointing, would continue to warrant a general belief in the system's justice and utility for advancing the general welfare and the other ends of the Preamble. Winners and losers alike would or could continually reaffirm the premises of ratification.

4

The Powers of Constitutional Government

IN CHAPTER 3 I AR-
gued that if fully conscious subjects of the Constitution are to make
sense of its transformation from mere practical proposal to supreme
law they must believe that they would reaffirm the Constitution's
ways as their best conception of the good society, a state of affairs
worthy of the nation's highest aspirations. This characterization of
the Constitution as a whole will influence an interpretation of its
parts. Consider, for example, Congress's power to enforce the guarantees of the Fourteenth Amendment: Does section 5 of the amendment authorize congressional initiatives to end racism in America?
This is one of the questions I discuss in this chapter; it has no simple
answer. But one can easily anticipate the general thrust of a satisfactory answer if the logic of the Constitution were to compel a
consideration of this question in conjunction with another: Would
Americans generally—even most racist Americans—be willing to proclaim a racist society as an American aspiration? The first step toward
a comprehensive picture of constitutional aspirations is a theory of
the powers granted by the people through the Constitution to the
national government, a theory of what kind of thing such grants of
power are; how rules embodying these powers should be applied by
judges and others who want to determine what the national government is authorized to do; and what the powers of the national gov-

ernment, as related to the powers of the states, indicate about the nation's values.

The Constitution embodies the principle of enumerated powers, most evidently in Article I, section 8. This is a list of what Congress is authorized to do. It says, for example, that Congress shall have power to lay and collect taxes, to regulate commerce with foreign nations and among the several states, to declare war, to raise and support armies. Although this list is a delegation of powers to Congress as the nation's legislature, it has always been understood as marking those areas of policy that were to be the concern of the national government as a whole. The list is supplemented by grants of power elsewhere in the Constitution, most notably the concluding sections of the Civil War amendments, which give Congress the power "to enforce" the amendments "by appropriate legislation."

The founding generation gave two potentially conflicting signals when it delegated powers to the national government. By *granting* powers to the government the founding generation implied that there were tasks to be performed, ends to be achieved—a positive, forward-looking implication. By *enumerating* the powers that were granted, however, the sovereign people implied that there were some things the national government was not to do. The authors of *The Federalist* were clear about this negative implication in several places.[1] Notwithstanding these assurances, the First Congress was pressured by public opinion to make this negative implication explicit, and the Tenth Amendment reads, "The powers not delegated to the United States by the Constitution, nor prohibited by it to the States, are reserved to the States respectively, or to the people." By this language it is clear that, in the main, the Constitution is the source of national powers, not state powers. In fact, the Constitution explicitly recognizes only a few state powers, such as the right to set "the Qualifications requisite for Electors of the most numerous Branch of the State Legislature" (Article I, section 3) and the right of two-thirds of the states to call a constitutional convention (Article V). If the Constitution in any sense "divides" power between the national government and the states, it does so indirectly and with virtually no affirmative allocation to the states, for it says simply that the national government shall do certain named things and the states or the people will be left with what, if anything, remains. The Tenth Amendment does not say explicitly that anything does remain. Nevertheless, the nation has always understood that the Constitution does leave some things to the states—or, better, that the Constitution does not grant all governmental power to the national government.

This method of telling the national government what it is authorized to do has contributed to the most protracted constitutional conflict in American history: the debate concerning the scope of national power vis-a-vis the rights or prerogatives of the state governments. Does Congress have the power to incorporate a national bank with branches in the states, contrary to the policies of the states? Can the federal courts review judgments of the state courts involving the meaning of the national constitution and laws? Can the nation's executive blockade the ports of states in rebellion against national authority? Can Congress work actively in the states against gambling, or prostitution, or polygamy? Can Congress end child labor and what it regards as substandard wages and working conditions in the states, contrary to the policies of the states? Can Congress force lunch counter owners to serve all customers, regardless of race, contrary to the policies of the states? Can Congress tax the wages of state employees, state-owned railroads, and state-owned liquor stores?

Questions like these once dominated constitutional discussion, and a states' rights debate has reappeared in the decisions of the Burger Court. But the frequency and intensity of these issues have declined sharply over the last fifty years because the reasons for supporting states' rights have seemed less respectable than the reasons behind national power in conflict with state policies. Some describe state and local governments as schools of civic virtue that provide more opportunities for citizen participation in government than are available at the national level. They say that by leaving matters to the states the nation becomes a virtual laboratory for experimenting with diverse governmental structures and policies. By permitting diversity, enhancing opportunities for participation, and experimenting with different governmental and social options, federalism contributes to our overall freedom of choice, thus revealing its connection with a concern for individual rights. So the defenders of states' rights have usually claimed. The states' rights argument is not a good argument, however, and for most of this century it has been widely regarded as disingenuous. The immediate question has not been whether the national government should close down schools of civic virtue and laboratories for social and political experimentation. The question is whether anyone can have good reasons for reading the Constitution in ways that permit some states to give racist policies an experimental try, or to use their laws to define virtue in sectarian ways or in terms of sharply contested moral beliefs, or to suppress unorthodox political views, or effectively to presume the guilt of criminal defendants, or to treat convicts inhumanely, or to obstruct policies aimed at the economic health of the nation and its people, including the weak and the chronically exploited—or, generally, to go their own way, contrary to what the nation's representatives believe is beneficial and right for the whole nation.

The answer to this question has been clear enough to most of the influential observers of our time, and states' rights have declined accordingly.[2] True, the right wing of the Republican Party is currently leading attempts to devolve some power to the states in a number of areas, such as education, environmental protection, welfare, and business regulation. But this renewed states' rights talk is a counterfeit of the original claim—the claim of a state's right to go its own way in areas allegedly left to its exclusive control, such as education, public morals, crime control, public health, land use, child labor, and labor relations generally. The current effort does not really manifest a principle that, somehow, federal power, per se, is bad and state and local power or control is good. In fact, current states' rights talk actually serves a particular version of the good society that the right wing would apply to the nation as a whole, and in a way that would actively work against the attempts of state and local governments to define the good society for themselves, as per the original states' rights claim. A good example of this counterfeit concern for states' rights is the recently proposed Family Protection Act.[3] As introduced in the United States Senate in 1981, the opening section of the bill finds that "certain Governmental policies have directly or benignly undermined the viability of the American family" and announces that henceforth "the policy of the Government of the United States should . . . be directed and limited to the strengthening of the American family and to changing or eliminating any Federal governmental policy which diminishes the strength and prosperity of the American family."[4] A section entitled "Rights of States and Local Educational Agencies" says federal funds shall not be withheld nor any federal law construed to prohibit any state or local educational agency from determining teacher qualifications ("including the right to make a determination that no certification requirement will be imposed"), from setting attendance requirements ("including the right to determine that no such attendance requirement will be imposed"), and from prohibiting "the intermingling of sexes in any sports or other school related activites."[5] Other sections prevent federal agencies from defining child abuse[6] and spousal abuse[7] more broadly than they are defined by state laws. In his formal introduction of the bill, Iowa's Senator Roger Jepsen spoke of these provisions as "[a] shift in responsibility from the Federal Government to the State and local government."[8] As cosponsor of the bill, Nevada's Senator Paul Laxalt claimed that "Federal intervention in the most intimate of family relationships" and "the vast array of Federal social programs" had "aroused the most hostile reaction of the American people."[9]

Paradoxically, however, Senators Jepsen and Laxalt were also calling for a new, *national* policy in behalf of "family values." Senator Laxalt termed the proposed act "an integral part of a process to develop a new awareness of the importance of the family to American society and to develop Federal policies designed to foster and encourage that family. . . . In essence today we are not merely introducing a Family Protection Act but we are reaffirming a family protection movement."[10] And, as one might expect from what would amount to an assertion of national power, provisions of the bill are designed to defeat state efforts to take a different view of family values and the educational practices appropriate thereto. Thus, there are provisions for withdrawing federal funds from any state program that provides contraceptive or abortion services or information to unmarried minors without prior parental notification,[11] or from any entity engaged in "advocating, promoting, or suggesting homosexuality, male or female, as a life style,"[12] or from any agency that excludes parents "or representatives of the community" from a part in curriculum decisions "relating to the study of religion,"[13] or from any agency requiring union membership of teachers,[14] or from any agency prohibiting "parental review of textbooks prior to their use in public school classrooms."[15] The bill prohibits use of federal funds for purchase of educational materials that "do not reflect a balance between the status role of men and women . . . [and] the ways in which women and men live . . . [and that] do not contribute to the American way of life as it has been historically understood."[16] Senator Jepsen later explained this last provision by attacking federally funded "human services professionals" for "recruiting females or males for employment in jobs not traditionally held by members of their sex."[17] The bill also provides that parents or other individuals aggrieved by state or federal agencies under the last four provisions may sue in federal court "for damages, or for such equitable relief as may be appropriate, or both," with costs and attorneys' fees as the courts choose to award.[18] This last provision should be particularly offensive to the pure states' rights view in light of conservative attacks since the era of Chief Justice Earl Warren on the use of the equity powers of the federal courts to promulgate sweeping and detailed rules for the operation of schools, prisons, and other institutions exercising public functions.[19] The courts have chosen to expand their equity powers far beyond simple injunctive orders rather than leave to uncooperative state agencies the job of correcting such unconstitutional conditions as segregated schools and overly crowded prisons. But the judicial orders remedying such violations of the Constitution look like codes of the kind that legislatures typically enact, and this has made the courts vulnerable to the charge that they are intruding into the discretionary, law-making authority of state and local governments. A federal judge so inclined would have clear authority under the Family Protection Act for this kind of rule making as a tool against recalcitrant state and local agencies. A legislative proposal with such provisions is hardly a genuine move to return power to the states.

One can easily have similar doubts about the states' rights *bona fides* of current proposals to restore state power in areas that have a direct effect on the economy, like land use, industrial safety, and environmental protection. Here again, those who are calling for restoring states rights do not seem to attach any special constitutional value to state regulation per se. They have not said, for example, that the states should have the opportunity for that sense of moral achievement and self-respect that comes from successfully repressing those demands for wealth that conflict with a respect for the health, safety, and dignity of other human beings and for the survival of other forms of life. In the absence of such arguments, one can presume that states' rights talk is being used to mask or legitimize a movement toward an even less restrained pursuit of wealth, probably on the assumption that acquisitiveness has more political leverage on the state than on the national level. It has happened before. Earlier in this century business interests regularly invoked the rights of the states as part of their opposition to federal attempts to compromise their desire for wealth with values like fair wages, decent working conditions, and opportunities for poor children to grow up in schools and playgrounds instead of mills and factories. But the solicitude of business for states' rights evaporated when the states did succeed in adopting policies favored by labor, consumers, and social reformers. On these occasions, businesses typically ran to the federal courts, claiming that the states had violated their federal constitutional rights, usually their Fourteenth Amendment right not to be deprived of their liberty and property without due process of law.[20] So our experience is that invocations of states' rights need not signify a genuine commitment to the right of a state to go its own way. Today's issues continue to implicate what has always been the real question: What kind of *nation* shall we be?

A central reason for the unpersuasive quality of the states' rights argument in this century is an apparent change in the popular under-standing of the constitutional rights of individuals from a more to a less community-oriented conception. Some of the framers may have been ahead of their time in this regard. The 10th *Federalist* makes clear the framers' recognition of a need to protect the rights even of the "obnoxious individual" against factious majorities, and the po-litical philosophy of *The Federalist* as a whole seems an appeal from the small, relatively homogeneous community to a nation whose large size and other features, like wealth, economic opportunity, social mobility, and secularism, would attenuate the individual's feeling of belonging to a whole community (i.e., a community large enough but not too large for one's mind and affections to grasp as a self-sufficient whole) and substitute attachments to groups or interests, mainly eco-nomic interests, of much smaller compass.[21] Belonging personally to a part, not a whole, this new individual would see constitutional rights primarily as claims to be made against the government, not as claims made by individuals as members and in behalf of their community vis-a-vis other communities representing more or less different values and, even, ways of life. To see the difference between this individ-ualistic and a more community-oriented conception of constitutional rights, contrast a right to consume pornography or to be free from racial, religious, or ethnic discrimination with rights (of individuals) to live in communities where pornography would not be found or where housing was not open to members of different racial, religious, or ethnic groups. As was consistent with the more individualistic conception of rights implicit in the plan for a large republic that he hoped would prevent tyrannical majorities, Madison proposed to the First Congress that it include in the Bill of Rights an amendment prohibiting the states from violating "the equal rights of conscience, or the freedom of the press, or the trial by jury in criminal cases."[22]

Congress did not adopt this proposal, however, and the federal courts did not begin to enforce the rights Madison defended against state and local governments until the twentieth century.[23] The initial defeat and subsequent vindication of Madison's position suggests that since the founding period Americans increasingly have come to view constitutional rights in more individualistic ways and to associate individual rights with national power exercised against local pressures in behalf of conformity and caste. This development has weakened the cause of states' rights among those who identify constitutionalism with the concern for individual rights.

Notwithstanding their recent quiescence and current artificiality, disagreements over the scope of national power have not only been the most troublesome of our constitutional history, they also involve issues that illuminate some of the most important questions of constitutional theory, including the leading question of this inquiry: the kind of country that ratification of the Constitution committed the nation to be. As an aid to isolating some of the elements of this issue I shall assume in this chapter that the only restrictions on the national government are those limitations expressed or implied by the enumeration of powers, as distinguished from limitations inherent in the internal organization of the government and imposed by constitutional rights. The conclusions of this chapter will therefore have to be supplemented by the findings of chapters 5 and 6, which discusss constitutional rights and constitutional institutions, respectively. How or whether the Tenth Amendment places restrictions on national power is addressed here, although I need not mention the amendment by name since its substance is already implicit in the enumeration of powers, whose logic I shall discuss. That discussion will confirm the consensus of twentieth-century commentary on the legal significance of the Tenth Amendment, as summarized in 1941 by Chief Justice Harlan Fiske Stone: "[The Tenth Amendment] states nothing but a truism that all is retained which has not been surrendered. There is nothing in the history of its adoption to suggest that it was more than declaratory of the relationship between the national and state governments as it had been established by the Constitution before the amendment."[24] This will make the scope of national powers depend solely on fair constructions of the national constitution and its powers, rights, structures, and purposes as a whole, without regard for any states' rights that do not fit that picture.[25]

The founding generation wanted a new constitution because it was unhappy about certain conditions in the country and because it felt a better government could do something about those conditions. These problems included the threat of commercial warfare resulting from the protectionist policies of some states; a decline in investor confidence due in part to debtor relief laws in the states and the reluctance of state legislatures to raise their share of payments on the national debt; and the presence of British troops in parts of the western territories, a presence the British tried to rationalize by citing efforts by state governments to obstruct treaty obligations respecting the property of British loyalists and debts due British subjects. Under the Articles of Confederation Congress could do little about these problems in the face of state intransigence because it had no workable power to pursue its version of the nation's economic health, to tax, to enforce treaty obligations, or to raise troops.[26] The "imbecility of our Government," Hamilton said in the 15th *Federalist*, had contributed to insecurity and unrest at home and a lack of respect abroad. This prompted him to ask: "[W]hat indication is there of national disorder, poverty and insignificance that could befall a community so peculiarly blessed with natural advantages as we are, which does not form part of the dark catalogue of our public misfortunues?"[27]

Against this background of social problems, *The Federalist* had a simple answer for those whose concern for liberty made them fear the extensive powers of the proposed government to tax, raise armies, and do other things sufficient to govern the nation's affairs: The people would not be giving the new government too much power in light of what the people wanted to achieve through government. In defending "[t]he necessity of a Constitution, at least equally energetic with the one proposed," Hamilton said the question of constitutional powers would "naturally divide itself" into the following questions: "—[1] the objects to be provided for by a Federal Government—[2] the quantity of power necessary to the accomplishment of those objects."[28] In an oft-quoted passage he went on to say:

> The authorities essential to the care of the common defence
> are these—to raise armies—to build and equip fleets—to pre-
> scribe rules for the government of both—to direct their opera-
> tions—to provide for their support. These powers ought to ex-
> ist without limitation: Because it is impossible to foresee or
> define the extent and variety of national exigencies, or the
> correspondent extent & variety of the means which may be

necessary to satisfy them. The circumstances that endanger the
safety of nations are infinite; and for this reason no constitutional shackles can wisely be imposed on the power to which
the care of it is committed. This power ought to be co-exten-
sive with all the possible combinations of such circumstances;
and ought to be under the direction of the same councils,
which are appointed to preside over the common defence.

This is one of those truths, which to a correct and unpre-
judiced mind, carries its own evidence along with it; and may
be obscured, but cannot be made plainer by argument or reasoning. It rests upon axioms as simple as they are universal.
The means ought to be proportioned to the end; the persons,
from whose agency the attainment of any end is expected,
ought to possess the means by which it is to be attained.

Whether there ought to be a Federal Government intrusted
with the care of the common defence, is a question in the first
instance open to discussion; but the moment it is decided in
the affirmative, it will follow, that that government ought to
be cloathed with all the powers requisite to the complete execution of its trust. And unless it can be shown, that the circumstances which may affect the public safety are reducible
within certain determinate limits; unless the contrary of this
position can be fairly and rationally disputed, it must be admitted, as a necessary consequence, that there can be no limitation of that authority, which is to provide for the defence
and protection of the community, in any matter essential to its
efficacy; that is, in any matter essential to the formation, direction or support of the National Forces.[29]

The first matter of importance in this passage for our purposes is
what it suggests about the general nature of constitutional powers:
Constitutional powers are means to ends; more precisely, constitutional powers are authorizations to pursue desirable states of affairs.
This view was not unique with Hamilton. Madison took it for granted
when he defended the several grants of power later in The *Federalist*
as serving "the following objects;—1. security against foreign danger—2. regulation of the intercourse with foreign nations—3. maintenance of harmony and proper intercourse among the States—4.
certain miscellaneous objects of general unity—5. restraint of the
States from certain injurious acts—6. provisions for giving due efficacy to all these powers."[30]

Now, of course, powers-as-means is a persuasive interpretation of constitutional powers in light of the instrumental aspect of the Constitution as a whole. The Constitution's Preamble, ratification provisions, amending provisions, and electoral provisions all suggest the familiar theory that the powers of our governments are delegated by the people without corresponding delegations of sovereignty. The sovereign people, which governs through the Constitution, has persuaded itself that it is good for the government to be accountable to an electorate that does not govern. In this context of instrumentalism and electoral accountability, the ends to be served by government are not the same as they would be among career public servants in regimes whose officials are not accountable to those who do not govern others. For example, the end served by the Constitution's powers to raise and support armies and to declare and conduct war is one of the ends of those predominantly civilian citizens who elect the civilian officials who are supposed to control the military. I will call this end "national security," even though it is not yet clear what that nation looks like whose security the Constitution envisions. What is clear now is that the career defense personnel of *this* regime—if they are to do their duty by it—must find ways to be "good soldiers" while accepting as the ultimate test of their performance the approval of men and women who, as civilians, do not value the honor of military victory above all else.

A similar point can be made about the commerce power, the power to tax and spend, the power to coin and regulate the value of money, and other powers relating to economic matters, like the powers to establish bankruptcy, copyright, and patent laws. Collectively, these powers point to the nation's economic health. Although, as I argued in chapter 3, those who fully accept the Constitution's supremacy must look upon the exercise of constitutional powers as forms of such intrinsically praiseworthy practices or states as autonomy, deliberation, and moderation, the founding generation did not grant powers to the government solely for the pleasure of seeing them exercised.[31] By creating conditions for investor confidence, removing barriers to trade among the states, and giving Congress power to establish a stable monetary system and laws on bankruptcies, foreign commerce, commerce among the states, and so forth, they obviously aimed at an ordering of the nation's energies that would yield something that the electorate would call prosperity, or progress, or material well-being, or something like that—I will call it "the nation's economic health."

Now, as we look through the Constitution's enumerated powers, we must ask what it is plausible to believe the founding generation expected or hoped would come of their proper exercise. Of course, "happiness" must be part of the answer. In addressing the people of New York the 1st *Federalist* referred to the Constitution as "the safest course for your liberty, your dignity, and your happiness."[32] A much more forceful statement of "the public happiness" as the overarching goal and test of our constitutions, prospective and established, is found in the following important, though prolix, passage by Madison in the 45th *Federalist*:

> The adversaries to the plan of the Convention instead of con-
> sidering in the first place what degree of power was absolutely
> necessary for the purposes of the federal Government, have
> exhausted themselves in a secondary enquiry into the possible
> consequences of the proposed degree of power, to the Gov-
> ernments of the particular states. But if the Union, as has
> been shewn, be essential, to the security of the people of
> America against foreign danger; if it be essential to their secu-
> rity against contentions and wars among the different States; if
> it be essential to guard them against those violent and oppres-
> sive factions which embitter the blessing liberty, and against
> those military establishments which must gradually poison its
> very fountain; if, in a word the Union be essential to the hap-
> piness of the people of America, is it not preposterous, to
> urge as an objection to a government without which the ob-
> jects of the Union cannot be attained, that such a Government
> may derogate from the importance of the Governments of the
> individual States? Was then the American revolution effected,
> was the American confederacy formed, was the precious blood
> of thousands spilt, and the hard earned substance of millions
> lavished, not that the people of America should enjoy peace,
> liberty and safety; but that the Governments of the individual
> States, that particular municipal establishments, might enjoy a
> certain extent of power, and be arrayed with certain dignities
> and attributes of sovereignty? We have heard of the impious
> doctrine in the old world that the people were made for kings,
> not kings for the people. Is the same doctrine to be revived in
> the new, in another shape, that the solid happiness of the peo-
> ple is to be sacrificed to the views of political institutions of a

different form? It is too early for politicians to presume on our
forgetting that the public good, the real welfare of the great
body of the people is the supreme object to be pursued; and
that no form of Government whatever, has any other value,
than as it may be fitted for the attainment of this object. Were
the plan of the Convention adverse to the public happiness,
my voice would be, reject the plan. Were the Union itself inconsistent with the public happiness, it would be, abolish the
Union. In like manner as far as the sovereignty of the States
cannot be reconciled to the happiness of the people, the voice
of every good citizen must be, let the former be sacrificed to
the latter. How far the sacrifice is necessary, has been shewn.
How far the unsacrificed residue will be endangered, is the
question before us.[33]

But the "public happiness" or the "real welfare of the people" or,
as in the discussion of chapter 3, our view of the "good society"—
these and similarly general ideas constitute only part of an answer to
the question of what the Constitution envisions, for the Constitution's
explicit grants of power indicate ends that are a little more specific.
That more specific ends are indicated does not begin to eliminate
disagreement on how constitutional powers should be understood and
applied, but it does show that whatever our best theory of what the
Constitution does envision, the Constitution cannot accommodate all
views of happiness and the good society. I showed this earlier when
I discussed the constitutional inflexibility that followed from the fact
that laws had to be recognizable to those who were less than completely virtuous, and when I rejected the notion that there could be
such a thing as a set of governmental procedures that is genuinely
"neutral" toward conflicting values.[34] We come, therefore, to the
question: What are the ends envisioned by the Constitution's several
grants of power? These will be the specific goals that constitute the
Constitution's version of the public happiness.

Bearing in mind the discussion in chapter 3 about the need to find
independent value in the practice of following the Constitution's procedures and what I said at the beginning of this chapter about ac-
commodating its conclusions to the findings of later chapters on constitutional rights and institutions, I submit the following as a more
or less defensible statement of the ends envisioned by the Constitution's various grants of power:

1. national security, including an image of respectibility among nations;[35]
2. a measure of law-abidingness in the pursuit of social goals;[36]
3. the nation's economic health;[37]
4. openness to the inclusion of other populations and territories as new states;[38]
5. a uniform code of naturalization, a single set of criteria of United States citizenship, and more or less uniform criteria of state citizenship;[39]
6. a nation of free men and women[40] enjoying certain personal rights (like speech and due process) against both their state and national governments,[41] and living in an equally protective state of affairs in which all feel that their achievements and stations are the fair results of what is or would have been their personal choices;[42] and
7. a society of aware and active citizens whose values fit them to see the ways of the Constitution as a reflection of some of their personal aspirations and as a model for their conduct toward each other.[43]

Consider this list as one observer's preliminary view of the ends envisioned by the Constitution's grant of powers, a hypothesis duly attended by the reservations and doubts mentioned earlier as characteristic of those who want fully to accept the Constitution's supremacy and therefore who seek to reaffirm it—those, that is, who continually aspire to improve their own conceptions of the good society and constitutional meaning.[44] Because this self-critical attitude is essential to a constitutional frame of mind, and because it can destroy any particular hypothesis, it is not a matter of immediate importance here for me to defend all the details of my particular version of the Constitution's ends. I hope the reasons for the general picture will be clear enough by the conclusion of this book. What is more important now is to show how general ideas like those in this proposed set of ends can influence decisions as to what the government is authorized to do. When I say that a certain end is envisioned by a constitutional power or group of constitutional powers, I mean that that end constitutes what, for now, seems to be the best reason for granting those powers in the first place. I address the question of why a whole community like the founding generation would vest a government with economic and foreign affairs powers, for example;

and the best answer—again, for now—seems to involve the economic health and security of the whole nation. With this in mind, let us turn to the central question in the area of state-federal relationships: Can the national government construe its powers in ways that authorize whatever measures might serve to bring about these general ends? Because of the nature of constitutional ends, I believe we must eventually answer this question with a qualified yes.

On different occasions different opponents of national power might contend that Congress cannot employ its powers in whatever manner it thinks necessary to achieve the ends indicated by its grant of powers because (1) under some circumstances Congress may feel that its authorized ends entail the violation of constitutional rights (consider the conflict between national security and free speech and press in wartime); (2) one institution of the government may believe the ends of government cannot be achieved without the suspension or abolition of another institution (thus, proposals have been made to suspend elections in emergencies, and to abolish the jurisdiction of the Supreme Court in controversial cases, like those involving busing, school prayer, and abortion); (3) to achieve its ends the national government may want to encroach upon the powers of the states (thus, the nation's economic health, as Congress sees it, may require that the state governments pay their employees the federal minimum wage). As I have suggested and as I shall argue at greater length in the next two chapters, we can remove the first two objections to a generous view of national power by conceptualizing the practices of honoring constitutional rights and following institutional norms as essential aspects of the government's authorized ends.[45] The nation whose security is sought would therefore be the nation that continues to honor constitutional rights and institutional norms, regardless of the sacrifices. Whether such a nation is viable in all circumstances is doubtful; but, as civil libertarians have pointed out, nations are at least partly constituted by what they say they stand for, and to that extent *this* nation is destroyed as much by violating constitutional rights as it would be by military conquest.[46] In its uncompromising form, this proposition may appear unrealistic—too idealistic, one might say. I remind the reader, however, that constitutional law is a complex of practices and beliefs and that this complex has its ideal dimension. One need only reflect on the fact that few would deny it would be better if national security could be achieved with no compromise of constitutional rights and institutional norms, or that as matters got progressively worse for constitutional rights and institutions, sooner or later most of us would agree that the nation was not what it used to be. Judgments like these are explained in part by the presence of a constitutional ideal in our thinking, and it is this ideal that I wish to bring to light in this book.

The question here, then, is whether the national government can lawfully pursue its authorized ends even when doing so conflicts with the policies of the states. The general answer to this question must be yes. If one agrees that Congress is authorized to pursue x; and if one believes x is what Congress is really after, the necessary and proper clause of Article I, section 8, and the supremacy clause of Article VI favor the conclusion that Congress may pursue x even if that should involve overriding or defeating the policies of the states. This was John Marshall's theory in *McCulloch* v. *Maryland* (1819).[47] I regard *McCulloch* as a case of unrivaled importance for the central problem of constitutional theory: the controlling values of American life. I may not persuade the reader to see this much in *McCulloch*. But virtually every student of this subject will agree that *McCulloch* is far and away the leading decision in the area of state-federal relationships, and most would also consider it the best theory, despite a recent, and apparently arrested, departure by the Burger Court.[48] I shall review in detail some of Marshall's argument in *McCulloch*, for as familiar as its outlines are, its implications are not always fully understood.

McCulloch asked whether Congress could incorporate a national bank despite the failure of Article I, section 8 explicitly to authorize the creation of corporations. *McCulloch* also asked whether the state of Maryland, whose policy opposed a national bank, could tax the Maryland branch of the national bank, as the state had done in an effort to put the branch bank at a competitive disadvantage with state-chartered banks. The Court decided that Congress could charter the bank as a means to authorized national ends and that Maryland could not tax the bank consistently with the supremacy clause, which mandates the supremacy of national laws "made in Pursuance" of the Constitution "any thing in the Constitution or Laws of any State to the contrary notwithstanding." *McCulloch* was concerned with the Second Bank of the United States, chartered by Congress in 1816. Congress had chartered an earlier bank in 1791. The First Bank had precipitated a major constitutional debate between two members of President Washington's cabinet—Treasury Secretary Hamilton, who favored the bank and who defended a loose or liberal construction of national powers, and Secretary of State Jefferson, who defended a narrow or strict construction of national powers from a belief that the prerogatives of the states might otherwise be destroyed and the national government might cease to be one of enumerated powers. Hamilton's views were more persuasive with Washington. The Jeffersonians were in power in 1811 when the charter was up for renewal, and Congress permitted the First Bank to die. By 1816, however, the nation's economic difficulties had moderated the strict constructionism of Jefferson's party, and Congress chartered the Second Bank with President Madison's approval.[49]

Marshall began his opinion in *McCulloch* by alluding to the history of the bank controversy up to that time. He made two preliminary but important observations, noting that the national bank had become a "practice of the government," and that in certain kinds of constitutional questions, though not in all, the fact that something had become a practice should be taken into account. Past practices should have some weight in doubtful questions involving the scope of constitutional powers, though, presumably, they should have less weight in easy questions concerning power and in questions involving what he called "the great principles of liberty." He noted that arguments favoring the bank had survived both a fair and open debate "in the executive cabinet" and the test of the nation's experience with the First Bank. "It would require no ordinary share of intrepidity," he said, "to assert that a measure adopted under these circumstances was a bold and plain usurpation, to which the Constitution gave no countenance."[50]

Marshall thus suggested that judges in doubtful cases of national power vis-à-vis the states should respect the considered opinions of Congress and the nation. He did not suggest, however, that judges should simply defer to others in doubtful cases of power, for he himself went on to give a carefully reasoned defense of what Congress had done, and he would not not have exerted himself in this way had he acted on a maxim of responding to doubt with simple deference.

What, then, might justify Marshall's suggestion that practice and the considered opinions of others are more weighty in some kinds of cases than others? One possible reason for this statement seems fairly obvious. We are typically more inclined to give others the benefit of the doubt in matters of lesser importance than in matters of greater importance. Marshall may have felt that questions involving the great principles of liberty had some special importance that should make judges less deferential to the opinions of others than they might be in other kinds of cases. We shall see a basis for this when I analyze the logic of constitutional rights in the next chapter. Having said what he did about considerations due the nation's past decisions, however, Marshall nevertheless went on to treat the question of Congress's power to incorporate a bank as if it were "entirely new."[51] By doing so, he indicated that even when deference is due a congressional act, the Court should be able to justify the act by finding a place for it within a theory of what the Constitution envisions.

Maryland had argued that the powers of the national government had been delegated by the states, but that the states had retained sovereignty, and therefore that national powers should be exercised in subordination to the states. Marshall disagreed. The powers of the national government, he said, had been granted by the people of the whole nation, who had followed Article VII and used conventions in the states to ratify the Constitution, thus bypassing the state legislatures as repositories of state sovereignty. Marshall also argued that Maryland's theory would give the representatives of a part of the nation the power to bind the representatives of the whole nation. He invoked the language of the supremacy clause to support his conclusion that "the government of the Union, though limited in its powers, is supreme within its sphere of action" and "must necessarily bind its component parts."[52] As for whether a given act was within Congress's power, Marshall suggested that grants of power should be understood as authorizations to pursue certain kinds of ends. Speaking perhaps not as clearly as he could have, Marshall said that the Constitution, unlike a legal code, marks only "its great outlines," designates only "its important objects . . . and the minor ingredients which compose those objects [should] be deduced from the nature of the objects themselves."[53] The meaning of this statement emerges in a passage closely following:

> Although, among the enumerated powers of government, we do not find the word "bank" or "incorporation," we find the great powers to lay and collect taxes; to borrow money; to regulate commerce; to declare and conduct a war; and to raise and support armies and navies. The sword and the purse, all the external relations, and no inconsiderable portion of the industry of the nation, are entrusted to its government. It can never be pretended that these vast powers draw after them

others of inferior importance, merely because they are inferior. Such an idea can never be advanced. But it may with
great reason be contended, that a government, entrusted with
such ample powers, on the due execution of which the happiness and prosperity of the nation so vitally depends, must also
be entrusted with ample means for their execution. The power
being given, it is the interest of the nation to facilitate its execution. It can never be their interest, and cannot be presumed
to have been their intention, to clog and embarrass its execution by withholding the most appropriate means.[54]

In the second sentence of this passage from *McCulloch* is a proposition
widely disputed by commentators on the Constitution: that the Constitution entrusts *all the external relations* of the nation to the national
government. Many have felt that if this were true the list of expressed
powers over foreign affairs would be longer than it is, that it would
provide for a great deal more than foreign commerce, war, ambas-
sadors, the military, naturalization, territories, and treaties.[55] The
document fails expressly to refer to deporting aliens, for example, or
purchasing territory from other nations, or intelligence gathering,
selling arms, paying ransom, foreign bases, international organiza-
tions, cultural exchanges, executive agreements, and so on. Are we
to infer, then, that power involving these other things is reserved to
the states, as the language of the Tenth Amendment might suggest?
Certainly not, say the commentators. Common sense supports the
need for uniformity in foreign affairs, and if common sense were not
enough, state incompetence in this area could be inferred from provisions of Article I, section 10, against states entering into treaties
or alliances, granting letters of marque and reprisal, taxing most
imports or exports, keeping troops and ships of war in peacetime,
and engaging in wars of their own. So, the commentators say, the
states cannot fill in the gaps in the foreign affairs powers, and it would
be unthinkable for the national government to have less than a full
complement of powers vis-à-vis other nations. Therefore, they conclude, powers are missing here, and the missing powers must come
from some source other than the Constitution, such as the right of
self-preservation, or the attributes of national sovereignty—that is,
the attributes people expect of any entity called a sovereign government.

   In contrast to this kind of thinking, Marshall's approach in *McCulloch*
eliminates the need for inventing a source of power other than the

Constitution. By holding that the Constitution grants power to the national government over all of the nation's external relations, Marshall reasoned as if the expressed grants of power authorized the pursuit of desirable ends and that power to pursue these ends implied the grant of other powers as means to the ends. One could say that the power to establish an air force, for example, is implicit in the general authorization to defend the nation, and the evidence for the existence of this general authorization is the expressed power to raise and support armies and navies. This, I think, is the best approach to deciding what the Constitution authorizes because, to continue with the example, granting the power to raise and support armies and navies would be perverse if it were motivated by no further objective or by some end other than national defense. If national defense were indeed the end in mind, it would be equally perverse to prohibit means to that end that were either similar in nature to or traditionally associated with the means expressly provided, as an air force or an intelligence operation would be to an army.

Perhaps few would quarrel with this derivation of Congress's power to establish an air force or an intelligence agency. But can a principle of general application be established through examples like these? In one of *McCulloch's* best-known passages Marshall attempted to state a general principle of state-federal power when he upheld the bank as a means to supporting the fiscal operations of the national government: "Let the end be legitimate, let it be within the scope of the Constitution, and all means which are appropriate, which are plainly adapted to that end, which are not prohibited, but consist with the letter and the spirit of the Constitution, are constitutional."[56] This famous statement is widely thought to favor a very enlarged view of national power. But, obviously, it is not as permissive as it would have been had it simply read, "Let the end be within the scope of the Constitution, and all means plainly adapted to that end are constitutional." As the language of *McCulloch* stands, some means might be good as mere means but inappropriate nonetheless or inconsistent with the letter and the spirit of the Constitution. What would we say, for example, if Congress nationalized the country's educational systems as a means to insuring good citizens—i.e., citizens who see the ways of the Constitution as a reflection of their attitudes toward each other, in accordance with the final end envisioned by my account of the Constitution's objectives. After all, the Constitution says nothing explicit about reserving the education power to the states, and if some states are determined, for example, to perpetuate bigotry and zealotry in derogation of the Constitutions's principles, the enforcement provisions of the Civil War amendments and the guarantee clause of Article IV could easily enable one to say that a nationalized educational system is a means to authorized national ends. Although one can say this and remain within the limits of constitutional language, however, one can still wonder whether such a move would be an appropriate means or one consistent with the spirit of the Constitution. Can the spirit of the Constitution be too far removed from historical understandings like the one concerning state responsibility for the development of young minds?

The typical situation in which we would have to confront this issue would find Congress attempting to displace the states in some activity the states are used to performing. But since we could say in such instances that most of the states were represented in the decision made by Congress, occasions for confronting state challenges to national authority are also those in which one state or a handful of states insist that they have a right to go their own special way, contrary to the considered preferences of the nation as a whole. Congress could decide to nationalize the education function, for example, only when the representatives of the nation and most of the states had decided that the time had come for that. If this decision were made in a fully constitutional way, those who voted for the move would believe that they were pursuing an objective they were authorized to pursue. They would believe the objective legitimate and envisioned by the Constitution; they would believe the means appropriate under the circumstances, plainly adapted to their objective, consistent with the letter (which, again, does not say that the states shall or that Congress shall not educate people) and also with the spirit of the Constitution, since their best understanding of that spirit would be precisely what would move them to act. As always, the representatives of the nation might be wrong, as they themselves would have to concede if their attitudes were fully constitutional, and the handful of states might be right. Under the circumstances of this hypothesis, however, to advance the debate in their direction the handful of states would have to appeal to more than the raw fact that they had grown accustomed to exercising a power over education.

Of course, the handful of states would not say, "We have always done this sort of thing, and therefore we have a right to do it." If that were a good argument no one would ever be right in changing the status quo. We could then have no idea of changing things for the better or even preserving things the way they are, for we do not think of actively preserving things until we perceive forces working for change, and since these forces are themselves parts of the status quo we could not exert ourselves against them consistently with our professed beliefs and principles about the status quo. The handful of states would have to find a different argument, therefore, and probably the first that would occur to them would be, "The states have traditionally exercised the education power, and the Constitution embodies our traditions." Before we could agree with this new argument, however, we would have to know what is meant by *tradition*, for the word could refer either (1) to a description of what we have always done or are used to doing or what we used to do, or (2) to a theory of what we stand for as a people—what we ought to have been doing and should continue to do whether we have, in fact, done it or will do it. If by "tradition" the states intend the first definition, they would lapse into the indefensible—actually, incoherent—proposition that they have a right to do whatever they have been doing. They would be confusing tradition with history in the sense of history as a generalized account of what has been done or what has happened. They might be brought to see the mistake of confusing history with tradition by reflecting on how they would react should someone say, "America has a tradition of bigotry and racial exploitation." This is a proposition they could and probably would reject even if they allowed that all or almost all Americans were bigots and gave every sign that they would remain bigots. One would find it easier to accept the proposition that we had a *history* of bigotry and racial exploitation; but to say that we have a *tradition* of these vices is to engage in critical irony or sarcasm, for it implies that we think this is what we have always stood for as a people. One could be excused for believing that we, in fact, do not have a tradition of bigotry and racial exploitation, partly because virtually no official document says this is what we stand for and partly because most Americans rationalize their prejudices whereas few, if any, have openly proclaimed pride in what they have admitted to be an indefensible hostility to others on account of race. We would surely be puzzled should someone say, "I am proud that [i.e., I feel others should honor me in a special way because] I have likes and dislikes I cannot justify to others."

History can hardly count as tradition, then, for if it did, we could not criticize our historical conduct in light of our traditions. It would make no sense to say that anything we have done or suffered conflicts with our traditions. Nor could tradition be invoked as a reason for acting in some ways as opposed to others, for, if tradition were merely the patterns, conditions, or events of our past, we would have con- flicting traditions, and therefore reasons for and against the same act. In appealing to tradition, therefore, the recalcitrant states would have to be understood as appealing not to historical facts of our past, but to a normative theory of what has always been and therefore still is best in us as a people. With respect to their position on the education power, they would be saying, "What remains best for the nation as a whole is a diversity of educational objectives." If they were incor- porating this proposition into a fully conscious constitutional argu- ment, they would be saying, "The Constitution envisions a diversity of educational objectives."

This would not speak to the problem under examination, however, because we are hypothesizing not mere diversity, but a clashing di- versity. In our hypothesis, the representatives of most of the states believe that a handful of states is using official power to impose beliefs on the young that would encourage opposition to the open and self- critical frame of mind essential to understanding and accepting the Constitution's authority, essential even to an informed and therefore free and voluntary rejection of the Constitution. The recalcitrant states would hardly claim that the Constitution envisions a state of affairs in which the states operate programs that destroy the possibility of constitutional government and a constitutional citizenry. If pressed, they would eventually claim that the Constitution envisions no par- ticular set of attitudes in its citizens—that the Constitution is a value- neutral set of procedures in the service of as many different attitudes as resources permit or, in principle, all attitudes. Since they would say they have the education power and Congress does not, the states in our hypothesis would claim that they, unlike the national govern- ment, could actively pursue illiberal styles of life. Of course, if acted upon, this claim would create serious constitutional problems in light of the guarantee clause of Article IV, the nationalization of the Bill of Rights, and other constitutional provisions and developments. It would only be a matter of time, for example, before the inculcation of religious values in the schools would result in state violations of the establishment clause outside the schools. Leaving these other problems aside, however, the hypothetical states' rights argument against the nationalization of the education power has been reduced to the theory of the value-neutral constitution and, therewith, to absurdity, for, as we have seen, that kind of constitution cannot exist—cannot even be imagined.[57]

So far, the argument I am presenting favors the following position: The powers of the national government should be construed in terms of authorized national ends, and if one agrees that Congress has the power to pursue a certain end, the national government may pursue it even if it should require overriding the policies of the states and displacing state agencies in the exercise of their accustomed functions. The states' rights advocates have not yet refuted this conclusion; but there are arguments they have not yet used. One line that remains open to them is that the nationalist position favored here would altogether eliminate from constitutional theory the old and honored idea of enumerated powers. Surely, they would say, if one can defend a move to nationalize power to educate the young, not much remains that one cannot rationalize as a national responsibility, given the right circumstances. Here is a serious attack on the nationalist view favored by my argument, and even though I think the attack will prove wrong, I concede immediately that there is much to it.

In *McCulloch* the state of Maryland argued that the Constitution did not authorize the making of all laws within the compass of its authorized ends. Marshall summed up Maryland's reading of the necessary and proper clause as follows:

> But the argument on which most reliance is placed, is drawn from the peculiar language of this clause. Congress is not em-powered by it to make all laws, which may have relation to the powers conferred on the government, but such only as may be *"necessary and proper"* for carrying them into execu-tion. The word *"necessary"* is considered as controlling the whole sentence, and as limiting the right to pass laws for the execution of the granted powers, to such as are indispensable, and without which the power would be nugatory. That it ex-cludes the choice of means, and leaves to Congress, in each case, that only which is most direct and simple.[58]

Marshall disagreed that the word *necessary* had to mean "absolutely necessary"; he argued that by consulting the common, everyday usage of the word *necessary* "we find that it frequently imparts no more than that one thing is convenient, or useful, or essential to another."

As for the fact that necessary sometimes means "absolutely necessary,"

> [s]uch is the character of human language, that no word con-
> veys to the mind, in all situations, one single definite idea; and
> nothing is more common than to use words in a figurative
> sense. Almost all compositions contain words, which, taken in
> their rigorous sense, would convey a meaning different from
> that which is obviously intended. . . . This word, then, like
> others, is used in various senses; and, in its construction, the
> subject, the context, the intention of the person using them,
> are all to be taken into view.[59]

With this, Marshall went on to argue that the very enterprise in which
the framers were engaged made it most implausible to say that they
intended to restrict the laws of Congress only to those that, in various
circumstances, had to be enacted lest the desiderata envisioned by
the Constitution be lost altogether:

> The subject is the execution of those great powers on which
> the welfare of a nation essentially depends. It must have been
> the intention of those who gave these powers, to insure, as far
> as human prudence could insure, their beneficial execution.
> This could not be done by confining the choice of means to
> such narrow limits as not to leave it in the power of Congress
> to adopt any which might be appropriate, and which were
> conducive to the end. This provision is made in a constitution
> intended to endure for ages to come, and consequently, to be
> adapted to the various crises of human affairs. To have pre-
> scribed the means by which government should, in all future
> time, execute its powers, would have been to change, entirely,
> the character of the instrument, and give it the properties of a
> legal code. It would have been an unwise attempt to provide,
> by immutable rules, for exigencies which, if foreseen at all,
> must have been seen dimly, and which can be best provided
> for as they occur. To have declared that the best means shall
> not be used, but those alone without which the power given
> would be nugatory, would have been to deprive the legislature
> of the capacity to avail itself of experience, to exercise its rea-
> son, and to accommodate its legislation to circumstances. If
> we apply this principle of construction to any of the powers of
> the government, we shall find it so pernicious in its operation
> that we shall be compelled to discard it.[60]

Marshall's theory of the necessary and proper clause is supported by Hamilton's statement in the 33rd *Federalist* that the inclusion of the clause had added nothing of substance to the Constitution because the power to exercise the powers of government was implicit in the very grant of powers. The necessary and proper clause had been added to the enumeration of powers in Article I, section 8, "only . . . for greater caution," said Hamilton, "and to guard against all cavilling refinements in those who might hereafter feel a disposition to curtail and erode the legitimate authorities of the Union."[61] *The Federalist,* then, testified against Maryland's contention that the necessary and proper clause was intended as a restriction on national power. Despite such support, however, opposition to Marshall's theory was strong: Here, said Marshall's critics, was a theory that would eventually consolidate all of the powers of government in Congress, contrary to the idea of enumerated national powers.[62] The critics may have had an unanswerable point.

To see why, one need only look a little further into what is involved in granting powers to a government—keeping in mind that powers must be understood as means to ends. Authorizing the doing of something is difficult to describe, and I do not have a full account of it to give. But it seems roughly true that when we authorize someone to do x (assuming we do so without reservation and that we really mean what we say) we tell him, at least, that we expect him to take steps that will get x done. As in every unequivocal case of doing x, we can tell in advance that the actor or agent will in some sense intend to get x done. We know in advance, for example, that wherever there is a clear and genuine act of window-opening someone intends to move a window from a closed to an open state. What cannot be known in advance is each move an agent will have to make to do anything as complex as effectively regulating commerce among the several states. This seems analogous to simpler acts, for even if we were to keep the same window over the years, never replacing it with a different or newer style, our agent could go through an indefinite number of physical moves in changing circumstances to get the window open, and it would not be possible for us fully to describe those moves in advance.[63]

It would be debatable, though correct, as I shall show momentarily, to say in advance that whenever Congress regulated commerce, Congress would be moved by something virtually everyone would describe, at first blush, as an economic purpose of some sort. In the terms of my proposed list of nationally authorized ends, it could be said in advance that Congress would be aiming at some version or other of the nation's economic health. But one cannot say much more than this in advance, for the steps that could be taken in pursuit of the nation's economic health seem unpredictable, especially in view of changing technologies, changing resource levels, and changing conceptions of what economic health is. If we really mean what we say, therefore, authorizing the regulation of commerce is authorizing any law whose most appropriate justification is the nation's economic health—it is authorizing Congress to act whenever Congress has economic reasons for acting. Taking no other constitutional authorization into account, this would come close to telling persons of a certain type—the type whose life is governed by the desire for economic health—that their kind can use government to do whatever they characteristically want to do. Recalling now the other authorized ends I proposed earlier and taking them all together in a rough way, the Constitution would be saying, in effect, that as long as they follow certain procedures (essentially designed to insure deliberation and moderation), people of a certain kind shall govern themselves and others—people, basically, whose governing desires put the secular values of economic health and the practice of honoring certain human rights above those versions of aesthetic, cultural, religious, and other values that come into conflict with economic health and honoring rights. If powers anticipate ends, superior powers imply superior values and the greater claim to power of those who have the right values. Those persons interested in profits, for example, are recognized as worthy of political power in this regime, whereas those who put the highest value on racial integrity and the love of God are not. I say this because the former can enact their typical preferences into law. The latter cannot—which is to say that the latter cannot form themselves into communities with a constitutional right to enact laws for their preservation, call those communities what you will: states, towns, company towns, Jonestowns, school districts, neighborhoods. If Marshall was right about the necessary and proper clause, therefore, the enumeration of powers may be something of an illusion, for the Constitution would have installed the undifferentiated rule of a certain kind of liberalism whose power depends solely on its remaining true to form.

Even if Marshall's position entails this result (and I think it does), his theory need not be inconsistent with the belief that the government is one of enumerated powers, for a sense of "enumerated powers" is preserved in the proposition that the government can act only if it has certain reasons for acting. When Marshall's critics attacked *McCulloch* as a harbinger of a completely centralized government, Marshall took to the newspapers under a pseudonym and reminded the critics that *McCulloch* had reaffirmed that the government was one of enumerated powers. He noted that a passage of the Court's opinion in *McCulloch* had even said: "Should Congress, in the execution of its powers, adopt measures which are prohibited by the Constitution; or should Congress, under the pretext of executing its powers, pass laws for the accomplishment of objects not entrusted to the government; it would become the painful duty of this tribunal, should a case requiring such a decision come before it, to say that such an act was not the law of the land."[64] Marshall thus recognized the possibility that Congress could abuse its powers by using them as means to unauthorized ends. This might be attempted through pretext—that is, through dishonestly pretending to pursue objectives one is not really pursuing in order to hide one's real purposes. Many examples of pretextual uses of power exist, especially in this century. Congress was hardly moved by what it and the nation understood as economic objectives on occasions when it employed the commerce clause against lotteries, immoral sexual practice, antiwar protest, and racial prejudice.[65] Neither Congress nor the nation had an efficient postal service in mind or improved communication between different parts of the country when it used its postal power as a tool against gambling, pornography, contraception, and abortion.[66] Congress did not have revenue, national security, the gross national product, or human rights in mind when it used its taxing power to regulate gambling and sales of marijuana.[67]

When I say that on certain occasions Congress used its powers pretextually, I allege a disjunction between what everyone knew Congress's purposes to be (from the way the problems were described in congressional and public debate) and what Congress chose to say it was doing when the time came to draft a statute in anticipation of the need to defend it later in court. I am not saying it is impossible for gambling and drug abuse to constitute problems for the nation's security and economic health, for I believe they do. When Congress comes to see such problems as obstructing the enjoyment of nationally authorized ends, it has power to move against these problems as long as it honors individual rights and the basic arrangement of institutions and offices. On occasions like these, Congress need not honor states' rights. But Congress still has no constitutional power to act when it is moved by reasons that only the states, if anyone, can lawfully invoke. These reasons concern educational practices and conditions that do not involve a threat either to the nation's economy or to national security and individual rights; sexual and other forms of personal morality not defeating nationally authorized ends; and ends like highway safety, to the extent that nationally authorized ends such as a favorable balance of payments and an independent foreign policy are not linked to safety-related policies, like the 55 m.p.h. speed limit.

To see what is wrong with pretextual uses of power, consider the appeal of Senator Winston L. Prouty before the Senate Commerce Committee when it was preparing to recommend passage of the 1964 Civil Rights Act as an exercise of the commerce power. Despite the effort of some of the bill's supporters to compile statistics about the economic impact of segregation in hotels, restaurants, and other public accommodations, those favoring passage of the bill were moved to vindicate a certain conception of human dignity; they were not really concerned about the gross national product, the distribution of property in American society, or other aspects of the nation's economic health. Senator Prouty wanted Congress to stand up and say so. Calling the results of discrimination "vicious affronts to human dignity," he saw "new affronts to dignity" in a bill based solely on the commerce clause. "Are we too timid," he asked, "to legislatively recognize the protection of the dignity and humanity of man as a lawful and proper objective of our powers?"[68] Congress, mindful of both principle and precedent, passed the bill as an exercise of the commerce power *and* of the power to enforce the Fourteenth Amendment. This gave the Supreme Court an opportunity to overrule the *Civil Rights Cases* of 1883,[69] which had held that under the Civil War amendments Congress could act directly only against state action, not private action—only, that is, to remedy racial discrimination by or under the authority of the state governments, not discrimination by the private owners of "inns, public conveyances on land or water, theatres, and other places of public amusement." The decision in the *Civil Rights Cases* had been problematic from the beginning for several reasons, including the difficulty of distinguishing private discrimination from what the Court called many kinds of "wrongful acts" supported by "State authority in the shape of laws, customs, or judicial or executive proceedings,"[70] and the arbitrary designation of decisions about the customers of one's business as "private" in a sense of "private" more appropriately applied to such decisions as whom to invite to one's home.

By 1964 the authority of the *Civil Rights Cases* had been eroded by Supreme Court decisions that had expanded the concept of state action to include a variety of discriminatory acts by individuals who were not officials of state and local governments and who were not acting "under color of law." Thus, in 1948 the Court refused to permit state courts in Missouri and Michigan to enforce agreements between property owners not to sell their houses to members of racial minorities. These "restrictive covenants," said the Court in *Shelley* v. *Kraemer*,[71] were not unlawful, but the state courts could not enforce them because it would be unconstitutional for the states to involve themselves in such private acts of discrimination. In 1961 the Court disapproved discrimination in a restaurant operating in part of a building leased from the city of Wilmington, Delaware.[72] In 1963 the Court reversed the trespass convictions of two groups of sit-in demonstrators because it found that state agencies had encouraged their exclusion from lunch counters on racial grounds through a segregation ordinance in one case and the public statements of officials in another.[73] These sit-in cases were in the spirit of *Shelley* v. *Kraemer*, at least insofar as they took a broad view of state involvement in order to combat discrimination. But the sit-in cases avoided saying that the states could not use their trespass laws to protect the property rights of proprietors who wanted to exclude persons from their businesses on grounds of race. Such a decision in the area of public accommodations would have raised questions about the availability of trespass laws for racially motivated exclusions from private homes, private clubs, private schools, and the like. This might have moved the Court to refine its views on the duty of government to protect a right to reject in one's personal life the values one must honor as a citizen of the regime envisioned by the Constitution.

By permitting the use of trespass laws to enforce racist exclusions from homes and private associations the Court need not have encouraged racism or pulled back from its commitment to do its part to end racism in public life or even in private attitudes. The Court could have recognized a sphere of privacy for racists as an unhappy concomitant of the reaffirmation process integral to the Constitution's supremacy. A constitution that depends on reaffirmation is a constitution that risks such failures as widespread racism. A society free of racism is envisioned by the Constitution because those who fully accept the Constitution's supremacy have to look upon themselves as parts of the self-governing sovereign that established the Constitution. This sovereign is both self-critical and sovereign—not willful, and not subject to any authority beyond its power to understand and reaffirm. Members of such a sovereign would strive above all else to be and to be recognized as reasoning creatures in the sense that they accept no authority higher than self-critical reason. The racist does not seek to be and to be recognized as such a creature. He joins the sexist, the zealot, the skeptic, the determinist—all who profess to believe that reason is subordinate to one or another species of imposition or command (e.g., historical, divine, genetic) allegedly beyond the affirming power of reasoning creatures. The patently unconstitutional status of racism, therefore, justifies a serious effort to end it everywhere—but to end it *constitutionally* or in a manner that befits those who are and want to be recognized as reasoning creatures.

The desire to be recognized as reasoning creatures moves constitutionalists to talk to racists in order to show them why it is a mistake to believe they want to be anything less than a part of the supreme authority that established and maintains the Constitution. Racists have to abandon their prejudice as indefensible before they can appreciate what it means to be a reasoning creature and before they can fully recognize other reasoning creatures. They cannot recognize opponents of racism as reasoning creatures if nonracists appear as willful exponents of another prejudice. So the ultimate success of constitutionalists depends on their capacity to enlighten and the capacity of racists to see the reasons why they do not really want to be racists. This requires a serious effort to end racism and other unconstitutional attitudes at the same time that they are permitted to exist if they will. Racists and their unworthy kin must have their place, therefore, despite our having to suffer the injustice of allowing them more of a place than they would allow their critics.[74]

The Civil Rights Act of 1964 gave the Court an opportunity to rethink Congress's role in combating racial discrimination. The act was consistent with the civil rights commitments of the Warren Court, and the Court wanted to uphold it, and did uphold it, unanimously. But the Court did not uphold it as an exercise of Congress's power under the Fourteenth Amendment, for it would have been difficult to do so without overruling or substantially reinterpreting the received reading of the *Civil Rights Cases*. The easy way out lay with the commerce power, and the Court took that course in *Heart of Atlanta Motel* v. *United States* (1964), citing with approval some of the cases in which Congress had used the commerce power as a tool against what the Court itself called "moral wrongs."[75] The separate concurrences of Justices Douglas and Goldberg contained words of regret that the act had not been upheld under the Fourteenth Amendment. From a states' rights point of view, of course, the act was no less offensive under the commerce power than under the Fourteenth Amendment. By 1964 the Warren Court's drive to complete the nationalization of the Bill of Rights was in high gear. So the Court was hardly moved to avoid a review of the *Civil Rights Cases* by a concern for states' rights. A more likely factor in the Court's choice of the commerce power over the Fourteenth Amendment was a sense that the *Civil Rights Cases* had sought to protect not only the rights of the states but also a sphere of individual privacy and freedom of association to which some constitutional value might attach. By failing to confront this problem the Court risked strengthening the charge that it had upheld a measure Congress had no right to enact.[76]

I have outlined a defense of the Civil Rights Act of 1964 that I consider faithful to the Constitution. I consider the act constitutional under the Fourteenth Amendment. We can say today, certainly, that since the states are free to outlaw discrimination in public accommodations, as the Court itself acknowledged in the *Civil Rights Cases*, no fundamental individual right exempts the proprietors of businesses from civil rights laws by government generally, and, as in *McCulloch*, the scope of Congress's power should not be determined with an eye to avoiding decisions the states are used to making. But if the Civil Rights Act is constitutional under the Fourteenth Amendment, the Court erred in upholding it under the commerce clause. As I defend this contention, I ask that the reader keep the purpose of this discussion in mind: Marshall's theory of the necessary and proper clause is a bad theory unless it can be made compatible with some sense of "enumerated powers." This can be done if one is prepared to invalidate pretextual uses of power, as Marshall said the judiciary should do. As enacted under the commerce clause the Civil Rights Act was a pretextual use of power. To permit pretextual uses of power, either by denying that one can usually distinguish the pretextual from the good-faith use of power or by inventing some rule that requires judges and others to abet pretextualism, is to defeat Marshall's theory of the necessary and proper clause by making it vulnerable to the fatal charge that it entails a proposition constitutional theory cannot allow: that ours is in no sense a constitution of enumerated powers. I shall have more to say against pretextualism after I show why the Civil Rights Act should have been treated as a pretextual use of the commerce power.

I have argued that the commerce clause, with other clauses, vests the national government with responsibility for the nation's economic health. I believe this conclusion is implicit in the Constitution. But I concede that the Supreme Court continued to have doubts about this generous view of national power until after the national government was forced by the Great Depression to assume responsibility for the economy. So I have defended a very liberal construction, and one that could easily be attacked for going beyond historical conceptions at the founding which divided commerce into what was later called "interstate" and "intrastate" commerce.[77] I will not defend my theory and the prevailing theory against such an attack beyond recalling what I have already said about construing powers in terms of authorized national ends and the limitations of historical conceptions in constitutional theory. After all, the problem with acts like the 1964 Civil Rights Act is not their suggestion of a more restrictive construction of the commerce clause than the one I am submitting. The problem is the suggestion that there is authorization in that clause for the pursuit of much more than the nation's economic health. Daniel Webster, as counsel for the defendant before the Supreme court in *Gibbons* v. *Ogden* (1824),[78] contended that the commerce power was as extensive as the concept of commerce itself, and that "[a]lmost all the business and intercourse of life may be connected incidentally more or less, with commercial regulations."[79] But though all intercourse (or "commerce," in the broadest sense) may be connected with commercial intercourse, that cannot mean Congress can use the power to regulate commercial intercourse as a means to governing other forms of intercourse. Even if the First Amendment had not been adopted, for example, Congress could not have used its powers over commercial intercourse for the sole or leading purpose of discouraging commerce in religiously, politically, or morally offensive publications. Thus, in the 84th *Federalist* Hamilton could say that the lack of a delegated national power to control the press was one of the reasons for opposing the adoption of a bill of rights:

I go further, and affirm that bills of rights, in the sense and in the extent in which they are contended for, are not only unnecessary in the proposed constitution, but would even be dangerous. They would contain various exceptions to powers which are not granted; and on this very account, would afford a colourable pretext to claim more than were granted. For why declare that things shall not be done which there is no power to do? Why for instance, should it be said, that the liberty of the press shall not be restrained, when no power is given by which restrictions may be imposed? I will not contend that such a provision would confer a regulating power; but it is evident that it would furnish, to men disposed to usurp, a plausible pretence for claiming that power. They might urge with a semblance of reason, that the constitution ought not to be charged with the absurdity of providing against the abuse of an authority, which was not given, and that the provision against restraining the liberty of the press afforded a clear implication, that a power to prescribe proper regulations concerning it, was intended to be vested in the national government. This may serve as a specimen of the numerous handles which would be given to the doctrine of constructive powers, by the indulgence of an injudicious zeal for bills of rights.[80]

The reason Congress cannot use the commerce power to govern all forms of intercourse is that the commerce clause is restricted in scope by its context: The clause appears in a list of *enumerated* powers. As it would be understood now, so it was understood at the time and later made explicit by the Tenth Amendment that the act of enumerating powers implied there were some things the national government could not do. Commerce in this context is a word used to designate a part of all that human beings can do, and therefore it can be assumed that some of the things they do fall outside its scope. If we allow that the word commerce in the commerce clause embraces all forms of human intercourse, the presence of other authorizations in Article I, section 8, cannot plausibly be explained. Moreover, if we concede that the commerce clause does not cover all species of human intercourse, the most plausible hypothesis is that it covers something roughly designated as "commercial" or "economic" intercourse, in the senses of these words that have to do with property, trade, the desire for money, and so forth.[81]

How then do we know if Congress is regulating commerce or if it is doing something else? Congress does not regulate commerce for constitutional purposes whenever it regulates acts of buying, selling, producing, and distributing. If it did, Congress could use the commerce power to enact special regulations for the production and sale of bibles. Under available judicial precedent, Congress could stop bible salespersons from crossing state lines, from using the mails to persuade people to live as the Bible says, and even from using a portion of the community's resources and purchasing power (i.e., their own labor and money) to print bibles for their own consumption.[82] Congress could do all this under the commerce clause and related clauses, and with an open hostility to what the Bible is supposed to stand for. Clearly, if the regulating of commerce is defined in terms of controlling the physical moves people happen to go through when money changes hands or the practices attending and affecting the making of money, the commerce clause would authorize laws controlling "almost all the business and intercourse of life." Because a constitution of enumerated powers could not admit this result, we are left with the alternative of defining the regulating of commerce in terms of Congress's purposes.

To say that Congress is constitutionally regulating commerce, as opposed to doing something else, like discouraging religion, one must believe that Congress's governing purpose is to increase, fairly distribute, or maintain the fair distribution of the wealth of the community. If Congress believes highway safety, to mention one desideratum, is more important than the immediate economic interests of the stockholders and workers of the auto and related industries, it can simply avoid passing laws that conflict with some of the safety policies of the states.[83] If the states are not interested in highway safety, Congress has to accept that choice unless or until the level of accidents begins to hurt the nation's economy, at which time, and to which extent, Congress can enact safety standards as a means to one of its authorized ends, the nation's economic health. As concerns in the area of public safety can become matters of economic concern, so can practices implicating protected rights. One can easily imagine religiously motivated activities that could hurt the economy and thereby come within Congress's reach. Think of possible boycotts against corporations that sponsor television shows with too much sex and violence or whose commercials portray Americans as brainless gluttons, swingers, clowns, and juveniles made not at all in the image of

God. The country would surely be in great economic difficulty if these sorts of boycotts were to catch on, and Congress might want to keep that from happening. In the process, however, Congress might intrude into what some would regard as areas of protected freedoms. Nevertheless, some religious practices can create economic problems, and if we were to confine our considerations solely to the commerce clause, without consulting the First Amendment, Congress could govern religious and other noneconomic practices under appropriate circumstances. Admittedly, this would defeat the enumeration of powers in one sense, for given the proper conditions, no aspect of social life would lie beyond the commerce power. The enumeration of powers in another sense would be preserved, however, because Congress could not act under the commerce power when moved by ends other than the nation's economic health. I say this despite what has happened many times for nearly a century now under a theory of judicial review of congressional acts that schizophrenically refuses to acknowledge that Congress sometimes does pretextually pursue unauthorized purposes.

Had the Court described Congress's acts in terms of what the public knew Congress's purposes to be, the Court could not have upheld uses of the commerce power like those that tried to reach unpopular political views, illicit sexual activity, and other practices whose regulation was unrelated to economic goals.[84] The Court could have upheld many of the social reforms of this century that were aimed at practices that had come to constitute economic problems. These included reforms in working conditions, product quality, advertising practices, and banking that were thought necessary for economic progress. Minimum wage laws, unemployment protection, social security, and other instruments of wealth distribution were also seen as essential for the nation's economic health. Ignoring equal opportunity and the fairness of wealth distribution as ingredients of the nation's economic health, some may have doubted the purity of Congress's intentions with respect to some of these policies and regarding laws against child labor, as well as race, sex, and age discrimination in employment. The facts relating to the implications of a given policy for production and competition may have warranted giving Congress the benefit of the doubt. Congress, however, could and should have removed such doubts by acknowledging responsibility for the national ends authorized by the Civil War amendments, ends that include our best conception of an equally protective state of affairs.

These last examples anticipate an objection to describing Congress's acts in terms of our perceptions of its purposes, for it is true that there is no such thing as a purely economic or even predominantly economic purpose, except, perhaps, among psychopaths. Wealth is usually desired for the sake of other things, like the respect and admiration of others, or the opportunity for play, or the enjoyment of beautiful, interesting, or pleasurable things. For this reason, it might seem impossible for Congress to regulate commerce as I believe we should understand that practice, for I have said one must believe Congress moves primarily by desires to increase, maintain, or distribute the nation's wealth in order to say it is acting under the commerce clause. But I have spoken in terms of what we call "wealth" against a background of values, some of which are usually too pervasive for us to be self-conscious about, rather than wealth pure and simple, whatever that would be. Notions of wealth do not exist in isolation from other values, as can be seen by reflecting on typical American attitudes toward misers and their unused hoards, or the "true wealth" or "true riches" of, say, fundamentalist Islam. Nor does the commerce power exist in isolation from constitutional logic and other constitutional provisions, like the requirements for reaffirmation, due process, and equal protection, all of which envision an equally protective state of affairs. In such a state of affairs all mature persons would feel that their achievements and stations are the results not of prejudice but of reasons they can understand and therefore of what is or would have been their personal choices as members of a common enterprise. Because the commerce power has to be exercised in concert with other constitutional provisions and with the meaning of the Constitution as a whole, and because this depends in turn on our best conception of what the nation stands for, the wealth of *this* nation need not be what other nations would call wealth—not if we take the Constitution seriously. One could not increase the wealth of *this* nation by permitting hunger and exploitation, even if such a policy would yield a higher gross national product. In any case, I do not presuppose a perverse singlemindedness when I say that for us to count what Congress does as a regulation of commerce we have to believe Congress moves primarily by what a broader cultural and constitutional context would permit us comfortably to describe as an economic objective.

I have argued that Congress's actions must be described in terms of what we believe Congress's primary purposes to be if we are to preserve some sense of enumerated powers without resort to the old states' rights doctrine that Congress must abandon its best conceptions of the nation's economic health, national security, and other ends and settle for those conceptions that do not require doing what the states are used to doing. In light of what the nation knew Congress's purpose to be, the public accommodations section of the Civil Rights Act was not an exercise of the commerce power. To say otherwise was to say what everyone knew was not so, thereby undermining the reputations of those who enacted and upheld the law while arming its opponents with evidence that its supporters had real doubts about its constitutionality. When courts and legislatures resort to pretexts like this they help to perpetuate the indefensible notion that the meaning of the Constitution is to be found in what we see as merely historical conceptions, for it was a nineteenth-century conception of Congress's power in the *Civil Rights Cases* that Congress and the Court were trying to get around by enacting the law under the commerce power. Calling the Civil Rights Act a bona fide exercise of the commerce power in 1964 was plausible only if one pretended that the Constitution means whatever the latest historical pronouncement of the Court would have it mean. Pretexts of this kind substitute the appearance of constitutionality for the reality, which reality, as I have shown, reveals itself only to those who accept the responsibility of trying to improve upon historical conceptions in a continuing effort to reaffirm the Constitution as supreme law.

As matters stood after *Heart of Atlanta* was decided, the Court had either (1) refused to overrule what it thought was an erroneous reading of the Constitution in the *Civil Rights Cases*; (2) joined in Congress's pretext to get around what it thought was a correct or partially correct reading; or (3) taken a prudent step toward what it hoped would be the eventual overruling of an old decision whose errors were still alive in the prejudices of Americans. Arguments are available for defending *Heart of Atlanta* as characterized by each of these descriptions. They could not be genuinely constitutional arguments, however, for in each case one or another authority would be placed higher than the authority of the Constitution: either (1) the authority of old judges or, as some might prefer, that of "the judiciary" as an entity that allegedly comes as close as possible in government to an institutionalization of reason itself—"the judiciary," in other words, as something of an alternative constitution; (2) the authority of present-day policy makers, including the present

Court; or (3) the authority of prevailing public attitudes, an authority that sets practical limits on how faithful one can be to the Constitution. Whatever virtue these arguments may have, they cannot claim to be constitutional unless they can be reformulated in ways that put the Constitution in a position of supremacy. Effectively denying that the Constitution can be real law in the here and now, a reformulation of the third argument might hold that the *Heart of Atlanta* Court did have the Constitution uppermost in mind, but as descriptive of an ideal to be achieved in a less than ideal world, and therefore to be achieved prudently, not through the suicidal affirmations preferred by constitutional zealots who scorn compromise and incremental progress for the pleasure of going down with principles ablaze. Obviously, this would be a respectable defense of *Heart of Atlanta* and even of some pretextualist methods generally, though it would not be a purely pretextualist defense because it would acknowledge the authority of a constitutional ideal that lies beyond the historical conceptions at the outer limits of what the pretextualist can see. But it still would not be a constitutional defense. Erstwhile constitutionalists might excuse it if they could prove that Americans are incapable of the self-restraint it takes to be true to their form of government— that, in other words, one can no longer reaffirm the Constitution as the most authoritative expression of this people. Surely there is much evidence that this is so. If this is our situation, however, those who are paid to seek and tell the truth about such things should say so, lest they abet those politicians on and off the bench who flatter people with fictions about their fidelity to their principles.

An adequate theory of nationally authorized ends would have removed much of the need for pretextual uses of power by correcting artificially narrow conceptions of what Congress was authorized to do. But judges and constitutional scholars have not developed such a theory, probably because most of them actually regard the Constitution as a set of commands of men long dead, to be followed or evaded, rather than as the adumbration of an ideal whose content becomes clearer as we strive to live by it. Because there can be no real reasons for obeying commands per se, the Court has made a practice of pretexts for getting around the Constitution when it thinks such moves good for the country. This is why the Court destroyed the enumeration of powers as a meaningful constitutional limitation. Through regulatory legislation or indirectly through its taxing and spending powers, today the national government can pursue virtually any policy it wants in relation to the powers of the states.[85] The nation began its constitutional history with three kinds of legal limitation on government (better, on itself)—powers, rights, and institutional norms. Only the last two remain, or seem to remain. Accordingly, we now understand ourselves in terms of how we should make decisions and what not to do to each other. We have no authoritative theory of constitutional ends or what way of life is worth pursuing or what we ought to be. We can be what we want to be, it is said, as long as we follow the right procedures and do not violate rights. Thus, it would seem, we can be a nation of zealots and racists, if that is what we happen to be, as long as the nation does not act in the manner of zealots and racists.[86]

Some observers believe that whether the collapse of the enumeration of powers is regrettable or not, it was unavoidable because judges should not tell a legislature that it is resorting to pretext. There is something to this argument. If the branches of government are "equal and coordinate," as is often said, judges will be reluctant to adjudge legislatures dishonest. This reluctance is understandable. That is one of the reasons I suggested judges might give legislatures the benefit of the doubt on some of the occasions when an enactment plausibly can be described in different ways, one making it constitutional, the other making it unconstitutional. This would have been enough to validate many of the legislative programs of the welfare state on commerce clause grounds alone, as I have indicated, because many of these laws did aim at what were regarded as economic objectives. Sometimes legislative pretext is undeniable, however, as it would inevitably be in an open society with an electorally responsible legislature and a great deal of discussion and reportage of what is going on in government. So one cannot say that a court ought not to call pretexts because it can never be certain as to when pretext exists. Pretextualists are left with the argument that the deference due equal branches of government in a system of separated powers puts pretext calls beyond judicial competence. This has been the Court's position on and off since the mid-nineteenth century and more consistently since the late 1930s, when it disavowed scrutiny of congressional purposes in order to get around artificial conceptions of "commerce" that had put labor conditions and other aspects of the nation's economic life beyond Congress's reach.[87] An especially regrettable example of this kind of judicial deference occurred in 1968 when the Court upheld a Vietnam wartime amendment to the

Selective Service Act punishing those who knowingly destroyed or mutilated draft cards.[88] It was enough for the Court that the act protected "the smooth and efficient functioning of the Selective Service System." The Court would look no further because "under settled principles the purpose of Congress . . . is not a basis for declaring this legislation unconstitutional." Such disavowals of inquiry into legislative purpose are typical of cases in which the Court knows or suspects something is wrong with the legislature's purpose. One cannot avoid imputing intentions or purposes when applying words that designate actions.[89] If confronted with a choice of competing descriptions of an act (say, "protecting the smooth and efficient operation of the draft" versus "punishing war protestors") one cannot truthfully say that Congress is doing one of these things rather than another unless one forms a judgment of what Congress wants most. A rule that says judges should take Congress's word for what it is doing is a rule that reads the enumeration of powers right out of the Constitution—not to mention the Bill of Rights. Judges who say they cannot call pretexts when they see them are saying that judges cannot apply constitutional rules honestly. The judge-made rule against inquiry into Congress's purposes surely does not enjoy the status of the constitutional principles it directly undermines.

The collapse of the enumeration of powers as a restriction on the national government has been an unconstitutional development. That is not to say, however, that it has been a bad development. On the contrary, error may lie instead with the earlier belief that dimensions of life can be parceled between governments and that the community's greatest power should be permitted to express itself only in military and economic terms. Indeed, madness may lie in separating responsibility for military and economic security from responsibility for moral, aesthetic, and intellectual health. Thus, there may be excellent reasons (or even excellence as a reason) for what has happened to the enumeration of powers. Nevertheless, the enumeration of powers is an essential principle of American constitutionalism. It informs constitutional theory with a hierarchy of objectives that enables us to identify a whole way of life, complete with affirmative commitments as well as procedures and proscriptions—commitments that enable us to transform mere procedures and proscriptions into objects of aspiration and pride. Those well-intentioned liberals who applaud what Court and Congress have done to the enumeration of powers inadvertently support indefensible historical conceptions of Congress's responsibilities and the Constitution as a whole. Most of them ignore Congress's affirmative substantive responsibilities under the Civil War amendments and the guarantee clause, and they do so primarily because they have acquiesced in the authority of old judges and academic value neutrality, despite the fact that there is nothing particularly special about old judges and little that is coherent in academic value neutrality. As they have substituted these strange authorities for the Constitution, liberals have substituted pretext for law and abdicated responsibility for efforts toward a better understanding of what those who accept the Constitution's supremacy are committed to become.

5

Constitutional Rights

$\mathbf{I}$N CHAPTER 3 I AR-
gued that if we are to make sense of the Constitution's transformation
from mere practical proposal to supreme law we must believe that
we would reaffirm the ways of the Constitution as our best conception
of the good society, a state of affairs worthy of our highest aspirations.
In chapter 4 I sketched some of the features of the society adumbrated
by the Constitution's principal grants of power. In general, this is a
secure and prosperous society of active men and women who feel
that their different stations and achievements are, or would have
been, the results of their personal choices and whose attitudes toward
each other are reflected in the structure of their government and its
arrangement of rights and powers. I said we could not complete this
picture without discussing constitutional rights and constitutional institutions. In this chapter I submit a general theory of the nature of
constitutional rights and discuss their influence on the public policies,
legal decisions, and private attitudes of those who really accept the
Constitution's supremacy. We shall see that those who are really
serious about their fidelity to the law would look upon honoring
constitutional rights as their highest political value. They would abandon the crude and unconstitutional notion that rights are interests
held by individuals in tension with the interests of society. They would
not regard the practice of honoring constitutional rights as one merely

of extending guarantees to individuals. Instead, they would see honoring rights as a virtue aspired to by the nation as a whole and all of its parts—that is, by each institution of government, not just the judiciary, and by the citizens as well, individually and collectively.

We have seen that a power of government, like the commerce power, is a rule authorizing the enactment of certain kinds of laws, like regulations of commerce. I have argued that we should determine the scope of governmental powers by asking ourselves what the social purposes are that best explain why people would grant a government powers in the first place. The activity of regulating commerce (as separable from the satisfaction we as autonomous creatures derive from the knowledge that it is our commerce that is being regulated by our representatives in our name) may be an end in itself for the career bureaucrat, but it is not an end in itself for the typical citizen in whose name the Constitution was ratified as supreme law. The power to regulate commerce, with other powers, points instead to the desideratum of a healthy national economy, just as the various war and military powers point to peace and national security. With an eye to the ends that explain and justify the powers of government, we are justified in believing that the Constitution implies powers other than those expressly enumerated. Hence, the implied powers to establish and operate an air force, military academies, and intelligence agencies, and to do thousands of other things not expressly mentioned in the document. Nevertheless, despite the notion of implied powers, the act of enumerating powers implies a limited number of authorized national ends. Thus, the enumeration of powers is itself a limitation on government. Indeed, when contrasted with the act of enumerating rights, enumerating powers can be viewed as the more fitting mode of constitutional limitation in a system of popular sovereignty because, as Hamilton argued in the 84th *Federalist*, the government of such a system is a mere agent whose activities are authorized only by the affirmative grants of the people.[1] As I have noted, Hamilton went on to caution against the adoption of a bill of rights partly because he felt those who would exceed constitutional limitations would construe an enumeration of rights to mean that government did not need to cite affirmative authorizations for its acts—the pretext, in other words, that government could do what it wanted to do short of violating explicit rights.[2]

Because the enumeration of powers is itself a method of limiting government to a few nationally authorized ends, one does not need an enumeration of rights for that purpose. If an enumeration of rights is to tell the government more than what it is already being told by an enumeration of powers, then rights must say more than "do not abridge freedom of the press," or "do not impose cruel and unusual punishments," and so forth. Even without the Bill of Rights the government would not have been authorized to regulate the press or establish a religion per se, as it would have been had it been empowered to pursue ends like excellence in journalism and the love of God. Nor, relative to the death penalty, is the government authorized to honor those ostensibly law-abiding citizens who are said to feel dishonored when the government fails to answer the cruelty of criminals in kind.[3] On the other hand, when the government pursues its authorized ends, it has an indefinite choice of means available to it by virtue of the necessary and proper clause. This choice of means might tempt some to see limitations of press freedoms, establishments of religion, and the imposition of cruel punishments as appropriate means—even, in easily imagined circumstances, utterly necessary means—to national security and other nationally authorized ends. If, then, an enumeration of rights is to do more than prohibit the pursuit of ends outside the enumeration of powers—something already accomplished by the enumeration of powers—then an enumeration of rights will remove certain means from those that would otherwise be available to the government in the pursuit of its authorized ends. In context, for example, the First and Eighth amendments will say something like, "You, the government, shall pursue national security and prosperity except as those ends are thought to require abridging press freedoms, establishing a religion, or imposing cruel punishments." At first blush, therefore, the Bill of Rights is a list of what the framers called various "exemptions" from what the government can do in pursuit of its authorized ends.[4]

This negative or proscriptive understanding is the more common understanding of the Bill of Rights. Constitutional rights, it is believed, are specifications of things the government cannot lawfully do. But if we remind ourselves that the Constitution is phrased less as a command directed to the government than as a declaration that "We the People of the United States" address to ourselves, we might prefer to understand constitutional rights as something different from specified exceptions to what government is authorized to do. The Constitution might be interpreted as declaring, for example, that "We the People seek the security and prosperity of a nation that permits

its policies to be criticized by a free press and rises above the desire for cruel retribution." The Constitution would imply that it is a good thing to be this kind of people. Thus, rights can be understood not only as exemptions from powers but also as ingredients of desirable states of affairs. I shall treat them both ways, and by doing so I can make two kinds of statements about rights. I can say, for example, that as long as the First Amendment is part of the Constitution, Congress cannot employ laws believed to abridge press and other freedoms of expression, even when Congress thinks those laws essential to the nation's security and economic health. This statement views the First Amendment as a set of exemptions from granted powers. I can also say that Congress must conceptualize the nation's prosperity and security in ways that honor freedoms of expression—that, in other words, Congress has a duty to work for the security and prosperity of this nation as a nation that honors the First Amendment. This last statement views the practice of honoring constitutional rights as an aspect of what the nation wants to be.

We recall that the enumeration of powers has an affirmative, forward-looking implication. It suggests desirable states of affairs to be achieved. The enumeration of powers has also a negative implication. Powers not granted are reserved; the government ought not to pursue unauthorized ends. Just as there are good reasons for recognizing the negative implication of the enumeration of powers, there are good reasons for recognizing the affirmative, forward-looking implication of the Constitution's enumerated rights. I argued in chapter 4 that by attending to the negative implication of the act of enumerating powers we would discover ends that, because they are limited in number, constitute a way of life that can be distinguished from other ways of life. The forward-looking implication of enumerating rights refines our understanding of that way of life.

An awareness of the affirmative implication of constitutional rights also enables us to see the weakness of an argument widely used to criticize the proposition that rights are genuine exemptions from the things government can do in pursuit of authorized ends; I call the argument in question the "suicide-pact argument." The suicide-pact argument contends that if we allowed real exceptions to the government's choice of means, government might not be able to do its job at all in many circumstances. Consider what would happen, for example, if domestic protest against an unpopular foreign war were eroding domestic support for the war to the point of making victory impossible in circumstances where the government fully accepted a domino theory of political-military expansion and was therefore convinced that our national security required a military victory. In circumstances like these the government could believe that restricting First Amendment freedoms was essential for the very survival of the nation. Let us assume that we ourselves believed this, for it is easy to imagine circumstances favoring this belief. In such circumstances being told that we cannot use our government to abridge the right to protest the government's policy might be telling us that we cannot save the nation from destruction. For that reason we might be very much opposed to viewing First Amendment rights or any rights as real exemptions from the powers of government. We might want to say instead that rights are values to be taken into account and balanced with other desiderata, like national security, and that if we do not temper constitutional logic "with a little practical wisdom," we will "convert the constitutional Bill of Rights into a suicide pact."[5] We might say, more generally, that by looking upon rights as real exemptions from granted powers we risk the defeat of our most important social goals.

The affirmative side of enumerating rights indicates the weakness of the suicide-pact criticism of rights as real exemptions from powers. Taking the Preamble at face value, and bearing in mind the interest here in explicating the ideal in constitutional law, everything in the Constitution is expressed by the collectivity "We the People of the United States." If we fully accept the Constitution's supremacy, we are prepared to reaffirm the Constitution as supreme law, and, in a way, when we believe we can reaffirm the Constitution we become one with the sovereign authority that established it. At the moment of reaffirmation we ourselves can both grant powers and recognize rights as exemptions from the powers granted. When we reaffirm the Constitution we indicate that honoring rights is an integral part of what we want—that, in other words, we seek security and prosperity not for just any people, but for the people that accepts the ways of the Constitution. The suicide-pact argument errs in assuming an unconstitutional notion of what it means to survive. The suicide-pact argument might be valid if one were to believe that the essentials of a people's makeup is something other than its principles. But the suicide-pact argument cannot be valid if one accepts the Constitution as supreme law. For if one accepts the Constitution one believes that the constitution of *this* people is given therein, and that the national security, domestic tranquility, and economic prosperity that the Constitution envisions—the usual indices of "survival," in other words—must be harmonized with or embody a commitment to honoring certain rights. As doctrinaire and foolishly idealistic as this might appear—and I cannot add to what I have already said in answer to that kind of criticism[6]—a people can commit suicide in several ways, including a retreat from the principles that constitute it as a people or from what it has said that it stands for.

Most of us would still shake our heads impatiently at this kind of talk and go right on begging important questions by insisting that ideals do have to be tempered with some otherworldly notion of reality that arbitrarily excludes the ideals that in fact are present in our understanding of ourselves. Some might even contend that by understanding constitutional rights as real exceptions to what the government can do, we weaken constitutional rights instead of strengthening them because we open the way to precedents for violating rights so conceived—precedents created by what we feel we will inevitably have to do when rights conflict with certain "vital interests." Yet there is no way to prove that we will inevitably violate rights when the going gets rough. Granting that very few of us, if any at all, are truly prepared to make real sacrifices for constitutional rights, that still does not mean it is *impossible* to make such sacrifices. Nor does that mean that those who will not make sacrifices cannot recognize the greater honor due those few who will. Our history, or folklore, certainly has its share of tales about heroic risks and sacrifices in the name of principles above and beyond what the average American would probably call prosperity and national security. The average American does not seem to tire of holidays, parades, monuments, and other observances celebrating these heroic risks and sacrifices. No matter what we might predict about our own behavior in the most dangerous of circumstances, therefore, we can still look down on regimes whose understanding of survival compels them to suppress their critics and stop people from reflecting on how to live and what to believe. Khomeini's Iran comes to mind as a leading example at this writing, along with the Soviet Union, Poland, and Cuba; some of America's past and present "friends," like Iran under the Shah, South Africa, the Philippines, the present regimes in Haiti, El Salvador, and Guatemala; and even this country in the aftermath of the French Revolution and the Japanese attack on Pearl Harbor, and during some phases of the Cold War and the Vietnam War. To the extent that we look down on such regimes and periods, we concede the possibility of acting as if our survival depended upon and included the survival of our principles.

We in fact do criticize regimes that try to survive by violating rights, even though it is not always clear why we do so and what violations of rights we believe we ought to condemn. Some of us criticize regimes that take property from the rich, and we do so because of an alleged right to keep all or most of the property one can get. But if there really were such a right there would be no reason for condemning a regime for keeping all the property *it* can get. Of course, the critics of property-taking regimes do not contend that there is a simple right to property; they say rather that there is a right to property rightfully acquired. When they say "rightfully," they usually refer to or pre-suppose some standard that they believe the holders of property or their representatives have accepted, or that they would have accepted had they been in a position to give the matter their best thought, or had they been in circumstances that would have forced them to give the matter their best thought. But at this point these critics are no longer talking about keeping whatever one can acquire; they are talking about what their best thinking says one ought to have a right to keep. That is often a far cry from what defenders of the rich have in mind. So if there is a right here, it is conditioned on our best thought about what one ought to keep or, better, how one ought to live. For this reason, one cannot always condemn regimes that take property.

Perhaps the regimes that really deserve condemnation are the ones that profess to have reasons to support the claims they make on the allegiance of their people but who nevertheless refuse to permit their people to examine and accept or reject those reasons. These are the regimes that try to silence their critics and eliminate that sphere of personal privacy and material self-sufficiency or independence which we usually presuppose when we think of someone reflecting on how to live or what to believe. We ought not only to fear the physical power of these repressive regimes when they are in a position to use it, we ought to look down on them for pretending to be what they know they are not. Insofar as they criticize other regimes, they imply that reason supports their principles, for it would make no sense to criticize others if there were no reason to believe that one regime is better than another. Although they criticize others, however, these regimes refuse to submit their claims to the test of reason, and this may betray their awareness that their reasons are not real reasons. They may defend suppression by saying that their people are not in a position to reason aright. But this will eventually prove to be an admission of failure to create or maintain the conditions for affirming the claims they continue to make. This failure itself will belie their claims to some degree because making claims presupposes that those to whom they are made are physically, emotionally, and intellectually competent to affirm them or deny them. Instead of submitting reasons, which is what one eventually does with reasons, these regimes would therefore impose ideology while acting as if they had reasons. They deserve our contempt because they pretend to be what they seem to know they are not. They seek the honors that they force their people to pay at the same time that they deny that their people have the competence to judge. I think this is the best justification for criticizing regimes that violate rights. But whatever our reason, the fact is that we do engage in such criticism, and when we do we presuppose either that a nation can make real sacrifices for rights or that it can understand its survival in terms of honoring rights.

At this point someone who wanted to push the suicide-pact argument further might contend that there is no real reason for criticizing regimes that violate rights. It might be said that these regimes cannot be other than what they are, that whatever they may profess, they do what forces beyond their control compel them to do, and that to the extent that our criticism of those who violate rights implies otherwise, our criticism is simply unfounded. But this view is difficult to accept, to begin with, precisely because trying to rise above "accident and force" seems so characteristic of human beings, whether the effort is based on illusion or not. One can wonder, moreover, whether it is fully coherent to say that people cannot act in ways other than the ways in which they are compelled to act by things beyond their control. Positing that very proposition is itself an act. If we were to ask the speaker why he performs that act he would say because he believes the proposition he affirms is true, not because forces independent of its truth compel him to call it true. Finally, in common with other normative statements, the Constitution itself presupposes that planning for the future is possible to some extent, despite the likelihood of events and inclinations contrary to plan. Those who accept the Constitution's supremacy accept this presupposition, whether it is ultimately defensible or not. So, again, one cannot accept the suicide-pact argument and constitutional supremacy at the same time.

Constitutional rights, therefore, are exemptions from granted powers; they remove certain means from those means available to the government for pursuing its authorized ends. That rights so understood will require extreme sacrifices in some circumstances is not enough to compel us to deny that rights are exemptions from powers, for it is not impossible to make such sacrifices. Indeed, the making of sacrifices seems compatible with other aspects of constitutional meaning uncovered in the process of this inquiry so far. I refer to the self-restraint characteristic of the act of making a constitution and the self-critical attitude of those who seek to reaffirm the Constitution's supremacy. A brief review of previous arguments will show that a commitment to honoring constitutional rights is an essential part of the constitutional attitude I have described.

Taking the Preamble at face value, we have seen that the Constitution is more than a law established by one generation for the sake of governing its posterity; it is also an imposition of the founding generation on itself. The language of the Preamble—and therefore at least one small part of its history and our constitutional consciousness—implies an act of sovereign self-restraint. The logic of the document indicates that a continuing practice of sovereign self-restraint is something of an end in itself—not simply something valued as instrumental to other ends. This conclusion resulted from an attempt to understand the supremacy clause. The body of the document was originally a set of means to what we believed would be the good society. However, on ratification this set of means became "supreme Law." Reacting to the anomaly of treating mere means as supreme law, Jefferson once called for new constitutions every nineteen years. While trying to justify the Philadelphia Convention's revolutionary disregard of the provisions for constitutional change in the Articles of Confederation, Madison cited what he called a rule of construction "dictated by plain reason, as well as founded on legal axioms," that where several parts of a commission "cannot be made to coincide, the less important should give way to the more important part; the means should be sacrificed to the end, rather than the end to the means." And so the Articles were sacrificed as inadequate "to the exigencies of the Union."[7] In asking how we could avoid applying this reasoning to the Constitution I argued in chapter 3 that the Constitution's claim to supremacy is at least potentially irrational (in light of its possible failure as an instrument) and unjust (as an imposition of one generation upon another). If we ceased to regard the Constitution as an effective means to the ends of the Preamble, we would be justified in challenging its claim to supremacy on its own terms, for we could say the only thing ratified was what we presumed was an effective set of means. To mitigate the anomaly of calling mere means supreme law we have to see the Constitution's ways as our best current understanding of the good society. Here, for example, would be a society in which it would be reasonable to believe that Congress was regulating commerce successfully while honoring speech, religious freedoms, rights to just compensation, and due process. The Constitution so conceived would not be altogether lacking in instrumental properties, for there would be a difference between what we believed to be our best conception of the good society and the good society itself, and the gap between the two would continue to justify criticism of the document, improvements through amendments, and improvements in our conceptions of the Constitution's general ideas and provisions. Our consciousness of the document as part of a defeasible conception of the good society would make its claim to supremacy depend on the belief that we could continually reaffirm the premises of ratification.

We saw that the Constitution thus presupposes a state of affairs in which it can be reaffirmed, for it is only in that state of affairs that its claim to supremacy approximates coherence. This state of affairs is something of an ideal in the sense of something aimed at but continually beyond final realization. It would be a mistake to view this ideal state of affairs as utopian. The Constitution could not be *law* in utopia, law presupposing as it does an inclination to, and thereby the possibility of, disobedience to what it prescribes. Since reaffirmation would take place in the context of this inclination to disobey (for law would remain the object of reaffirmation), meaningful reaffirmation would presuppose the possibility of the Constitution's rejection. On the other hand, we saw that the Constitution does envision its own reaffirmation—it would remain law, and it would remain law in the face of inclinations contrary to its terms. Accordingly, the reaffirmation presupposed by constitutional logic is performed by those who are aware of their inclinations to disobedience and who, accepting the law's supremacy, seek to reaffirm the law itself and not their conceptions of it. Accepting the Constitution's supremacy in the face of one's inclinations to the contrary could not be done unless one recognized a distinction between one's preferences and the law. Would-be subjects of the Constitution would seek to reaffirm, say, procedural fairness as descriptive of the good society while being sufficiently distrustful of their conceptions of procedural fairness to open them to criticism. Reaffirmation, therefore, entails a self-critical search for the best conceptions of constitutional norms— a search, in other words, for the best in us—and a continuing criticism of constitutional norms as ingredients of the good society—a continuing willingness to ask whether the best in us is good enough.

   In light of the manifold self-criticism integral to reaffirming constitutional supremacy, the maintenance of the Constitution entails a desire really to be good or to achieve goodness as a society rather than merely to proclaim or assert our righteousness. Of course, the Constitution cannot successfully command this desire, but it does presuppose it as a condition for its supremacy, and the desire is felt by those who fully accept the Constitution's supremacy. We want to achieve goodness as a society, and the Constitution implies that the good society is one that does not suppress criticism as a means to national security or deny fairness as a means to personal security and social quietude, no matter how strongly we incline toward these comfortable ends. This forces us to work harder for the end we seek, thereby improving our chances of getting the real thing, not just the appearance thereof.

   Honoring rights is thus an aspect of the larger practice of self-restraint in which those who would reaffirm the Constitution participate. For this reason, one can appropriately call honoring constitutional rights a virtue, by which I mean a self-restraining of the desires for security, comfort, and pleasure. This self-restraint is believed to be an end in itself or an aspect of a self-fulfillment that deserves the admiration of others. This is really the law, and it is possible for us to accept it as law. Whether we will accept it is another matter, to which I shall attend in due course. But let us first consider how these conclusions bear on what many consider the most vexing of constitutional problems: ascertaining the activities protected by constitutional rights.

   Should we say that our state and national governments offend the establishment clause of the First Amendment when they spend some of our tax dollars to help parochial schools and colleges survive in a national educational system dominated by secular public and private educational institutions? Would a state violate the establishment clause by requiring public schools to teach the Bible's story of the origin of the species? Consistently with the First Amendment's freedoms of speech and assembly, can a small number of peaceful and orderly war protestors be excluded from privately owned shopping centers in suburban and other areas where there are few other places of daily congregation for the general public? Can the government, consistently with the Second Amendment, prohibit people from keeping guns designed to kill or stop the aggression of other people? Should the government exclude from criminal trials good evidence obtained through inadvertent failures of the police to follow the law for obtaining search warrants? Should the government be permitted to compel a person to be a witness against himself in exchange for a promise not to prosecute? Is capital punishment consistent with the Eighth Amendment? Does the government have to have a good reason for stopping a person from having an abortion, or from paying employees a substandard wage, or from smoking marijuana?

We look upon these as difficult questions because we do not agree on their answers. There are at least two reasons why most of us regret the occurrence of difficult questions like these: first, because they are difficult, they make us work, and second, until they are answered to everyone's satisfaction, the official answers will appear wrong to some, who then will think that they are deprived of some good thing, contrary to the law of the Constitution. Thinking that such disagreement is a bad thing, judges do their best not just to decide lawsuits, but also to provide answers in ways that aim at eliminating future disagreement. Confronted with disagreements as to what claims are favored by general constitutional ideas, judges and scholars develop formulas, tests, theories, or doctrines to stand in the place of the Constitution's general ideas. These doctrines are then considered successful or not, depending on how well they reduce the disagreements.

Not everyone believes that disagreement about general legal ideas is always regrettable, however. H.L.A. Hart has written that "we should not cherish, even as an ideal, the conception of a rule so detailed that the question whether it applied or not to a particular case was always settled in advance." A rule like this, says Hart, would not serve us well in light of our inability to predict all that will happen in the future and in light of not really knowing what we want until we have had a chance to weigh our original aims against the unanticipated costs. This is why Hart believes a general legal standard often may be preferable to one that is highly detailed.[8] Ronald Dworkin has suggested a better reason, perhaps two, for welcoming constitutional disagreements: These disagreements give us opportunities for making ourselves better people, and the Constitution is worth following because, or to the degree that, it forces such opportunities upon us. This, at any rate, is what I take from a well-known passage in which Dworkin criticizes so-called strict constructionists, who impose on the Constitution a principle of interpretation that confines the meaning of general ideas to particular historical versions of those ideas. Dworkin says:

> But the theory of meaning on which this [strict constructionist] argument depends is far too crude; it ignores a distinction that philosophers have made but lawyers have not yet appreciated. Suppose I tell my children simply that I expect them not to treat others unfairly. I no doubt have in mind examples of the conduct I mean to discourage, but I would not accept that my "meaning" was limited to these examples, for two reasons. First I would expect my children to apply my instructions to situations I had not and could not have thought about. Second I stand ready to admit that some particular act I had thought was fair when I spoke was in fact unfair, or vice versa, if one of my children is able to convince me of that later; in that case I should want to say that my instructions covered the case he cited, not that I had changed my instructions. I might say that I meant the family to be guided by the concept of fairness, not by any specific conception of fairness I might have had in mind.[9]

Dworkin errs in suggesting that his distinction between concepts and conceptions is a philosopher's distinction, not a lawyers's distinction. In fact, lawyers and judges have often made this distinction or equivalent distinctions, as is to be expected from the perfect familiarity of the distinction to common sense, where it is likely to be termed something like the distinction between general ideas and particular versions thereof.[10] I mention this because eristic or even dishonest "strict constructionists" (I put the term in quotes because people who apply it to themselves do not read the Constitution strictly and have little interest in doing so) might seize upon the difference between lawyers and philosophers and say with some justification that they take an oath to be governed by the norms of the former, not the latter. That, of course, would not be the whole story. American lawyers take an oath to be governed by those norms of judging and lawyering that are consistent with constitutional supremacy, and the Constitution, strictly speaking, is an expression of the people, not of the judges and lawyers. So, to the extent that judges and lawyers deny common-sense distinctions or employ distinctions common sense cannot penetrate, they stray from the perspective necessary to see the Constitution for what it is. To those who take "constitutional law" to refer to whatever judges and lawyers say about the Constitution, one can only respond that constitutional law is not always constitutional. But I have already defended my view of why we must distinguish between the Constitution and its judicial gloss, and in the last chapter I shall show why we should reject the doctrines of judicial infallibility and finality.[11] What I want to focus on now is what Dworkin's words suggest about the authority of the father in the preceding passage.

Surely, the father Dworkin talks about is a very good father. He does not play the game of father knows best. He seems to sense that there is something conventional about his authority over his children. He wants the conventional aspect of his authority to be understood in light of what he thinks is really authoritative, and that is fairness itself, in this case—not *his* notion of fairness or anyone else's notion of fairness, but *fairness*. So, he is open to his children's arguments about better conceptions. In fact, he expects his children to have their own views because he expects them to be fair to others in dealings he has not anticipated. Even though Dworkin does not say so, it is obvious that this is a father who is more interested in his children's welfare than he is in flattery for himself, and this because he wants them to grow up to be what others can respect and admire, not what he alone can respect and admire. How much more attractive such a father is by comparison to what some have in mind today when they talk about a restoration of "family values"! I am not saying this merely to express a personal preference or to appeal to the reader's personal preference. I say this because I believe we would all accept it given sufficient thought and because the Constitution favors this preference—even dictates it, and in a way not altogether different from some of the "family values" people seem to have in mind.

Father often refers to a normative notion of what a father ought to be, a notion not at all congruent with whatever one finds men doing to their children. People speak from normative notions of *father* when they say, "he is like a father to me" and when they speak of "founding fathers." Since we must assume that fathers want to be fathers—for *real* fathers, as we say, could want nothing else—then fathers want to be what fathers are supposed to be, in accordance with one or another understanding of what fathers are supposed to be. Let us assume that two alternative understandings confront us: (1) a father as someone who wants what is best for his children but who does not fully know what is best, and (2) a father who knows what is best. The first alternative presents no problem for the preference I have expressed, and though the second alternative might appear to conflict with that preference, it does not have to. For if we treat the second alternative as a normative notion of *father*, then *father* would be *the one who knows what is best*. In that case, the children cannot be sure that one who claims to be their father is really their father unless he is also the one who knows what is best, and this they cannot know unless they have an independent knowledge of what is best. They would therefore have to think for themselves in order to recognize one who claimed to be their father for what he claimed to be: the one who knows what is best. In either case, therefore, if the family in question is that headed by the "founding fathers," we were meant to think for ourselves. This is especially true if we are to understand the document embodying their claim to patrimony. On the basis of what they said, either they intended that we think for ourselves or we have to think for ourselves if we are to recognize them as fathers. In trying to verify their claim we must continue to treat our conceptions of what is best as mere conceptions, as we have seen, not as final answers beyond the challenge of others. In this way we imitate "the fathers'" own approach to constitutions, and by becoming chips off the old block we behave at least in one respect as preferred by those who preach "family values."

It would appear, therefore, that disagreements over constitutional meaning are not altogether regrettable. Ending disagreements is hardly a way to insure the supremacy of a law whose supremacy necessitates a process of reaffirmation generated by disagreement. Disagreement is essential because the Constitution's supremacy is visible only through disagreement. This raises the question of how to regard the theories and legal doctrines that judges and scholars produce in their efforts to resolve constitutional disagreements. The Constitution requires that the effort be made because it requires that its provisions be applied to concrete disputes as the law of the land. However, those who accept the *Constitution's* supremacy cannot permit any other norms to take the place of the Constitution's provisions and that includes the doctrines judges produce in their efforts to answer constitutional questions. As I argued in chapter 2, there is no successful way to deny the distinction between the Constitution itself and its judicial gloss, and as long as that distinction is made, interpretations of the Constitution can always be criticized as falling short of its meaning. The Supreme Court acknowledges this insofar as it is prepared to abandon old judicial doctrines and overrule its own prior decisions in light of what it claims to be better conceptions of constitutional meaning.

The same applies to the answers submitted in academic commentary on the Constitution. Academics who want to answer constitutional questions from a perspective that takes seriously the Constitution's claim to supremacy must treat their answers as hypotheses or matters for discussion. This is not to say that constitutional controversies cannot be resolved, for the possibility of resolution is presupposed by the very controversies themselves. But those who are perfectly happy with their answers lose all inclination to question their best judgment of what the Constitution says, and when that inclination is gone, they can no longer understand themselves as subject to the Constitution as law. We would not consider ourselves subject to that which we do not have to think about, that which is perfectly congruent with our inclinations. The point at which the Constitution becomes congruent with our inclinations occurs in a place beyond the Constitution as law. One who has arrived at that point is not to be confused with one who would ordinarily be described as virtuous in accordance with a constitutional model of virtue, for we do not ordinarily speak of virtue where there are no tendencies to repress or overcome. Where there is no inclination contrary to the Constitution, there is no constitutional need for restraint or striving and therefore no virtue in accordance with constitutional criteria. One could say that insofar as the Constitution requires that its provisions be applied to concrete controversies, it requires efforts to find answers to the questions of how it should apply, and therefore it requires movement toward that point where what we want to do is in perfect, unthinking, easy conformity with what the Constitution says we ought to do. Better (for then it would be meaningless to talk about what the Constitution says we ought to do), one could say that the Constitution requires movement toward a complete unification of what we ought to do with what we want to do in an area beyond human affairs as we know them, for here there would be no thought about what to do. Thus, a world of difference remains between moving toward perfect congruence and arriving at the point at which congruence occurs. If the Constitution requires the former, it is still not made for the place at which the latter happens. As Madison said, "If men were angels, no government would be necessary."[12] The Constitution is good, therefore, insofar as it requires the disagreements that make us better. But the Constitution cannot comprehend the agreement that it itself anticipates.

The intractably provisional quality of the answers submitted in constitutional debate should cause us to shift our concerns from answers qua answers to the kinds of questions we should be asking in constitutional cases and the attitude with which we should proceed. As important as it is to seek an answer to the question of the scope of the First Amendment's freedom of speech, for example, it is more important to have an idea of the kind of thing we are looking for when we try to determine the scope of constitutional rights and what our attitude toward conflicting answers should be. I have argued that when we inquire into the scope of congressional powers, we are looking for ends whose desirability can make the grant of powers intelligible. Since desirable ends are the objects of this kind of inquiry, we should construe congressional powers accordingly, as constitutional language permits. I have argued that understanding powers in terms of ends leads to a liberal view of the scope of national power, although it does not justify going as far as the Supreme Court has sometimes gone. Such is the character of inquiries into constitutional powers. What kind of thing, then, are we looking for when we inquire into the scope of constitutional rights? How should we feel about the various answers proposed? How will our aims and attitudes influence the answers we favor? These are the questions I will try to answer here, and without attempting anything beyond mere proposals for the meaning of specific constitutional rights.

I have argued that the Constitution requires us to conceive constitutional rights as exceptions to the means available to the government in the pursuit of its authorized ends. Since rights so conceived can be expected to require what most would call sacrifices, honoring rights must be looked upon as a virtue—that is, as some form of self-restraint valued as an end in itself and as intrinsically praiseworthy. From this it would seem to follow that at least one of the factors to be consulted when ascertaining the scope of constitutional rights is what one believes the nation either does or can and should come to regard as praiseworthy. The other factors are the language of the constitutional rights in question and the logical status of rights in general as exemptions from granted powers. Thus, should we be confronted with equally plausible constructions of a constitutional right, that one is to be preferred which would make us more praiseworthy as a people. As for what would make us praiseworthy, that cannot be known without a successful theory of what is admirable per se, modified to accommodate rational creatures whose imperfections as actors and knowers put them in need of government even though they are capable of some degree of self-government. Short of such a theory, we can only put provisional reliance on what appears to be more or less widespread, if not universal intuitions. Thus, we seem to admire individuals who are collected and self-controlled; men and women who do not lose their nerve, bearing, or composure when the going gets rough—unless, perhaps, they pretend to do so as a device for tricking wrongdoers. We admire people who consider lying, misrepresentation, and affectation beneath them—unless these faults are intended as harmless sport, perhaps, or to save the weak and innocent from pain. We seem to admire strong people who do not hurt others, unless they are forced to do so as a means to educating others (in which case one can deny that they are hurting others) or as a means to combating encroaching harm. We admire those who are or would be accepted as governors by those they regard as their equals, rather than those who want to rule persons they regard as underlings of one sort or another. We admire people who accomplish difficult things.[13] These seem to be the kinds of attributes we find admirable in people, and I mention them to evoke considerations that will enter into our constructions of constitutional rights if we are to follow what I believe their underlying logic to be.

To illustrate the truly constitutional approach to the meaning of constitutional rights, I will begin with the guarantee made in both the Fifth and Fourteenth amendments that neither the national nor the state governments shall deprive "any person" "of life, liberty, and property without due process of law." No language in the Constitution has caused more controversy. The debate in the cases and commentaries over the last hundred years and more has involved many themes concerning federalism, the separation of powers, nature, and the nature of: democracy, reason, choice, tradition, history, consensus, morality, and human opinion about all these things.[14] I interpret the leading problem as follows. On its face, the due process clause guarantees that the government will not hurt a person unless it follows procedures prescribed by law.[15] Obviously, this provision assumes that following the prescribed procedures will tend to insure that no one will be hurt unfairly by the government. However, some affect to read the clause in a more narrow way. They say that what is fair is determined entirely by the prescribed procedures—that, in other words, as far as the due process clause is concerned, government can do whatever it wants to do to a person as long as it goes through the prescribed motions. It is doubtful that anyone seriously holds this narrow view of the due process clause, but this view is suggested from time to time in the cases and commentaries by judges and scholars who appear to believe that the governmental actions being challenged are somewhere between desirable or tolerable without being fully defensible in ways that one feels able to explain or wants to try to explain to others. "I know you think what has happened to you is unfair," says the oblique defense of what the government has done, "but where there is so much disagreement about what is fair, we have got to put our faith in the prescribed procedures, and whatever they yield has to count as fair."[16] In response to this comes a broad interpretation of the due process clause which holds that intrinsic to the very notions of constitutional government and law are assumptions and expectations that prevent a person from believing that unjust and unreasonable governmental action is really lawful. This broad interpretation can apply either to the procedures used by courts in trying criminal and civil defendants or to the laws enacted by legislatures. When applied to trials in court, it requires that the procedures measure up to our best theory of what procedures are fair. When applied to legislative acts it says that if a legislative act hurts someone without a defensible reason, the government has violated the due process clause.[17]

When judges who accept the broad interpretation apply the due process clause to a legislative enactment, they have to judge whether the legislature has a defensible reason for the law. Other judges say that judges have no business telling a legislature that its proffered reasons are not its real reasons or that its real reasons are not good enough to justify the harm it is doing to those who complain about the law. These judges often profess to be moved by a theory of the judiciary's proper role in the separation of powers, a theory that says the judiciary should defer to the other branches of government for the meaning of contested constitutional ideas. (I shall show why this is a bad theory of judicial duty in the next chapter.) Along with their theory of the judiciary's proper role, they tend to invoke the narrow reading of the due process clause. As far as the due process clause is concerned, these judges say, in effect, that whatever the law says is just is just, be it the law of the Constitution that keeps judges in their inferior place, or the law that is created when legislatures go through their prescribed motions. Some academicians propose an argument to justify this judicial policy. One reason is as good as another, they say, for human beings act ultimately to satisfy subrational wants; they do not really act for defensible reasons.[18] Academicians who propose this argument as a justification for a policy of judicial deference to others tend to agree (although to avoid inconsistency they would have to concede they have no reason to agree) that the government can do what it wants to do to people as long as it goes through the prescribed motions.

Those on the other side of the debate take some consolation from the fact that, as toughminded as they initially appear to be, those who take the narrow view of the due process clause inevitably back down. Some are forced to concede that due process is denied when government does something downright shocking.[19] Others say the due process clause of the Fourteenth Amendment "incorporates" all of the Bill of Rights because the framers of the amendment intended that it do so even though the amendment itself does not explicitly express that intention.[20] Still others cannot go so far as to say that all of the Bill of Rights should be incorporated, partly because they do not want to read the history of the Fourteenth Amendment that way, and partly because they think that some or all of the ends served by government (crime control, for example) are more important than honoring some constitutional rights (like freedom from self-incrimination or unreasonable searches and seizures). This last group believes that some rights are established as fundamental by Western and Anglo-American tradition and others are not, and that due process is denied only when the government violates the former—without good reason, that is.[21] A third group is aware that the others inadvertently concede a connection between what is lawful and results one can defend independently of what is lawful. They point out that one does not have to read the history of the Fourteenth Amendment any one way and that there is no noncontroversial way to tell a right that is fundamental from one that is not. They call for a return to a reading of the due process clause as strictly procedural. But this group compromises its toughmindedness, too. Thus, John Hart Ely, a leading critic of substantive due process or the proposition that fair procedures must produce independently defensible results, believes that other clauses of the Fourteenth Amendment can prevent most of the bad results that a broad reading of the due process clause has been used to prevent.[22] Ely also argues that the processes of the Constitution in general are democratic processes and that as such they should stop government from reaching results that a knowledge of community attitudes would lead one to recognize as *prejudiced*—i.e., as unsupported by good reasons.[23] Thus, Ely restores a connection between lawful processes and substantively defensible results on the level of what he calls the Constitution's broader themes, a connection he denies in his discussion of the due process clause.

Accompanying this debate among jurists and academics about the connection between lawful process and defensible results is a pattern of judicial decision that has been called a mess, and aptly so. The Supreme Court requires that our state and national governments have strong reasons for hurting people who make certain demands, reasons so strong that some speak of a right to these things. To hurt people who make other demands, however, government needs only weak reasons, so weak that they amount to no reasons at all, leaving government free, for all practical purposes, to do whatever it wants. Thus, we appear to have the right to use contraceptives, to have abortions on demand, to send our children to parochial schools, and to instruct our children in a foreign language.[24] If government stops us from doing these things, government deprives us of due process, whether or not it goes through the prescribed procedures. But there is no violation of due process, says the Court, if government forces us to pay our employees for time off to vote in elections for governmental officials, or if government falsely damages our good reputations, or if government arranges it so that some public employees can be fired on the whims of their supervisors, or if government prohibits homosexual practices among consenting adults.[25] Government, according to the Court, is thus free to do some things that hurt people for any reason or no reason at all. But why? Why, for example, should teenagers be free to have abortions on demand when consenting adults can be deprived of their liberty and property for private homosexual acts? The Court's answers to such questions have left large segments of the public and the profession unpersuaded.

A satisfactory theory of the due process clause must acknowledge that we do presuppose a connection between laws and defensible reasons. But it must also accommodate the fact that the language of the due process clause is concerned with how government reaches certain results. One may have to concede, in other words, that the Constitution does not recognize general rights to life, liberty, and property, and that the due process clause does imply that one can be deprived of these things as long as one is accorded due process of law. The Constitution also permits the government to take private property for public use as might be needed in the pursuit of its authorized ends, so long as just compensation is made. If rights are to be defined as real exceptions to what government can do in pursuit of its ends, we have a right to due process, not to the things that government can deprive us of if we get the process due. There is therefore a right against deprivations without due process; there are no simple and general rights to life, liberty, and property. On the other hand, there is no purely procedural test for laws under the Constitution because the laws in question have to be *constitutional* laws. Constitutional laws of Congress not only have to aim at conceptions of the authorized ends of government, they have to be perceived as such by those who are subject to the laws because the enumeration of powers provides a set of criteria by which the public can measure the actions of government. Although this does not mean the subjects of the law need approve the particular policies that the legislature has enacted, they nevertheless must be able to see those policies as versions of the ends of government in order to say that they are authorized by the Constitution. They must be able to say at least this much, for example, "I do not agree that this policy [say, the promotion of nuclear power] is good for the country, but I can understand why Congress sees it as a means to the economic health of the nation." Such judgments cannot be made if the enactments of the legislature are predicated on beliefs or pursue ends too far removed from those who observe what the legislature is doing. Thus, as conditions got worse for the poor, we would have trouble recognizing cuts in social services coupled with tax advantages for the rich as good-faith efforts to serve the common interest of rich and poor alike. This need to perceive enactments as good-faith and reasonably competent versions of the ends of government results in a substantive notion of rationality or reasonableness as part of the meaning of a constitutional law. The same can be said for the enactments of the states, for even though the states' powers are not enumerated as those of Congress are, the state governments are obligated to serve the common good of their people by virtue of their theoretical origins in acts of popular sovereignty. This understanding is reflected in a number of constitutional provisions, including the equal protection clause and the guarantee to the people of the states that they shall enjoy republican forms of government.

The Constitution does not support a theory that law is merely the command of some sovereign law-making power. Quite the contrary; the document was originally proposed as a means to desirable ends, ratified after what was claimed to be a representative process of deliberation, and binding only on those whose representatives accepted it. Logically, the document is less a willful assertion of power than an act of sovereign self-restraint in behalf of a hierarchy of values that would find us willing to adjust our notions of economic well-being and national security as needed to honor constitutional rights. Moreover, the Constitution provides an elaborate process of representation, deliberation, and moderating checks as partial tests for the legitimacy of popular demands. To recognize the enactments of this system as unequivocally constitutional laws, people cannot be so mistreated or neglected by the government that they cannot reaffirm the system as a means to the good society. In other words, the system as a whole must do good things for people or enable all to do good things for themselves in order for them to be able to understand the Constitution for what it claims to be.[26] We have seen that those who fully accept the Constitution as supreme law must see the body of the Constitution as the prescriptive counterpart of their best conception of the good society. The Constitution is fully law only when it meets the continuing test of reaffirmation, which is the condition for its status as supreme law. For these reasons admittedly irrational or unreasonable laws cannot be viewed as pursuant to or consistent with the Constitution, and the only laws that are authoritative with those who accept the Constitution's supremacy are *constitutional* laws.

In light of the reasonableness inherent in our concept of a constitutional law, courts have an obligation to decide appropriate cases by declaring acts of legislation invalid if they believe them beyond identifiable versions of the public interest. Exempting legislative enactments from a constitutional requirement of rationality suggests that legislatures and those they represent can do no wrong by their own standards. Constitutional supremacy implies otherwise.

This leads to a difficult question, which we might want intially to frame as follows: "How is one to tell a good reason from one that is not good enough for purposes of settling controversies under the due process clause?" This would be a careless way to frame the question, however, since it assumes that no answer is good unless it is beyond controversy. This assumption is inconsistent with constitutional supremacy, as we have just seen. A better way to phrase the question would be, "What should we take into account in deciding whether government is making responsible proposals concerning the public interest?" One cannot successfully object to this way of putting the question by pointing out that responsible proposals do not settle controversies and that judges have to settle controversies. Judges do have to hand down final decisions in the cases before them, but the answers in these individual cases need not be, and in fact are not, treated as irreversible precedents for future cases in constitutional law. What seems reasonable under some circumstances need not be declared reasonable for all future circumstances. As for the particular controversies before them, judges who take an oath to be guided by the Constitution owe the litigants only their best effort. Indeed, this is as much as the Constitution permits, for the Constitution cannot be understood to put judicial precedent on a par with the general ideas of the Constitution itself.[27]

How, then, do we approach the question of what is reasonable? Recalling the preceding part of this discussion, we begin with the understanding that the due process clause tells the government that it cannot hurt anyone unless it has a reason—a reason, that is, to believe that what it is doing serves the common good. If the government believes it has a reason, however, it believes that all who can reason aright will agree that it has a reason. The government would believe, for example, that even thieves and drug addicts would agree that reason supports laws against theft and drug abuse if the thieves and drug addicts were only in a position to give these matters their best thought. Thus, the government would believe that there would

be virtually no thieves and drug addicts if impediments to clear thinking were removed. It would believe at least that theft and drug ad-
diction could be eliminated as social problems of significant magni-
tude, as, for example, religiously motivated snake handling and mass
suicide are not significant problems for us today, despite what occurs
now and then. If this government were a government that fully accepted and effectively pursued its duty to maintain the Constitution,
it would work hard to remove conditions obstructing clear thinking
so that persons who would otherwise be thieves and drug addicts
could find evidence in a lawful environment for the Constitution's
claim to prescribe ways that constitute their best conception of the
good society. The government would therefore study and try to correct the conditions it believes lead people to reject the testimony of
reason when they become thieves and drug addicts, conditions like
poverty, unemployment, poor schools, and, ultimately perhaps, the
boredom of those who find insufficient moral, intellectual, or artistic
challenges in money making and its normal cultural concomitants.

Suppose that this government thought it knew with certainty that
its laws served the common good, and suppose further that it thought
it had removed all obstacles to reasoned choice by those subject to
its authority. In that case, the government would not expect theft
and drug abuse to continue as problems of any significance. If these
problems did continue, however, our perfectly competent government would be in a perfect quandary, for it could no longer comprehend the assumptions of its own existence and actions. It could
not explain the defeat of its expectations by concluding that those
who become thieves and drug addicts are incapable of reasoned choice,
for this would be inconsistent with its holding thieves and drug abusers
responsible to the criminal law. After all, one does not pass laws
prohibiting people from catching unavoidable diseases; one does not,
or should not, punish people for having bad luck. If the government
reached the more general conclusion that reason can have no decisive
influence on the way people act and live, it could not believe it had
real reasons for its own policies, and this it would have to believe
unless it was prepared to concede that it was violating, or that it could
not conform to, the due process clause. Faced with the continuing
failure of its policies, then, the government would have no choice
but to begin questioning its assumption that it was a good government.
It could no longer be confident that its laws really did serve the
common good. It would have to doubt that it had done its duty to

remove the obstacles to an appreciation of its reasons. As I said earlier, one does not impose reasons, one eventually submits them; this is why a truly constitutional government could never be altogether certain about its competence or rectitude.

This is not to say that constitutional governments are chronically indecisive, that they must always stew and fret about whether they are doing the right thing, that they cannot ever have the capacity for difficult things, a quality I spoke of earlier as a characteristic of persons whom we admire. After all, some policies do work, and the government is not always called upon to give reasons, partly because most criminals do not challenge the aims of the laws they disobey. Few thieves, for example, will question the aims of laws against theft, not the professed aims, at any rate. When people do challenge the reasonableness of a law, they are implicitly offering a different version of the common good from that upon which the law is predicated. They are saying something like, "This will be a better place for all if you decriminalize the activity for which I am being punished." The government may be convinced that its version of the common good is superior to deviant versions, and it may believe this without being confident that it will continue to affirm all aspects of its present version for all time. Sometimes, in defending the reasonableness of its policies, the government can invoke generally established ways of the community and more or less widespread community attitudes, presuming as it does so that those who want things done differently do not have a better vision of a truly *common* good.

If, however, a government believes it is actively pursuing the common good, which pursuit would include removing obstacles to reasoned choice, and if it believes that the bulk of those who are subject to its authority are capable of reasoned choice, the persistent failure of its policies should lead it to question its version of the common good. Doubt is especially warranted where failure is accompanied by persistent and articulate opposition to the government's policies. After a certain point, the government will no longer have reason to be as confident as it once was that it is working toward the common good. The government's appeals to established practices and dominant opinions will not help at that point because it is the established version of the common good that has failed in some respect and that the government must now try to improve if it is eventually to satisfy itself that it is acting for what all can appreciate as a reason. If the government cannot find better policies and accompany them by what it believes to be new and ultimately more persuasive reasons than the old reasons, then the government simply cannot do what the due process clause says it must do. It cannot base its actions on what it itself has reason to believe is a defensible version of the common good.

From the late 1890s to the mid-1930s the Supreme Court was intent upon using the due process clause as a weapon against governmental regulation of what businesses charged their customers, the wages, hours, and working conditions of employees, and other business practices.[28] The Court defended business interests by treating such legislation as constitutionally suspect and requiring the state and national governments to persuade the Court that they had exceptionally good reasons for enacting the regulations. Sometimes the Court was persuaded, typically when the government could show that it was aiming at what the Court could appreciate as goals in the areas of public health, safety, and morals. But the Court would not accept most attempts to improve the economic position of consumers and workers as such, and the Court was quick to spot such legislation masquerading as health laws or safety laws. The Court of this period, often called the Old Court, apparently felt that reason favored a more or less healthy, chaste, and safe society, where industry was rewarded, property was secure, and where businessmen made the controlling decisions respecting the distribution of wealth. The nation rejected much of this view as a result of the Great Depression, probably for a very long time to come. Even after the return to power in 1980 of the right wing of the Republican party, it was widely taken for granted that what happens to the economy is still the responsibility of government, and that the test of economic policy is not a natural right to keep what one can acquire, but what the progressive critics of the Old Court said it should be: a general prosperity, equal economic opportunity and mobility, and a distribution of the nation's wealth that would eventually be held fair by all social classes and political groups.[29] While there is an element of hindsight in the judgment, most observers agree today that the Old Court erred in refusing to recognize progressive aims as elements of a responsible version of the common good.

That does not mean, however, that all aspects of the Old Court's thinking were irresponsible. The Old Court did not err in requiring government to defend laws that appeared harmful to business. Whether one is probusiness or antibusiness on those occasions when business contends that going along with its pursuit of profits will lead the nation to all that makes life worth living, business is part of a common enterprise in America, and the Constitution does not permit policies reducing business to a lesser status. That the Court came to accept the progressive version of the common good as a responsible version did not make it impossible thereafter for government to hurt business interests for no good reason. Progressives can act unjustly, too. Officially, the modern Court says it is aware that arbitrary actions against business are still possible, and it acknowledges the principle contended for here when it says that it will strike down arbitary actions against business should they occur.[30] But the course of decision since the mid-1930s belies this official acknowledgment of judicial duty, and the Court has approved legislative actions that appear oblivious to the due process requirement that government should strive for arrangements that are in the common good—arrangements beneficial to everyone who can reason aright and to every pursuit that is a part of the common enterprise, in other words.[31]

A notorious instance of this hypocrisy is a 1955 case in which the Court upheld an Oklahoma enactment requiring a prescription from an optometrist or an ophthalmologist before one could have an optician replace a broken lens or put old lenses into a new frame or even "fit lenses to a face."[32] From all appearances, the law was an attempt to force the people of Oklahoma to spend more than their health required them to spend on the services of ophthalmologists and optometrists. This policy might have been justified had the legislature been moved by the picture of a better life for its people, or had the legislature believed that if the eyeglass wearers and the people of Oklahoma generally could reason aright they would prefer more or richer ophthalmologists and optometrists to more food, better clothing, and other things they could buy with the money they would save by having lenses replaced, framed, and fitted by opticians. It is conceivable that the legislature might have been moved by such a theory. Thus, it might somehow have based its policy on the connection between vision and knowledge as that good which is truly common and which its people would eventually see as better than more food, better clothing, and fewer or less prosperous optometrists and ophthalmologists.[33] But on the surface, at any rate, no such vision seemed apparent. The enactment appeared to be what C. Herman Pritchett calls it: "a statute which was the product of an interest group

struggle in the Oklahoma legislature, . . . a victory for the ophthalmologists and optometrists of the state over the opticians."[34] Such a
description was virtually conceded by Justice Douglas's opinion for
the Court when he observed that the enactment "may exact a need-
less, wasteful requirement in many cases."[35] But this did not stop
Justice Douglas and his brethren from going ahead and overruling
the appearances by inventing hypothetical reasons why someone could
support the act in the public interest—reasons admittedly less hypothetical than the one I just offered, but hypothetical nonetheless,
and obviously so to all who were expected to take the claims of
constitutions and judges seriously, not to mention the claims people
generally make for themselves in other contexts.[36] The court did not
help its own implicit claim to authority in this case, for Justice Douglas's opinion is fodder for the view that the only difference between
a reason and a rationalization is one's personal preference for the
result. A corollary of that proposition is the view that government
can hurt someone for any reason or for no reason at all—really, that
it is up to government to decide what life, liberty, and property are
and therefore whether someone has been hurt or not. Justice Douglas
and his allies opposed thought heading in that direction when it appeared later in some of the opinions of younger men on the Burger
Court, men who had inherited their opinions about the essentially
arbitrary nature of law from older men.[37]

In 1973 the Supreme Court held in *Roe* v. *Wade* that there is "a
right . . . to choose to terminate pregnancy" comprehended by a
more general "right of privacy" in "personal" relations like marriage,
procreation, contraception, family relationships, child rearing, and
education.[38] The Court said that physical, psychological, economic,
and social "harm" would be imposed upon women should the states
deny this right to terminate pregnancy altogether. The state must
show a "compelling state interest" before it can impose such harm,
and, said the Court, the state of Texas had made no such showing
in this case. The state said it was protecting life, which, it had decided,
begins at conception. But the Court, in effect acknowledging some
of the conditions for counting something as a reason, took notice of
"the wide divergence of thinking on this most sensitive and difficult
question" among physicians, philosophers, theologians, and members
of different generations, and it said that, in light of this divergence
of thinking, the state could not override the right to have an abortion

simply by enacting a definition of life into law.[39] Reaching for what would count as a reason, the state said also that it sought to prohibit abortion as a means to protecting the health of the pregnant woman. The Court accepted this as a permissible aim of the state, but the Court felt that a government really moved by that end would seek only those restrictions on abortion reasonably calculated to achieve that end. Accordingly, the Court indicated it would permit special regulations beyond the normal licensing of physicians so long as the aim was safe abortions, not burdening the right, after the first trimester of pregnancy, the statistical point at which abortion was more dangerous than childbirth.[40] A final reason proffered by the state was the protection of potential life. That, too, was a permissible aim, said the Court, but only after the second trimester, the point of the fetus's "viability . . . outside the mother's womb."[41] Doubtlessly sensing the limits of what can count as a reason among a people with our constitution, the state did not say it opposed abortion as a sin or a manifestation of a morally corrupting sexual revolution or anything like that.

Few decisions in constitutional history have catalyzed as much bitter controversy as *Roe* v. *Wade*. Religious considerations fuel most of the attacks, despite the reluctance of the states to say so in court.[42] Such reluctance bears witness to the durability of a constitutional psychology opposed to religious impositions, a "genius," to use a term of the founding period, that seems to survive the periodic pressures of religious zeal. As I suggested in the last chapter true believers will have difficulty fully accepting the Constitution's claim to supremacy. That claim can only be understood by men and women who continually subject both their beliefs about what should be supreme law and the Constitution's claims to supremacy to their best critical effort. Such is not the way of those who do not admit a need for inquiry into the highest authority.[43] My argument is an inference from the notion of constitutional supremacy. Historical testimony is available for the same conclusion, however. An oft-quoted passage from a letter by Jefferson regretting his inability to attend the celebration of the fiftieth anniversary of the Declaration of Independence relates the central significance of the revolution and what the nation said it stood for at the time:

> I should, indeed, with peculiar delight, have met and ex-
> changed there congratulations personally with the small band,

the remnant of that host of worthies, who joined with us on
that day in the bold and doubtful election we were to make
for our country, between submission or the sword; and to
have enjoyed with them the consolatory fact, that our fellow
citizens after half a century of experience and prosperity, continue to approve the choice we made. May it be to the world,
what I believe it will be (to some parts sooner, to others later,
but finally to all), the signal of arousing men to burst the
chains under which monkish ignorance and superstition had
persuaded them to bind themselves, and to assume the blessings and security of self-government. That form which we have
substituted, restores the free right to the unbounded exercise
of reason and freedom of opinion. All eyes are opened, or
opening, to the rights of man. The general spread of the light
of science has already laid open to every view the palpable
truth, that the mass of mankind has not been born with sad-
dles on their backs, nor a favored few booted and spurred,
ready to ride them legitimately, by the grace of God. These
are grounds of hope for others. For ourselves, let the annual
return of this day forever refresh our recollections of these
rights, and an undiminished devotion to them.[44]

On the basis of historical statements like these together with the
implications of the establishment clause and the arguments I made
in chapter 3, we can assume a constitutional preference for a secular
society—a society that acknowledges that there is nothing beyond
truth itself that is sacred to inquiring minds: no gods, no creeds, no
taboos, perhaps not even the "inquiring mind," as is evident from
our willingness to entertain the reduction of mind to ultimately un-
knowable . . . what? . . . "matter?" . . . and from our openness to
the criticism of true believers themselves. Surely all this counts as an
argument against religiously motivated bans on abortion. On the
other hand, there may be a genuinely secular justification for the
sexually repressive moralism that fuels much of the attack on *Roe*.
Students of Plato's *Republic* may recognize the following: Let us
assume arguendo that young people schooled in sexual indulgence
are less likely than their repressed counterparts to acquire the intellectual tools, attitudes, and personal habits necessary to love and
follow the ways of the truly inquiring mind. A mind that is always
asking whether the apparent good is really good is not part of a soul
that stops to smell the roses, as the popular song recommends. One
might add to this that the truly inquiring mind must be distinguished

from those who deflate the community's dogmas for the hell of it or in quest of excuses for "breaking away" from repressive "moral codes." This last group of self-flattering swingers, moved as it is by pleasure and pain, is both cowardly and potentially authoritarian, and therefore it can and should be frightened into repressing drives that lead much more often to moral nihilism, degradation of self, and exploitation of others than to a dedication to replace the community's myths with genuine knowledge of the good. So, the argument would run, while a repressive moralism provides us with a basis for disciplining those who ought to be disciplined, it also provides tests or obstacles to rising above the community's dogmas. These tests can be passed only by those whose love of truth overpowers an aversion to the varieties of pain attendant upon the community's disapproval—the only ones who can be trusted not to use knowledge for the sake of destructive private pleasures.[45]

This could be a good argument. I am not going to reject it with any confidence here. It may provide some direction toward reconciling liberty with decency, and it suggests a way to explain our admiration for those who seem able to rise above "accident and force." On balance, however, this argument faces several problems as a policy that can be comprehended by the Constitution (which, incidentally, may be enough for us to reject the Constitution). It would require that the government lie to those ordinary folks whose passions are not strong enough to withstand the pain of breaking away from the security of the community's dogmas. The government could not tell people that the repressive moralism they are taught to look upon as simply right is but a contingent instrument to a life of intellectual pleasures beyond their capacities.[46] Thus, the plan would not result in the people's appreciation of the claims of inquiring minds—indeed, the greater likelihood is that the latter will be forced underground. A general appreciation of the best minds will not exist because there will not be many of them and they will be quite overpowered politically by those who will not be able to recognize them. The best minds, loving truth as they do, can hardly be expected to serve either the established myths needed by lesser minds or the mindless pleasures lesser minds indulge when liberated from the old myths.[47] This will force the best minds underground because they cannot make themselves known to the community without exposing the fallacies on which the established order rests. Ludicrously or tragically enough, therefore, if the best minds consult their own interests first, they may

settle in places where something like the "Playboy Philosophy" prevails.[48] Although one can debate whether a love of knowledge has
less in common with a love of pleasure than with repressive moralism,
the latter is much less tolerant of those who are not its true believers.
So, it is not clear that a policy of repressive moralism is justified as
a means to raising the young to their intellectual potential.

Still other secular arguments against abortion may be available.
One, ostensibly, is predicated on the belief that abortion is murder:
The state has a duty to prohibit abortion along with other types of
murder. Let us try to assume that this view need not represent religious zeal or sexually repressive moralism. Of course, such a view
holds that the fetus is a person, and that proposition is most controversial. Nevertheless, some judges say, a "reasonable man" can believe it. With that, many leading constitutional lawyers conclude that
the Court made a mistake in *Roe* v. *Wade*. But in the context of the
abortion issue in America today, these critics are wrong, for their
argument inclines toward an overly narrow, purely procedural, and
ultimately incoherent reading of the due process clause. They hold
in general that if a "reasonable man" can believe such and so, the
necessary connection between law and defensible reasons has been
satisfied for purposes of the due process clause standing alone and
apart from other constitutional provisions. To see why that rendition
of due process is untenable we need only recall the upshot of the
judiciary's current message to legislatures as to what passes for due
process in the area of business regulation: "Give any reason, or no
real reason at all. Do what you want, just go through the motions,
albeit motions originally prescribed with an eye to channeling what
people want in directions they can recognize as what they ought to
want." This, in effect, is what some would say to legislatures opposed
to abortion.

What does it mean, however, to say that reasonable people can
believe such and so? Is the reasonable person the ordinary citizen
who pays taxes, goes to work, and does not get excited about many
things? Some thinkers might say so, either because of the way we
sometimes use the expression "reasonable man," or because of out-
ward connections between reason and some of the calmer affections.[49]
But there is no compelling reason to accept this as the controlling
sense of "reasonable man," for reasonable people so defined can be
and often are bigoted, superstitious, and willful, albeit calmly so. Is
it not more reasonable in the present context to define a reasonable

person as one who can believe such and so if he or she believes there are good reasons for concluding such and so? Now, again, such a person need not have good reasons for all that he or she believes because most of what we believe is never challenged—because, in other words, we are not expected to have reasons for all that we believe. But a person who has no reasons or who gives no reasons when others are looking for reasons cannot be recognized by them in any sense of reason that enables us to distinguish reason from unreason. So, if a reasonable person can believe abortion is murder, then that person must have reasons to give to those who believe it is not murder, especially when large numbers of people—people who seem reasonable enough by the model of "reasonable man" on which critics of *Roe* v. *Wade* rely—believe that an early fetus, or a young one, is not a living person.

Now, from the perspective of the proabortion opinion in this country at this time, who can say that in *Roe* v. *Wade* the state of Texas gave reasons to dispel the appearance of a simple, arbitrary antipathy to abortion? Who also can deny the religious entanglement and the probability that those who cannot give nonreligious reasons in this and related areas are moved by religious views? I shall show in a moment why the Court has an affirmative obligation under the First Amendment to do all that it can to prevent pretextual impositions of religious dogma.[50] But focusing on the due process clause for now, and bearing in mind the way we must define a reasonable person in this context if we are to distinguish reason from unreason, what reason do we have for believing that reasonable people can believe that all nontherapeutic abortion is murder? Clearly, we have none because the antiabortion people have not yet given the proabortion people anything that the latter recognize as a reason. Should the critics of *Roe* v. *Wade* respond that those in power do not have to give reasons to those numerous and persistent groups who believe they are being treated arbitrarily, I would repeat what I have already said about what it means to tell a popular government it cannot hurt people without a reason. To say that the mere fact of enactment by a representative legislature is proof enough that good reasons exist is to ignore what we all know about the possibility of the best schemes of representation going wrong. It is to beg the important question whether the system as a whole is to "represent" more than some mathematical total of whatever we might want it to represent. It is to ignore the fact that despite what our representatives want from time to time, the Constitution "represents" an act of sovereign self-restraint, including the restraint of religious zeal. It is to deny the unavoidable distinction between what is constitutional or just and what is represented as constitutional or just. Rending procedure from its inevitable substantive context, it is to make incomprehensible the idea of a written constitution whose normative force continues beyond that moment when it brought governmental procedures into being. Indeed, it is to render incomprehensible exactly what it was that was created, since distinguishing it from the surrounding chaos and giving it a name, like "representative government" or even "government," would not be possible without the continuing influence of the substantive vision in which it originated. In sum, it is to read the due process clause out of the Constitution and the Constitution out of the due process clause.

If critics of *Roe* v. *Wade* are mistaken about what the due process clause requires of government, however, they are not altogether mistaken in saying that the Court was wrong to declare, in effect, that a right to abortion is something to be honored on a par with, say, freedom of speech or freedom of the press. What I have said here should not be taken as contending for a right to abortion as such. I have argued only for a right to feel that one is not being hurt by the mere wants, resentments, and religious beliefs of those who control the government—a right to what one can appreciate as a real reason, no less but no more than that. In light of what I have said about constitutional rights as real exemptions from the powers of government, the so-called right to an abortion is not really a constitutional right because abortions could be prohibited if government were to have what those who are asking for a reason can recognize as a reason. As matters now stand with the abortion controversy in America, the old reasons given by the antiabortion forces are largely pretextual, or so they appear to those who want to leave the abortion question to the individual. It is not likely that new reasons from the old antiabortion groups will be looked upon as more than a cover for the imposition of religious beliefs which one cannot support in a forthright fashion before someone who does not already share them. Since religious impositions are among the most resisted, for they concern the highest and most pervasive matters, a victory by antiabortionists would probably divide the country more deeply than it already is on this issue. New reasons against abortion would have to come from new sources in order to have a chance of appearing even arguably constitutional to those who favor abortion. Such reasons may exist, and I have not mentioned all the possibilities. But reasons of the kind I have suggested are not at all those associated with today's antiabortion groups. So for the time being, and for a long time to come, as far as I can see, the right to abortion will, or certainly should, appear to be a constitutional right.

Nevertheless, to digress from *Roe* v. *Wade* for a moment, an apparent constitutional right is not a real constitutional right. A real right is a real exemption from granted power. That means we cannot have a constitutional reason for violating a constitutional right no matter what the sacrifices. Because there will be sacrifices when real constitutional rights are involved, honoring them must be seen as an end in itself, higher in value than the desiderata sacrificed—higher than what are usually called life, liberty, and property. That is why honoring rights must be seen as something that can be praised as a virtue. This makes us want to know the activities at the limits to what we can honor as constitutional rights if we are to see ourselves as worthy of praise. What is included in the constitutionally protected freedoms of speech and press, for example? What punishments are humane; what trial procedures fair? But when dealing with general ideas like these we cannot know the limits of what we can honor as constitutional rights without knowing *the* best conception of those rights, as opposed to *our* best conception for the time being; and we cannot be certain that we know the best conception as long as we conceive ourselves subject to the Constitution as supreme law. The reader will recall the reason for this uncertainty: Fully conscious subjects of the Constitution would be aware of their inclination to disobey the Constitution, and a desire to combat that inclination would lead to a continual and self-critical quest for the best conceptions of constitutional provisions. This leaves us only with general ideas about the provisions of the Constitution and a certain attitude about ourselves in relation to those ideas. We know that honoring constitutional rights is a virtue, and we know that there have to be limits to what we can honor and still be virtuous, but we do not know exactly what those limits are, and we are aware of the danger of substituting our preferences for the law. One can illustrate the point in the terms of the familiar debate about whether First Amendment rights are "absolutes." These rights can be called absolutes because it is possible for us utterly to defeat the exercise of constitutional powers in honoring them. But the rights that are absolutes are only those that jurists now call "core concepts." It is not any and every claim of First Amendment rights that can override conflicting conceptions of such ends as national security, tranquility, and prosperity. These rights are not absolute with respect to the range of practices they protect.[51] Thus, we know from the logic of the First Amendment's relationship to the powers of government that there is an understanding of, say, free religious exercise that is an absolute; but the Constitution does not protect all understandings of free religious exercise. Surely we can be excused for doubting that protecting Jonestown-style free exercise, for example, is descriptive of the nation's aspirations. We can say the same when racist religious schools seek tax subsidies. More generally, we believe a constitutional right exists when we believe there is an x of sufficient worth to defeat prosperity, order, and security if necessary, whether or not we concur in a particular conception of x. We cannot avoid debate in formulating conceptions of x because of our aspirational relationship with the ideal state of affairs of which x is a part and because of our disinclination to obey the law in which x is couched. As we have seen, consciousness of this disinclination should make us cognizant of—and troubled by—the possibility that it is our conceptions rather than the best conception of x that we seek to honor. This, then, is an absolutism of the self-critical, not of the self-righteous. Those of us who accept the Constitution's claim to supremacy accept an obligation to find the best conception of x by subjecting our conceptions to critical examination.

Scholars fitting Hart's description of disappointed absolutists might say of this thesis that it recommends more of an attitude toward constitutional decision than a method of decision. This I might concede, though I could hardly take it as criticism in light of what legal realists rediscovered about the importance of attitude in legal decision. Granting the absence here of technical instructions for making constitutional decision easy, I still propose an attitude derived from the Constitution to be contrasted with the unconstitutional attitude that treats rights as interests to be balanced in avoidance of serious social risk and sacrifice. Nor is this constitutional attitude uncontroversial as an attitude; it will not suit those liberals who would give many social interests some constitutional insulation from majoritarianism but no right sufficient dignity to justify real sacrifices. It would be missing the point to contrast this constitutional frame of mind with some mechanical model of decision that would eliminate debate. Debate is intrinsic to the constitutional attitude because of the continuing reaffirmation required to accept the Constitution's supremacy. Moreover, a constitutional attitude and its supporting logic can make a difference in constitutional decision because they will often favor some decisional alternatives over others.

We can see this by reflecting on our reactions to what went on in Jonestown under the thralldom of the Reverend Jim Jones. Can such activities qualify as free religious exercise? When we seek the best conceptions of what constitutional language and logic will permit, we should not forget that by some accounts, and potentially by anyone's, the best in us may not be good enough. It could very well be that prophets could persuade us that God is man's only salvation and that acts such as suicide and the killing of one's children are fitting expressions of a faith in God and a god-fearing contempt for the mundane. Perhaps, by their account, if one could succeed in proving the free exercise clause does not protect extreme testimonial acts of true belief, so much the worse for the Constitution as just another futile expression of human arrogance. Arguments like this should make us aware of the way our backgrounds influence the hypotheses we put forward in constitutional interpretation. So, in the case of Jonestown, we have to ask, Who is prepared to say that the political progeny of Jefferson can begin with his general ideas and, through a process of dialectical progression and refinement, end up taking pride in their toleration of Jonestown-style free exercise? Could such a people reaffirm the establishment clause, which effectively rules out government by priests as such? Could they agree to a document that prohibits religious tests for public office and thereby refuses to require religious faith of officials while permitting government by atheists? Could they agree with what we have found to be the implications of the supremacy clause concerning the posture of critical thought toward all forms of authority?

Now, unlike the attitude of people in Jonestown toward others, those of us who want to accept the Constitution's supremacy may have some doubts about our presumably negative attitude toward Jonestown. That is why I approached the Jonestown question by asking other questions, not by giving answers. Again, unlike that of the people in Jonestown, our willingness to concede that we may be wrong in our reaction to what happened there is one of several arguments for letting Jonestown exist as a community in speech. Thus, the People's Temple can continue to exist and, if it wants, its congregation can talk about Jonestown and even advocate its reestablishment. But, if I may make a proposal about the limits of its activities, I do not think we can aspire to be a nation that challenges its best thought about the free exercise clause at the same time that we would acknowledge a right of zealots actually to establish legally protected enclaves where people are physically and psychologically forced and programmed to believe that thinking for oneself about religious matters is a sin. To the people who live in these and similar enclaves the rules governing them are at least as authoritative and coercive as the laws of duly constituted governments. A government that protects these places is using its resources to help maintain the practical equivalent of legally coercive societies that the Constitution itself prohibits the government from establishing.[52] If Jonestown could exist under the Constitution, no constitutional objection would lie against a countryside covered with Jonestowns, Klantowns, and other de facto coercive communities whose ways are directly contrary to the liberal values embodied in the Constitution. In that case it would make no sense to talk about a constitutionally ideal state of affairs, and unless we assume a constitutionally ideal state of affairs we cannot solve the anomaly of elevating means over ends, a problem we have to solve if constitutional supremacy is going to make any sense. Allowing Jonestown-style free exercise takes us back to the incoherent idea of a constitution that, in principle, can accommodate any and every state of affairs.

On the other hand, our commitment to self-critical thought and our desire to be recognized as reasoning creatures requires some toleration of illiberal private associations because it is from these associations that some of the premises of self-criticism come and because reasons as such are eventually submitted, not imposed. However much the government might try to keep the public informed about their threats to constitutional values, illiberal private associations would have a place as long as they remained credibly voluntary and adhered to the criminal laws, compulsory school laws, and other public policies. One might also defend a governmental concern for the survival of those private parochial schools and colleges that in fact do not promote racism, zealotry, and other illiberal attitudes. Of course, this kind of support would not have the advancement of religion as its aim; rather, it would seek to keep a self-critical and open society from becoming complacent or from degenerating into a closed, dogmatic, and therefore false secularism—false because a true devotion to reason would continually probe the nature and test the claims of reason itself. But the overall aim of any program of support for parochial education would be to help keep self-critical thought alive in the community. That aim would make us willing to err on the side of withholding support from parochial institutions, as in fact the Supreme Court is willing to do today, unless it can be shown that, among other things, governmental aid to parochial schools has a secular purpose.[53]

As for a general constitutional right to privacy mentioned in *Roe v. Wade* and other cases, no such right could exist under the due process clause, and the reason for this is the same reason that a real right to abortion cannot be found in the due process clause. Honoring a real constitutional right has to be seen as a virtue; violating a real constitutional right, a moral wrong. Thus, there is evidence in our traditions, combined with constitutional logic and the language of amendments four through eight, that it is morally wrong to condemn persons as criminals without stringent efforts to get at the truth of their conduct in ways that comport with our awareness that our suspicions could be wrong, with our recognition of their dignity as rational subjects of the criminal law like ourselves, and with our refusal to let our own conduct toward them attest that rational creatures can ever have reasons for degrading themselves to anything less. There is also evidence in the Civil War amendments and the First Amendment that racial, ethnic, and religious intolerance are wrong, along with other attempts, like sexism, to classify those who resemble us, and therefore ourselves, as other than rational creatures. In cultural and larger constitutional context, the First Amendment suggests that coercing belief, silencing criticism, and compelling pledges to flags are wrong, for these practices would degrade us as a nation by implying that we are so incompetent and insecure that we would eventually have to govern creatures that resemble us as incapable of acting from reason and example and distinguishing displays and appearances of patriotism from the real thing. The electoral provisions and the whole structure of separate and coordinate institutions of government can be taken to suggest that unaccountable and precipitous decision is wrong, and wrong essentially for the same reason as the rest: its inconsistency with the claim that human beings can act on the basis of what reasoning among themselves reveals as good.

There is no evidence, however, of a constitutional belief that it is morally wrong to prohibit abortion per se or deny obtrusive sexuality the status of exemplary adult conduct. One does find in the due process clause a general presumption in behalf of individual liberty strong enough to require that liberty be abridged only in accordance with legal rules pursuant to the decisions of more or less representative deliberative bodies and with what all who are recognized as capable of reason can see as good-faith versions of the common good. This general presumption in behalf of liberty does allow for large amounts of privacy in property, sexual preference, the nurture of one's body, and so forth. It should certainly prohibit persecution or any active discrimination against homosexuals per se, for example. Moreover, even after liberties are abridged by constitutionally enacted laws, the Fourth and Fifth amendments recognize limited rights to lock our doors and refuse disclosure of our activities to others. So the Constitution maintains a de facto privacy far beyond those forms of privacy it exempts from legislative decision by right. For better or worse, however, many of the liberties we enjoy in actual privacy can be abridged constitutionally when we make them visible enough to constitute obstacles to the desiderata envisioned by the grants of power to our national and state governments. We have to recognize, for example, the possibility that obtrusive sexuality of any variety and assertive associational preferences born of "private" race prejudice can seriously reduce the effectiveness of public agencies like the armed forces and the public schools while burdening the nation's effort to achieve an equally protective state of affairs. Despite occasional periods of forgetfulness, we have known for a very long time that unrestrained liberty to accumulate and use property can defeat any conception of the public's economic health. Because the nation did and should have given the government the powers to pursue certain ends, the due process clause constitutes no barrier to legislative determinations beyond requirements for due deliberation by constitutionally competent bodies that act through established lawmaking procedures productive of constitutional laws—i.e., laws embodying recognizable versions or conceptions of ends that one or another of our governments is empowered to pursue.

What about the Ninth Amendment and the equal protection and privileges and immunities clauses of the Fourteenth Amendment? Can they shelter privacy rights other than those subsumed by specific constitutional guarantees? I have discussed Ely's recent argument that these three clauses are open-ended delegations to the future.[54] If he is correct, one could contend that new social values could achieve constitutional status despite the commitments of the framers. One must agree with Ely and others that historical practices and conceptions are not dispositive of constitutional meaning. The due process clause, for example, commits us to the general idea of fairness, not to any particular historical conception, and we have seen that there is no compelling reason to believe the framers would not have recognized the potential unfairness of their own particular conceptions and thus the constitutional obligations of future generations to substitute better conceptions of the same general idea.[55] Moreover, to insist upon historical conceptions of these general ideas, as Raoul Berger and other conservatives have done, is to overlook the aspirational aspect of the Constitution.[56] We would have no aspirations if we were perfectly content with prevailing attitudes and practices or if we felt the self-satisfaction of having realized our goals.[57] When law incorporates aspirations, the meaning of the law cannot be ascertained merely by pointing to historical attitudes and practices, for if we had no prior idea of the aspirations in question we would not know where to point; and, by the logic of aspirations, we could not point at anything and everything that was said and done. We recall here that the historical fact of slavery did not prevent Lincoln's reasoning from an aspirational view of the Constitution respecting the intentions of the framers about slavery.

One can agree with Ely in part, therefore, about the need for "constitutional growth"—more accurately, about the need for maturing conceptions of constitutional norms. This kind of growth not only can occur, it must occur lest one lose evidence of those normative distances between one's inclinations and constitutional provisions on which the Constitution depends for its status as law. The Constitution ceases to be law for us when we stop trying to live up to it and when we come to feel that any of its subjects is always right, including the Supreme Court, and including ourselves. But constitutional logic cannot support Ely's notion of open-ended delegations to the future without abandoning altogether the idea (to which Ely himself subscribes) that nothing is constitutional except that which has been ratified in some sense.[58] In short, new conceptions must be understood as better conceptions of old ideas—expressed or implied, in specific provisions or in the Constitution's authentic tradition, structure, or broader themes—but old ideas nonetheless. And to satisfy the logical requisites of constitutional rights as real exemptions from the powers of government, those who hold new conceptions must believe them worthy of great, even heroic, sacrifices. Perhaps privacy rights beyond those in the penumbras of explicit constitutional guarantees, like the freedoms of speech and religion, can reveal themselves in the logic of the Constitution as a whole and thus find a place in what Ely calls the open-ended provisions of the Constitution. But if I may give a personal judgment without pretending to settle the matter, I do not see anything in the historical claims of this nation, in its aspirations, in the nature of reason, in constitutional language, or in our ordinary views of what is admirable that would yield true constitutional status to a right to abortion per se. I say this notwithstanding my approval of permitting early abortions as a matter of public policy and my conviction that antiabortion policies of any kind at this period of our history, including discriminatory funding decisions, are violations either of due process or the obligation to provide equal protection of the laws.[59]

For an additional illustration of the difference a constitutional attitude can make, I shall briefly outline a theory of the general scope of the First Amendment's freedom of speech, and I shall deliberately develop an initial hypothesis as to the content of that guarantee in a way that conservatives and so-called strict constructionists could approve. I shall not begin, as my argument so far would have suggested, with an eye to the intrinsic value of a nation that never flinches from the risks of testing its claims. Instead, I shall initially defend a relatively conservative conception in order to show how the logic of the Constitution and a corresponding constitutional attitude would transform such a conception. We would begin, then, by asking what form or forms of speech the founding generation aspired to place above prevailing conceptions of such ends as national security and economic health. The language of the First Amendment and the logic of its relationship to the powers of government compel the conclusion that *some* form or forms of speech are so elevated. Some may feel that artistic expression and commercial speech are as valuable as any other form of expression. But a necessary condition for believing a form of speech truly exempt from governmental power is a belief that it is worthy of supreme sacrifices. Equally important for constitutional purposes is whether one believes the founding generation did or, if it had been fully conscious of its own aspirations, could have aspired to protect a form of speech regardless of competing social costs. Of course, as a historical matter one can doubt the commitment of the founding generation even to freedom of political expression, given its own suppression of dissent during and after the American and French revolutions.[60] But here again, we are entitled to rely on the founders' most authoritative word, and that word clearly implies transcendent value for some form or forms of speech, no matter what the subsequent judgments of their legislatures and courts about the constitutionality of their efforts to suppress dissent. Although some people may well have aspired to more, our conservative beginning would lead one to say that the enormous strength of the right we seek limits its scope, and we risk error by imputing to the framers a real commitment beyond peaceful and even public-spirited expression on matters of public concern.

Why *peaceful* expression? Did not the founding generation defend a right of revolution? Do not conservative groups incorporate that right in their liberal interpretation of the Second Amendment right to keep and bear arms?[61] Does this qualification undermine the claim that the Bill of Rights points to values higher than prevailing conceptions of personal and national security? It could be said that the Constitution protects all forms of political expression, peaceful or otherwise, were it not for Congress's power under Article I, section 9, to suspend the writ of habeas corpus when "public Safety may require it," "in Cases of Rebellion or Invasion." The power to suspend the writ is at least the power to suspend opportunities for asking judges to declare that rights have been violated, if not the power to suspend the rights themselves. The existence of this power argues for a conception of honoring rights as a practice that takes place in a context of minimal physical safety. Hence the theory that the Constitution protects only *peaceful* political expression. But even so, the language of the writ-suspension power signifies a great deal less than a general power to defeat constitutional rights for the sake of domestic tranquility and national security. What is protected here is a much more limited interest in the physical safety of the population in cases of rebellion or invasion. When there is no rebellion or invasion the First Amendment leaves people free to work for the reversal of particular conceptions of national security in times of peace or war at home and abroad by such acts as peacefully organizing, speaking, and petitioning for the adoption of one's views, however hateful they may be to others.

Of course, a mandate to protect "peaceful political expression" is too general for mechanical application. But the belief that *some* acts of speech fall within that category creates a certain thrust toward the solution of the specific problems of applying the First Amendment. One might accept a two-level theory in which government can punish obscenity, libel and slander, fighting words, incitement to violence, disclosure of defense secrets, commercial fraud, disruptions of normal governmental activities, breach of the peace, and other items on a list of unprotected forms of speech. Nevertheless, the language of the First Amendment and the logical relationship of rights to enumerated powers indicate that somewhere there will be a core First Amendment freedom that must not be sacrificed to any other good. And that implies it is ultimately better to sacrifice all the desiderata within the affirmative powers of government than to suffer the blame or other loss attendant upon the forbidden act. Doing *that* wrong is worse than all the harm we ourselves might suffer if we do not do it. This is where the logic of the document leads, and if we are willing to follow that logic we will surely find ourselves tolerating forms of speech that we may believe unworthy in principle but whose protection seems necessary to insulate a core that is protected in such an uncompromising way. Thus, even though there would be no First Amendment protection for obscenity, libel, or fighting words per se, we would try to narrow the scope of these categories to avoid any possibility of inadvertent suppression of well-intentioned efforts to criticize, inform, or otherwise educate the public. We might find ourselves distinguishing between obscene expressions that do and do not have "redeeming social value."[62] We might conclude that "public figures" should not have the same right to defend themselves against defamation as private persons do.[63] The category of "fighting words" might be confined to such narrow, face-to-face situations that one could employ the most offensive of expletives and the most hateful of symbols to communicate political points of view.[64] Moreover, if we really believed that no greater evil could befall us than the dishonor of suppressing peaceful speech designed to enlighten the public as to its true interests, we would protect artistic and commercial forms of speech insofar as they arguably serve the same purpose, and we would resolve in behalf of liberty and against suppression most doubts as to the classification of expressive actions as "peaceful or not," or "speech or action." Thus, political protest would be permitted to take the form of destroying draft cards and "desecrating" flags, along with nonviolent marches, sit-ins, and other bids for public attention, even to and, inevitably, sometimes beyond the brink of disrupting official functions.[65]

Truly hard doctrines would eventually suggest themselves, and truly difficult cases would eventually occur, especially if the inevitable protection of penumbral forms of speech intrinsically unworthy of sacrifice spread forgetfulness of the worthy core. One would have to grant, for example, an absolute freedom from prior restraint for communications whose would-be speakers claimed with any degree of plausibility that what they were about to make public would enlighten public decision and that they were publishing their information for that purpose. Even if we were to grant the constitutionality of subsequent punishment for malintentioned speech, we could not always know whether the communication in question was protected expression, as its hypothetical author would claim, without its content being revealed to those with the right to ascertain its nature. The Supreme Court has acted on this principle in other areas by giving judges power to review the substance of certain presidential assertions of executive privilege and the decisions of motion picture censors.[66]

A question would remain whether a court could declare itself absolute censor of what the public would be permitted to see and evaluate. Ordinary citizens with the right to be governed only under constitutional acts surely have a right to know enough about a governmental decision to ascertain its constitutionality. A court that would claim a power to hide from the public all of the materials of its decision to permit censorship would claim infallibility, in effect, for it would withhold information the public would need to assess the constitutionality of its decision. One can imagine the reaction had the courts decided for President Nixon in the tapes controversy or had they asked the public to settle for their word on the contents of the tapes. One day the public may be asked to place absolute trust in the government's or the courts' judgments about information concerning the nature of weaponry or troop movements even though there are historical examples of unlawful troop movements and weaponry shocking to the civilized conscience. Logically, there can be no constitutional justification for unconstitutional troop movements and weaponry, that is, troop movements and weaponry that would make us unwilling to reaffirm the Constitution's supremacy. One must ask, then, how the Constitution can permit the kind of censorship that would make it impossible for us to know whether certain acts of the government are constitutional or not. These considerations justify the conclusion that where it is plausible that publication is sought for the purpose of influencing public policy (a qualification that could often preclude publication of technical details, the specifics of troop movements, and other information) there can be no *constitutional* prior restraint, no matter what judges may think about the threat of irreparable harm.

"But," (one can hear it now) "to hold that we must be content with subsequent punishment because we cannot ever prevent irreparable damage by use of prior restraint is to hold the kind of nonsense that only discredits the claim to proper freedom."[67] I have already discussed some of the problems of what it means for a nation to commit suicide, and I concede the need to try to avoid construing the Constitution as a "suicide pact," to the degree that one can. But then I would ask why we are not free to call spades spades. If public opinion and other political pressures force judges to rationalize the unflattering facts of public life in constitutional terms, why must academic observers and other citizens do the same? Like it or not, there are absolutes in the First Amendment, and the First Amendment is law. But asserting this does not deny that people in and out of government disobey laws of all kinds, and with considerable frequency. Nor does it deny that people can have excellent reasons for disobeying laws. Just because the First Amendment says something does not mean that we can or should do what it says, not even that we should act on our best conception of what it says. Nor can one successfully argue that those who would keep the Constitution alive as effective law would look for workable conceptions of constitutional provisions beyond the Constitution's language and logic if need be. That is not a defensible position because those who accept constitutional supremacy commit themselves to a process of continuing reaffirmation, as we have seen, and that process is pointless unless one admits the possibility that the Constitution may not meet the tests for survival, despite one's wishes that it will. Those who see constitutional interpretation and reaffirmation as forms of rationalization do not really accept the *Constitution* as supreme law, and, despite the pretexts, they know that they do not accept the Constitution as supreme law. When they face a choice between admitting that the government violates the Constitution and pretending that the Constitution is so flexible that the government cannot violate the Constitution, they opt for the latter on the strength of the slogan that "there are no absolutes." But this slogan cannot translate into a constitutional principle.

If the First Amendment contained no absolute it might effectively read, "Abridge speech only when there are good reasons for doing so." Such a rule would be better than no rule at all because it would provide a warrant for judicial entry into legislative decision and thereby an additional obstacle to precipitous actions affecting speech. Here one would invoke Ely's argument that there is no constitutional basis for judges to deny the institutional implications of constitutional provisions;[68] a First Amendment requirement that the government abridge speech only for good reasons would still be the judiciary's to enforce in appropriate cases. If, however, all the First Amendment requires is good reasons, then the constitutional concept of free speech amounts to the right to have one's day in a court that wants to do its duty, and this because the only effective freedom we would have is that which the courts would believe unreasonable to deny us. Freedom of speech would fluctuate with the authoritative reasons for abridging speech.[69] At best, First Amendment claims would be due process claims of sorts, and the First Amendment would have succeeded in forcing policy makers to regard those whose speech is abridged as parts of a common enterprise that all would approve if they could but reason aright—again, no small safeguard for the individual, as we can see in past and present controversies over property and abortion rights. As with the other substantive values protected by the due process clause, however, the First Amendment so conceived would not really be an exemption from the powers of government.

I have said that if the First Amendment were not an absolute it might be equivalent to a requirement of good reasons for abridging speech. But why "good reasons"? Why not "any reasons," or "no special reasons at all"? Aside from what I have said about the requirements of the due process clause, those who deny the existence of constitutional absolutes cannot very well cite the text of the First Amendment as a basis for requiring good reasons, because the text of the amendment says nothing about good reasons. Of course, by citing the text of the amendment one would implicitly acknowledge the uncompromising language that makes "good reasons" preferable to "any reasons." Spotting the inchoate contradiction in references to the First Amendment's text, liberal nonabsolutists move to other grounds for requiring good reasons for abridging First Amendment rights. The principal nontextual arguments for strict judicial review of First Amendment claims as opposed to, say, property rights claims, have been that special protection for speech (1) keeps open the avenues of political redress, (2) protects minorities not effectively represented in the legislature, and (3) expands the policy alternatives available for democratic choice. Yet, as Wallace Mendelson once pointed out in opposition to these arguments: (1) Communists and their sympathizers were not prevented from working through the political process for repeal of the Smith Act; (2) some ideological positions are better represented in the legislatures than some economic interests; and (3) one may well contribute to eventual restrictions of popular choice by vetoing the suppression of speech threatening to the democratic process itself.[70] So these grounds need not support a strong First Amendment. As it turns out, no absolutes means no absolutes—not even an absolute requirement for good reasons in First Amendment cases. That leaves us with the uncompromising language of the amendment's text and the general logic of constitutional rights as a better basis for requiring good reasons for abridging speech. A strong First Amendment is defensible only against the background of an absolute First Amendment.

Does this mean we would have to permit all plausibly public-spirited publications concerning troop movements, intelligence activities, weaponry, and the like? How fortunate the nation that can evade this question! Sooner or later, however, we would have to say that the First Amendment prohibits prior censorship regardless of the costs. Of course, we probably would say at that point that we simply could not honor the First Amendment. "Necessity" would win out, as it does most of the time—one could say all of the time if human beings did not have and insist on having tales about gods and heroes. But if it is true that the nation probably would not honor constitutional prohibitions in the face of truly great risks and sacrifices, is there any remaining sense in which the Constitution can govern our behavior? The answer depends on the attitudes of those who believe they have been forced by events to violate the law. Those who settle for the mere appearance of legitimacy will gloss such failures to live by the law with a spurious constitution inconsistent with the very concept of failure. For them the Constitution will not have been violated when events force violations because the Constitution contains "no absolutes." But this is not the only way to react to failure. When government proves unable to avoid violating the Constitution, there is nothing impossible about facing that fact, deploring the conditions that bring it about, and committing the nation to change those conditions. With this attitude, the Constitution, while no longer effective law, could still be an effective ideal despite our lapses. Even in the breach, an aspect of the Constitution could remain alive in our public life as a set of standards for self-criticism and self-improvement. In light of its aspirational properties the Constitution will die in the attitudes of its subjects before it is killed altogether by events external to those attitudes. In any case, a living constitution is one that remains normative for events; it is hardly one that is dragged along behind events. The "no absolutes" slogan cannot be a constitutional principle.

One of this century's most important constitutional developments has been the application of most of the Bill of Rights to the states through the due process clause of the Fourteenth Amendment.[71] This development has overcome much of the effect of John Marshall's holding in *Barron* v. *Baltimore* (1830) that the framers intended to apply the Bill of Rights solely to the national government.[72] Marshall's opinion about the intentions of the framers is widely accepted as accurate. Yet, one could argue that, historical conceptions aside, the best evidence for what the framers intended was what they said and that the language of all but one of the first nine amendments is general enough to apply to all levels of government in America. But even if one accepts this argument the First Amendment expressly applies to Congress with no mention of the states, and this reinforces Marshall's view of the original intention regarding the Bill of Rights as a whole. Nevertheless, Marshall's theory remains problematic, for the general normative properties of the Constitution have to be taken into account in deciding between alternative interpretations of the framers' intentions, and Marshall's theory offends both the need for consistency among constitutional provisions and the aspirational aspect of the Constitution as a whole.

When we refer to First Amendment rights today, say, the right to free speech, we think of one right, applicable to all agencies of our governments, national and state. We do not think of a right against *this* government or agency as distinguished from a right against *that* government or agency. We think of the right as a human right applicable to all governments everywhere, though honored only by few, and we criticize those regimes that fail to honor the right. In this we are in tune with Jefferson when he said of such rights that they are "what the people are entitled to against every government on earth, general or particular."[73] As long as we think of constitutional rights this way, the refusal of the founding generation to apply the First Amendment rights to the states seems to involve a contradiction. The contradiction appears when we recall the logic of constitutional rights generally and the supremacy of national policies over those state policies in conflict with national policies. If constitutional rights can trump the powers of the national government, and if national policies can defeat state policies, it seems anomalous to conclude that state policies can defeat constitutional rights. It is like holding free speech more important than the national goal of national security, national security more important than the state goal of litter-free streets, and litter-free streets more important than free speech. This would have been a valid result had the Court and the nation generally continued to view the First Amendent as an exemption from national power only.[74] If the framers' views could have supported such results, were the framers not simply confused or wrong?

When we form judgments about the beliefs of individuals we cannot say they believe all that is implicit in a prior belief. We cannot say that x is weightier with them than z because they feel x outweighs y and y outweighs z. One need not believe the implications of one's beliefs because one need not be aware of those implications. But whether or not the framers were aware of the implications of their beliefs, one who is aware of what one is doing cannot accept the premises of an argument without accepting the conclusion. If we believe the values of the Bill of Rights more important than conflicting conceptions of nationally authorized ends that, in turn, are more important than conflicting state policies, we cannot deny that the values of the Bill of Rights are superior to conflicting policies of the states—not, at any rate, if we want consistency for our beliefs about the meaning of the law, something we must have if the law is to guide our conduct. Marshall's beliefs in this regard were simply inconsistent, for despite his refusal to apply the Bill of Rights to the states he held a strong nationalist position in most other respects. By refusing to apply the Bill of Rights to the states Marshall inevitably, if inadvertently, suggested the broader constitutional view in which that refusal makes sense. This was the old states' rights view that the quality-of-life concerns of the states were more important, if not always more urgent, than the narrow objectives of the national government in commerce and foreign affairs, objectives that could supersede state policies when absolutely necessary to maintain minimal economic and international conditions needed by all, whatever their differences in styles of life. From this view it is not irrational to say that it is up to the several states to decide basic questions of human rights, that the national government must for the most part accept whatever enjoyment of rights the states decide to permit, but that in some areas, principally commerce and international affairs, the national government can on urgent occasions overrule the states, as long as it does not violate individual rights as defined by its own courts.

This, of course, was not Marshall's broader constitutional view. Had Marshall believed national powers superior only in the sense of greater urgency but not in the sense of higher value, he would have adopted the states' rights construction of the necessary and proper clause in *McCulloch* v. *Maryland*. But Marshall could not agree with Maryland's position that the national government could encroach on matters reserved to the states only when absolutely necessary to avoid nullifying national objectives. He held instead that Congress could do things otherwise reserved to the states whenever such moves were merely "appropriate" or "plainly adapted" to authorized national ends.[75] One would not compromise higher (though less urgent) values so lightly.

One might say in defense of Marshall that as a mere judge he had no choice but to accept a contradiction that originated not with him but with the framers of the law. But this cannot be a complete description of a judge's duty, for insofar as a law is contradictory it cannot guide our conduct and therefore is not really a law. Nor are its framers really framers of a law. For this reason, fidelity to the framers as framers would require that one try to resolve their contradictions in accordance with a theory of their higher values. As is evident in his *McCulloch* opinion, Marshall himself appreciated the need for construing parts of the Constitution to harmonize with broader themes of the Constitution as a whole. This brings us back to the aspirational character of the Constitution. The document must have more than the internal consistency of a law. To be the supreme law it purports to be, its ways must continually be reaffirmed as descriptive of our best current conception of an ideal state of affairs. First we must seek and then we must ask whether we can reaffirm our best conception of the framers' aspirations. Of course, we can err in these judgments, and our consciousness of this possibility should result in an attitude of self-restraint and self-criticism, as I have argued. But we cannot avoid judgment. In this case, the question is whether (1) constitutional language, logic, and tradition lead us to believe that the framers as framers aspired to a regime in which the highest social values were served by the states with only the most urgent tasks left to the national government, and the Bill of Rights a limitation on the latter only, or (2) the framers aspired to a society in which the values of economic prosperity and liberal toleration would defeat the culturally exclusive, comparatively illiberal societies in the states.

This is an old question. Walter Berns once found it at the heart of the debate between Jefferson and Hamilton on the bank bill.[76] He contended that the nationalist aspiration is more plausible as an imputation to the framers partly because the nation has been set on a firm nationalist course since the founding and partly because there is no institutional support for the states' rights position comparable to the institution of judicial review.[77] Had the framers been states' righters, in other words, the Constitution would have recognized the right of the states to enforce the Constitution against the national government, something Berns said it does not do. But the issue is complex. The nationalist aspiration may not last indefinitely for a variety of psychological and economic reasons, and as I shall contend in the next chapter, constitutional logic may not support the current judicial monopoly of constitutional review, a monopoly presupposed in Berns's argument, at least as far as the states are concerned. Aside from secession and nullification, which, let me assume here, we can dismiss as constitutional powers, the notion of interposition that Madison defended in his later years is unobjectionable on constitutional grounds.[78] Madison's critics say that when he spoke out against the nullifiers of the 1830s he retreated from the strong suggestion he had written into the Virginia Resolutions of 1799, the suggestion that the states could actually nullify national laws. Looking back on the Virginia Resolutions some thirty years later Madison said that, beyond the natural right of revolution, they had claimed little more than the legal right of state legislatures to communicate informal judgments about the constitutionality of national laws. Madison insisted that he had not really intended interposition by state legislatures as a substitute for judicial review. Perhaps this was a shift from a strong claim to a weak one, but it does not have to be construed this way, for an informal power of interposition need not have been an insignificant power. One should not overlook the influence of informal institutions in the American system, nor should one assume that the judicial monopoly is as formally accredited as other institutions. Indeed, because the Constitution does not expressly provide for the judicial monopoly, one could cite that monopoly as an example of just how powerful an informal institution can become. In any event, the states can still establish an informal practice of interposition, which could become an important influence on our constitutional law. For all the risks it would involve (and they seem forbidding to me at this writing) one might even defend an informal practice of interposition as a step toward creating a constitutional frame of mind among state officials generally.

Although an adequate discussion of Madison's thought on interposition is beyond the concerns of this book, I mention Madison's later theory lest we take for granted the constitutionality of the nationalism that prevails today. Nationalism is decidedly more plausible than states' rights as an imputation to the framers. But in holding this view we may be revealing more about ourselves than the Constitution, and we should be sufficiently disturbed by that prospect to be critical of our view. On the other hand, Berns's inference from the practice of judicial review may hold even if we come to deny a constitutional warrant for the judicial monopoly of today.[79] A pluralist approach to constitutional review would still find judges looking to their best constitutional conceptions when exercising their functions, for while legislatures would do the same in performing their functions, legislatures could not decide concrete judicial cases and controversies. As I shall argue in the next chapter, legislatures might refuse cooperation with unconstitutional judicial acts without thereby supplanting judicial decisions in particular cases or obviating the need to propose new amendments for controlling the future decisions of courts. Some independent form of judicial review would survive because of our notions of constitutional supremacy and the different functions of legislatures and courts.

Assuming, then, that nationalism was the authentic intention of the framers, we should approach the Bill of Rights accordingly. We could pattern our arguments after Lincoln's theory about an original constitutional commitment ultimately to end slavery. We could say that, despite the flawed perception of the First Congress, a nationalized bill of rights was always implicit in the logic of the system. The integrity of the document as a whole of compatible parts would depend on its adumbrating a future state of affairs in which liberal toleration would pervade the nation at large. We would view the Fourteenth Amendment as a step toward the fulfillment of an original commitment in that it provides the legal categories for removing the contradiction of allowing the inferior powers (and values) of the states to defeat superior national values.

In general, therefore, from 1925 to 1972 the Supreme Court helped the nation realize its constitutional aspirations in nationalizing most of the Bill of Rights.[80] Nevertheless, the precise manner in which First Amendment rights were nationalized has brought about results offensive to the Constitution. The courts should have protected these substantive rights under the Fourteenth Amendment's privileges and immunities clause, not under the due process clause.[81] The due process clause does not really exempt life, liberty, and property from governmental power; it only protects persons from being hurt by government without due process. Incorporate First Amendment rights into the due process clause and the amendment effectively reads, "The states [and Congress, too, if the same rights apply to both] can deprive persons of their freedoms of speech, press, and religion if they have compelling reasons for doing so." Substantive rights so conceived have become "liberty interests" to be balanced by the courts against interests the legislatures serve in exercising their powers. This downgrades constitutional values that should be protected with unqualified force and deprives these rights of their status as real exemptions from the powers of government. Worse, the resulting view of constitutional rights distorts our view of the proper ends of constitutional powers.

Hamilton cautioned in the 84th *Federalist* that bills of rights would provide little more than illusory protection for the rights themselves and that "[w]hatever fine declarations may be inserted in any constitution . . . [rights] must altogether depend on public opinion, and on the general spirit of the people and of the government."[82] This raises the question whether our governments are empowered actively and directly to shape attitudes favorable to constitutional rights. Can a constitutional government seek to make its people virtuous in accordance with a constitutional model of virtue? Of course, a great deal can be done to shape public attitudes simply by the conduct and statements of public officials and by the liberal or illiberal nature of governmental policies. But aside from education by example, public exhortations, and the character of what people try to achieve through government outside what is usually called the field of education, what about that field itself? Can the government instruct and train young people to believe that things like bigotry, self-righteousness, vindictiveness, greed, superstition, self-indulgence, and pretext are ugly and wrong? Part of the answer to this question depends on whether the Constitution presupposes certain qualities of mind in those who fully accept its authority. I have argued that the Constitution is not open to any and every way of life, that we must understand the Constitution in terms of certain kinds of ends, that constitutional questions must be approached with a certain attitude, and that we cannot fully comprehend the Constitution's claims if we do not have that attitude. So, it would seem, the Constitution does presuppose and depend on certain attitudes and beliefs, and to the extent that one can reaffirm the Constitution's supremacy, perhaps one can feel justified in promoting those attitudes and beliefs.

Of course, the problem with this suggestion is that one who accepts the Constitution's supremacy knows that reaffirmation has to be repeated over and again. As I have observed, the moment one loses all disinclination to follow the Constitution, one can no longer see the Constitution as an ideal to be achieved or as a norm of any kind. An attitude perfectly congruent with the Constitution is not properly described as one conforming to the Constitution's model of virtue, because virtue implies self-restraint in accordance with some standard, and, relative to the Constitution as a standard, a perfectly congruent attitude has nothing in it to restrain. Those who accept the Constitution's supremacy must be committed to that through which they perceive constitutional supremacy: a process of thought through which they examine their values and their best understanding of the Constitution. It is precisely this commitment to thought that undermines the idea of molding the character of children because it is always possible that thinking people will reject the constitutional mold. Because genuine reaffirmation is possible only for those who are prepared to reject the Constitution, I have argued that we undermine constitutionalism itself when we affect to believe what we know is not so: that the Constitution can take any form, serve any value, survive any environmental change. It might seem, therefore, that to the extent that one accepts the Constitution's dependence upon thought, one cannot feel justified in promoting a particular set of attitudes and beliefs, for we may find reason to reject it.

It may not be true, however, that thinking individuals can succeed in rejecting all attitudes and beliefs. The attitudes and beliefs I have in mind are those favoring reason itself. Aside from wondering about the nature and adequacy of reason, can someone arrive at a reasoned decision to live without thinking any more? Can there be a successfully reasoned rejection of reason itself? Let us assume here that an affirmative answer to these questions would be absurd, or at least beyond public defense or proof, for then we would have the paradox of self-styled irrationalists giving reasons for believing that they had rejected having reasons for what they do.[83] If one cannot give reasons for rejecting reason, we could justify the government's inclining children in the direction of honoring at least some rights or the ideas they embody if we could accept one additional proposition: that certain rights flow from the value we find in giving and exchanging reasons about what to believe and how to live. I have already suggested why I believe this to be the case for the general ideas embodied in the First Amendment, the due process clause, other provisions of the Civil War amendments, the Nineteenth Amendment, and the basic rights of criminal defendants. Thus, I suggested that our criminal law presupposes that its addressees are rational, that rational creatures would accept the criminal law if they were in a position to reason aright, that it is fair for the government to hold those who violate the law responsible for their acts, and that the government itself cannot have a constitutional reason for breaking the law. If this is a good argument, then the government cannot ever have a constitutional reason for failing to honor the basic rights of criminal defendants, no matter how strong the provocation to do otherwise. For not only do we degrade ourselves when we contribute to the degradation of people who resemble us, as do all who are subject to the criminal law, but their rights are embodied in what the nation said it would respect as the law. A niggardly approach to the rights of criminal defendants challenges the proposition that we human beings are capable of living in accordance with our conclusions as to how we should conduct ourselves. This is so because the Constitution embodies conclusions of this nature and because constitutional logic opposes a niggardly approach to constitutional rights. Our own pretensions require that we do our utmost to assure ourselves that we are trying to live by our best and most authoritative conclusions when events pressure us to find excuses for doing otherwise. When we fail to do our best we challenge the idea that thought can govern events. This is one reason a niggardly view of the rights of criminal defendants is an affront to the supremacy of thought in human affairs, as is a niggardly view of the First Amendment, the due process clause, and other rights.

One can at least argue, therefore, that some rights do flow from or accompany the values of reflecting and reasoning with each other about how to live in the world in which we find ourselves. To this extent a government may be justified in orienting its people toward respecting the claims of thought when those claims conflict with the specious claims of the status quo, race, religion, sex, physical comfort, safety, and so on.[84] Under ideal conditions and the solution of very difficult pedagogical problems, which I am assuming in order to hasten the point at which this argument is heading, the nation would try to educate its children to believe that they were born to think about what to do and believe more than to enjoy such obstacles to thinking as luxurious living, the approval of those who do not think, and the false comforts of dogma, narcissism, vengeance, and sophistry. We would try to make it hard for them to close their minds in later life to the representations of other thinking creatures who happened to be different in race, religion, sex, social status, or any other way except the ability and the willingness to give and exchange reasons. By developing such attitudes one would incline young minds against different kinds of prejudice, not against thought. Nor would such an attitude be receptive to the propaganda of "patriotic" groups in behalf of the Constitution, for since those who would reaffirm the Constitution must allow the possibility of its failure, a constitutional attitude would be open to evidence against assumptions on which the Constitution's authority depends. This openness applies even to the assumption that virtually all adult human beings are sufficiently capable of thought to be classified as rational creatures for the purposes of government—the assumption that under the right circumstances virtually everyone has the capacity for an active part in a self-restraining sovereign authority. The Constitution stands or falls on this assumption, as we can see from the logic of the due process clause. One would be free to reject the Constitution because the Constitution leaves one free to reject this assumption. But, if I may say something to evoke what Ely regards as one of his most important observations, we could not trust ourselves to exclude any person or group from the family of rational creatures until our best effort to avoid that result had failed, unless we considered favoritism of anything other than the truth to be immoral, and unless we valued the truth above all other values.[85]

The remaining constitutional obstacle to an effective governmental concern for the character of its people would be the view that the national government has not been granted a substantive power over education with which to displace state efforts to subordinate reason to one or another variety of "family values" different from that of the family of all rational creatures. When Congress believes it does not have an expressed or implied substantive power over some area, like education, Congress sometimes resorts to the powers to tax and spend as tools for imposing the nation's will upon states that would otherwise go their own way. Consider how the national government took advantage of the fear of losing federal funds in its recent pursuit of racial justice in the states. Notwithstanding the Supreme Court's approval, however, using the powers to tax and spend as means to ends the government is not supposed to pursue through direct regulation is improper because it is a pretextual way to circumvent the enumeration of powers.[86] Congress has gotten away with such pretextual uses of the powers to tax and spend for most of this century, as one can see in the far-flung scope of federal grants-in-aid to the states, and this has led the nation to expect that Congress will play a role in deciding many questions of policy in areas otherwise reserved to the states. But the liberals who created this expectation in our century failed to support it with good arguments of constitutional principle, and this has strengthened the belief of some conservatives that most of the grant-in-aid programs are unconstitutional. These conservative critics of the scope of modern national government are not altogether wrong; I have already discussed the corrupting influence of pretextualism in constitutional law. But merely because a given area of state concern does not contain a problem for an authorized national end at a given period does not mean that it will retain its local character for all time. Clearly, the local problems of one era can become the national problems of another. This is true even if national problems are defined in terms of a fixed set of authorized national ends. At the time of their adoption, some, though not all, of the existing federal grant-in-aid programs could have been justified as means to the nation's economic health, if not the narrow requirements of interstate trade, and supporters of these programs could have answered constitutional doubts by showing their critics why a genuine commitment to constitutional supremacy calls for understanding Congress's powers in terms beyond historical conceptions like interstate trade. Had this happened the nation might not have felt the need for a theory that Congress can tax and spend for whatever purpose, authorized or otherwise. As for areas beyond Congress's authority, Congress should have restrained itself until it could give a forthright justification for its intervention in terms of its authorized ends, as it did, for example, in the National Defense Education Act of 1958 and as it could do today in view of the military and economic implications of the current crisis in the nation's schools. While the nation's circumstances have not always favored an awareness of them, justifications for a broader intervention in the educational policies of the states have always been present in the guarantee clause and in the enforcement provisions of the Civil War Amendments, for these provisions impose affirmative duties on the states and imply that where Congress believes the states have failed in these duties, it has an obligation to do the states' jobs for them.[87] The Court might have been moved to see these provisions in light of legitimate national concerns beyond military and economic needs had it recognized the extent to which the performance of constitutional duties depends on a constitutional attitude among the public at large. Consider, for example, how difficult it would be for the government to pursue policies that would be accepted as reasonable by all segments of public opinion if a majority or even a significant minority were eager to employ government as an instrument of its religious convictions. One can also wonder how an electorate of greedy and prejudiced individuals could support the variety of welfare and affirmative-action programs that a genuine commitment to equal opportunity requires, or whether the various segments of our society could trust each other's policy preferences as responsible versions of the public interest if all had not been persuaded that fraud, indolence, and self-indulgence were wrong.

A pervasive constitutional attitude would make the performance of constitutional duty more feasible by weakening the impression that constitutional rights can conflict with each other. Those who are aware of the Constitution's logic will agree that although some rights expressed or implied by provisions of the Constitution's text may not be real constitutional rights, and that although litigants and others invoking particular conceptions of constitutional rights may conflict with each other, the rights themselves do not conflict. That the constitutional document may contain mistaken rights follows from what the document itself implies about the possibility of errors on the part of the framers. Thus, some see no virtue in honoring the right to keep and bear arms. I am inclined to disagree with this view, but I would agree that the implied right of property in slaves was a mistake, to be honored, if at all, only because of extraconstitutional considerations, not because one could have a coherent view of slavery as part of a constitution whose broader themes are found in the Preamble, the process of constitutional reaffirmation, and the due process clause.

That litigants or conceptions of constitutional rights can conflict with each other would be evident even in a constitutionally ideal state of affairs, for this would not be a utopian state of affairs, and wherever the Constitution would be obeyed as law there would be disinclinations to follow it. Aware of these disinclinations, those who accepted the Constitution's supremacy would recognize the need for government to remind them of their better selves. Losers in legislatures and courts that functioned as the Constitution envisions would leave these struggles at least with the feeling that their initial conceptions of justice and the common good could be wrong and that, all things considered, the government was probably closer to the mark than not. They would not confuse conflicting conceptions of rights with conflicting rights because they would appreciate the distinction and they would acknowledge the potential error of their conceptions. Such, of course, is not the attitude of racists, sexists, religious zealots, ideologues, determinists, and others who, in one way or another, deny or try to deny that reasoning with others is the best way to determine what to believe and how to live. This is why these attitudes cannot predominate in a constitutionally ideal state of affairs.

That constitutional rights themselves cannot conflict is indicated by my earlier argument that honoring real constitutional rights is a virtue. If the rights themselves could conflict, then one right could defeat or compromise another. To the extent that honoring one right involved defeating or compromising another, honoring that right could not be a virtue. Thus, to the extent that honoring the freedom of religious exercise resulted in the practical equivalent of officially established school prayer, one could doubt that honoring the right of free exercise was a virtue. Added to the Constitution's dependence on the supremacy of reason, this would suggest, let us say, a more moderate conception of the free exercise clause. One could conclude that it is a mistake to hold conceptions of free exercise that guarantee much more than the freedom of religious belief already implicit in the establishment clause and elsewhere. We would have to alter our conception of one or another right in this way in order to avoid the impermissible conclusion that constitutional rights themselves can conflict.

To illustrate further unacceptable consequences of believing that constitutional rights can come into conflict, let us assume that the indisputably best conception of the freedom of the press embraced the right of reporters to shield the identity of their news sources. On this hypothesis one might compromise or otherwise abridge the right to shield sources, but one could not deny that it is a constitutional right that is being compromised. Assume further that the defendant in a hypothetical criminal trial had the undeniable right to know the names of the reporter's sources as part of the right to a fair trial. Here, then, would be what we would call a real conflict of rights or the best conceptions thereof, not a mere conflict between persons holding contestable conceptions. Should a judge try to resolve this conflict by honoring one right at the expense of the other, he would fail to honor his oath to honor all constitutional rights. He might say, however, that he has no choice because conditions make it impossible for him fully to comply with his oath. But that would amount to a concession that the Constitution had ceased to be applicable to events as law—that, strictly speaking, the Constitution was no longer the law it says it is.

To avoid this result our judge might consider dismissing the prosecution against the defendant. Arguing for dismissal would be the fact that compromising the reporter's right would force that right to yield not to the defendant's right but to some of the objectives of the criminal law, objectives authorized by the government's granted powers. If the judge had no interest in advancing these objectives he would dismiss the prosecution, for the defendant would have no right to a fair trial per se, but only as a condition for losing life, liberty, or property.

Does it follow, then, that our judge would have to dismiss the prosecution in order to avoid violating his oath? How could he do otherwise consistently with his obligation to treat constitutional rights as real exemptions from granted powers? Many would oppose dismissal because they would place the highest value on the aims of the criminal justice system. But theirs would be an unconstitutional view of the ends of the criminal law under the Constitution, ends that must be defined to include honoring defendants' rights. Their position also suggests that what they see as constitutional ends can be pursued through unconstitutional means. They might try to defend this assumption (or equivalent assumptions, like "no absolutes") by arguing that it is necessary for the Constitution's survival. But this would suggest that there is always a constitutional way to get whatever the nation might want, and we have seen that this assumption denies constitutional supremacy by eliminating the need for the reaffirmation on which the Constitution's supremacy depends. Nevertheless, it is true that the Constitution does envision its own reaffirmation—it envisions a state of affairs where all would agree that the government can deprive the guilty of their liberty without violating their constitutional rights. And, in addition to violating constitutional rights, government can defeat the Constitution by acting in ways that convince people that it is impossible to live as the Constitution envisions. Even if constitutionalism could survive the conviction that time had run out on the Constitution of 1789, it is this constitution that our judge is sworn to look for ways to preserve. He would make a dubious contribution to that objective by an action that would deepen the feeling that a real respect for constitutional rights is incompatible with any acceptable version of personal security and similar desiderata. So our judge would run into objections on either of the options considered so far.

The judge may have an alternative other than resigning and taking leave of the entire matter, perhaps looking for a better place to be altogether: he may try to honor his oath by persuading the parties to restrain their demands against each other. To succeed he would have to show them that their attitude toward each other forces him and others in government to act in unconstitutional ways. He would make them see that constitutionalism itself and therewith their highest aspirations are illusions without a pervasive commitment to honoring constitutional rights as a collective and personal achievement. The judge could properly understand this educational work to be a part of his function as a judge. Indeed, there is no good reason why judicial exhortation of the public should exclude appeals for a better understanding of constitutional principles and the dissemination of a constitutional attitude. If it is proper for judges to make the public aware of crowded dockets and other problems of judicial administration, it is proper for them to speak out about the attitudes and other conditions that give rise to these difficulties. Should he fail in his attempt to persuade the parties to restrain themselves, our judge would be unable to try the case without violating what, by hypothesis, is someone's constitutional right. Multiply this and similar situations enough times and the government would be seen as unable to achieve the immediate ends of granted powers while honoring constitutional rights. To the extent that the government could not follow the Constitution, the Constitution would cease to be effective law, and the people would have failed to constitute a self-restraining and therefore truly sovereign authority. Here, then, would be another reason why constitutional maintenance necessitates a concern for the formation of constitutional attitudes.

6

Constitutional Institutions

W E HAVE SEEN THAT
the Constitution makes sense only in light of an ideal state of affairs
to which those who fully understand and accept the Constitution's
claim to supremacy aspire. In chapter 4 I began explicating that ideal
by discussing the ends envisioned in the grant of powers to the national
government. This effort was carried forward by the discussion of
constitutional rights in the last chapter. At the center of what the
Constitution envisions are men and women whose desire for the best
conceptions of the Constitution and the good society moves them to
self-criticism and an antipathy to everything that stands in the way
of giving and exchanging reasons with each other about how to live
and what to believe. For those who accept the Constitution's authority, the ideal society seems to be that in which we enjoy just
those amounts and kinds of other good things (security, comfort,
etc.) as are compatible with honoring constitutional rights, a practice
that manifests our devotion to thinking and therefore our concern
for all who are capable of thinking.

How does this picture affect our general understanding of the
institutions established by the Constitution? I have already discussed
the most important aspects of governmental institutions: their objectives and the attitude of officials and private citizens toward those
objectives. Thus, at the bottom of those institutional problems under

the heading of "federalism" lies a question of the kind of community we want to live in—and by "we" I mean those of us who want, above all else, to give and exchange reasons about the way to live, or who would want to do so if we were in a position to think clearly about what we wanted. I have shown how the desire to be and to be recognized as reasoning creatures favors what the national government stands for, as opposed to the relatively illiberal commitments historically associated with the rights of the states. In light of all this, Marshall's reading of the necessary and proper clause is superior to Jefferson's, and the general shape of state-federal relationships follows from that. This chapter submits a few additional comments on other institutional concepts and problems, including the concept of checks and balances, executive power in emergencies, and, finally, judicial review.

The Constitution's institutional provisions are easier to point out than to delimit by a definition that would separate them sharply from provisions we call constitutional powers and constitutional rights. Institutional provisions reveal something of what the patterned motions of governing are to be and who shall have the authority to go through these motions. We know from these provisions that there shall be certain offices, who is eligible to occupy these offices, how these persons get there, and how long they can stay there. At least a superficial difference can be discerned between the normative force of institutional rules on the one hand and rules specifying powers and rights on the other. More so than institutional rules, powers and rights seem closely associated with praiseworthy practices or desirable objects, like national security, a prosperous economy, fair treatment of criminal defendants, and openness to criticism. Powers and rights are often couched in evaluative language, here authorizing the "necessary and proper," there forbidding the "cruel" and the "unreasonable." By contrast, institutional rules are more descriptive in tone. They contain many quantitative expressions, and their meaning is less controversial than the meaning of powers and rights. In fact, most of the problems concerning their meaning have involved their implications for the powers and rights of governmental bodies—that is, their implications for the kinds of things specific institutions are authorized to do on their own or relative to each other. Thus, the nation has debated whether the executive should have the power to remove administrative officials without Senate approval and whether the sole possession of the judicial power gives the courts the sole power of constitutional review. In the historical background of this difference in normative tone between institutional provisions and powers and rights, *The Federalist* suggests as part of its argument against the adoption of a bill of rights that these three different kinds of provisions would be maintained in practice by different forces. Consider a passage from the 84th *Federalist* to which I have referred:

> On the subject of the liberty of the press, as much has been said, I cannot forbear adding a remark or two: In the first place, I observe that there is not a syllable concerning it in the constitution of this state [New York], and in the next, I contend that whatever has been said about it in that of any other state, amounts to nothing. What signifies a declaration that "the liberty of the press shall be inviolably preserved?" What is the liberty of the press? Who can give it any definition which would not leave the utmost latitude for evasion? I hold it to be impracticable; and from this, I infer, that its security, whatever fine declarations may be inserted in any constitution respecting it, must altogether depend on public opinion, and on the general spirit of the people and of the government.* And here, after all, as intimated upon another occasion, must we seek for the only solid basis of all our rights.
>
> There remains but one other view of this matter to conclude the point. The truth is, after all the declamation we have heard, that the constitution is itself in every rational sense, and to every useful purpose, A BILL OF RIGHTS. The several bills of rights, in Great-Britain, form its constitution, and conversely the constitution of each state is its bill of rights. And the proposed constitution, if adopted, will be the bill of rights of the union. These remarks are designed to support an earlier observation that, unlike the situation that obtains in a monarchy, bills of rights have no application to constitutions professedly founded upon the power of the people, and executed by their immediate representatives and servants. Here, in strictness, the people surrender nothing, and as they retain every thing, they have no need of particular reservations. "WE THE PEOPLE of the United States, to secure the blessings of liberty to ourselves and our posterity, do *ordain* and *establish* this constitution for the United States of America." Here is a better recognition of popular rights than volumes of those aphorisms which make the principal figure in several of

our state bills of rights, and which would sound much better in
a treatise of ethics than in a constitution of government.[1]

Here, then, is a prediction that the restraining influence of constitutional rights will depend on the public's and the legislature's sense
of what is beneficial and right. The prediction could apply to states'
rights as well as individual rights and therefore to the restraining force
of the enumeration of powers as well as a bill of rights. Nevertheless,
in a previous argument *The Federalist* rejects a reliance on a sense
of what is beneficial and right when it comes to maintaining the
separation of powers, and the reason given is that there is little hope
that the public will regularly repress unconstitutional demands. In
the 48th *Federalist* Madison criticizes the poor knowledge of history
exhibited by those who hold that it will be "sufficient to mark with
precision the boundaries of these departments . . . and to trust to
these parchment barriers against the encroaching spirit of power."[2]
In the 49th *Federalist* he dismisses Jefferson's proposal for recurring
to popularly elected conventions in cases of boundary disputes between the branches of government. The reasons he gives amount to
the view that an almost inevitably prejudiced public opinion cannot
be expected to decide such constitutional conflicts on their real merits.[3]
Madison's general point is that the nation cannot rely on virtue for
maintaining the separation of powers, either virtue in the electorate
or virtue in the officials of the government. But if that is the case,
one must ask whether there is any realistic way to maintain the separation of powers. And if a constitutional self-restraint is unavailable
for maintaining the separation of powers, what will maintain the
Constitution generally?

Madison's famous answer to the problem of maintaining the separation of powers is usually summed up in the term *checks and balances*, an idea that still has to evoke at least a little wonder in anyone
who tries to lift it from the history books, grasp the theory behind
the cant, and apply it seriously to the problems of political life as we
know them. Madison's answer amounts to the thesis that human
beings can so arrange their intercourse with one another that they
can be counted on to do the right thing even if they do not want to.
He says in the 51st *Federalist*:

> But the great security against a gradual concentration of
> the several powers in the same departments, consists in giving
> to those who administer each department, the necessary con-

stitutional means, and personal motives, to resist encroach-
ments of the others. The provision for defence must in this, as
in all other cases, be made commensurate to the danger of attack. Ambition must be made to counteract ambition. The interest of the man must be connected with the constitutional
rights of the place. It may be a reflection on human nature,
that such devices should be necessary to controul the abuses of
government. But what is government itself but the greatest of
all reflections on human nature? If men were angels, no government would be necessary. If angels were to govern men,
neither external nor internal controuls on government would
be necessary. In framing a government which is to be administered by men over men, the great difficulty lies in this: You
must first enable the government to controul the governed;
and in the next place, oblige it to controul itself. A dependence on the people is no doubt the primary controul on the
government; but experience has taught mankind the necessity
of auxiliary precautions.

This policy of supplying by opposite and rival interests, the
defect of better motives, might be traced through the whole
system of human affairs, private as well as public. We see it
particularly displayed in all the subordinate distributions of
power; where the constant aim is to divide and arrange the
several offices in such a manner as that each may be a check
on the other; that the private interest of every individual, may
be a centinel over the public rights. These inventions of prudence cannot be less requisite in the distribution of the supreme
powers of the state.[4]

At the end of the 51st *Federalist* Madison repeats the conclusion of
the 10th *Federalist* about finding the security of civil and religious
liberties not in public and official virtue but "in the extended republic
of the United States, and among the great variety of interests, parties
and sects which it embraces." With this great variety of interests "a
coalition of the majority . . . could seldom take place on any other
principles but those of justice and the general good."[5] But according
to Madison, what moves majority coalitions to good results is not a
desire to do the right thing; it is rather the "uncertainty" and "insecurity" of the members of the majority as to the long-range impact
on themselves of a general atmosphere of injustice—the same impulses that prompt strong individuals "in a state of nature" "to submit
to a government which may protect the weak as well as themselves."[6]

So, it would seem, rights can be protected by processing demands in a certain way even in the absence of a genuine desire to honor rights on the part of those who make the demands. Ambition checking ambition is the thing to rely on, not a careful enumeration of "do's" and "don't's." Relying on the latter is banking on what history exposes as the weak to nonexistent influence of virtues connected with reason, philanthropy, public-spiritedness, and other sources, like religion.

As we reflect on the old and familiar theory of checks and balances we might wonder whether its point was that, despite the logical character of the Constitution as an expression of sovereign self-restraint, no constitutional limitation could be successful which proved inconsistent with the public demands for security and prosperity.[7] Hindsight certainly warrants this conclusion as we look around us to see how the three species of constitutional limitation—powers, rights, and institutional rules—have fared over the last two centuries. The separation of powers retains some value in the nation's constitutional consciousness; this is evident from the occasional attempts to compensate for the principle's continuing breach. The usual case for an effective separation of powers is not persuasive in times of crisis. This is to be expected, of course, for the public loses much of its apprehension of tyranny when facing serious foreign threats, civil convulsion, or economic collapse. The nation respects the separation of powers more during normal times—but not too much more, as is attested by the triumph of the administrative state and by such current controversies as those involving "legislative vetoes" of administrative decision and proposals to strip courts of their jurisdiction in cases on abortion and school prayer. The most salient recent attempt to reassert the principle in an area of policy where it had been neglected occurred in the aftermath of the Vietnam War with the passage of the War Powers Resolution of 1973 over President Nixon's veto. Several years after Congress had abdicated responsibility for the decision to Americanize the war, the growing unpopularity of the conflict had finally made it politically safe and even advantageous for Congress to insist on shared responsibility with the president for national commitments. The act was hardly an extreme claim of congressional war power, for it still gave the president a virtual blank check to act on his own for up to ninety days, time enough to effect a national commitment in all but the clearest of executive blunders. Yet the act itself was ignored, in an election year, when President

Carter announced that America would go to war in case of Soviet advance beyond Afghanistan toward the Persian Gulf, and when he moved the navy into position to prevent the war between Iran and Iraq from closing the Strait of Hormuz to oil shipments. At this writing Congress is artfully avoiding a clear position for or against what is more often called President Reagan's policy than national policy in El Salvador and other parts of Central America. The president also is resisting appeals to seek congressional approval for a peacekeeping contingent of marines in Lebanon. So goes the story of Congress's grand reassertion.[8]

As for the enumeration of powers, it has clearly ceased to be an effective constitutional limitation. On the basis of arguments in the last two chapters, I believe that some, though not all, of what has happened to the enumeration of powers is justified by the injustices historically associated with states' rights in America. This is not to say, however, that the defenders of states' rights erred in all respects. For, as I have argued, there was wisdom in the idea of a community committed to an identifiable way of life and actively concerned with the character of its people. Along with other aspects of the states' rights view, this idea succumbed to the same demands for security and prosperity that weakened the old separation of powers. These same forces had a large part in defeating the claims of states and local communities in behalf of the character and taste of their members. The economic passions liberated on the way to the urban-industrial society produced a psychology that often blended self-interest with indifference to others. It left to individuals the care of their own souls while demanding their liberation from a variety of repressive norms that would have inhibited an increase in the goods and services of an indulgent, permissive society—precisely the kind of society that really is committed to an ever-expanding gross national product, with diminishing concern for the cost in other values. The effect on the public's constitutional sense is clear. Mention "constitutional limitations" to the average American today and the first thought is of "constitutional rights." It is this species of limitation alone that appears to have been strengthened since the founding, and for the obvious reason that the wants of consumers are couched easier in rights than in other norms. Today, constitutionalism is not understood as governmental and popular restraint in behalf of the nation's aspirations. Rather, constitutionalism is said to be governmental responsiveness to public demands in ways that allow persons to do as they wish short of interfering with the wishes of others, with no real reasons for self-restraint if one is strong or clever enough to be confident of getting and keeping what one thinks one wants. It is said, typically, that the First Amendment should be supported for purposes of maintaining means for testing the usefulness of social proposals and because everyone can imagine situations in which one might put forth an initially unpopular proposal. Honoring free speech is rarely held to be a practice that is admirable in itself, as it would be among those who aspired to be reasoning creatures and to be recognized as such.

The prevailing attitude makes it difficult to see constitutional rights for what they really are: exemptions from the governmental and private impositions we make upon each other, exemptions that flow from a desire to be the kind of people who have the moral and intellectual strength to give and exchange reasons for the ways in which we want to live with each other. A certain willfulness occupies the place of dignified self-restraint. This willfulness is revealed in the Supreme Court's current approach to litigation involving constitutional rights. Here, says the Court, are contests of a kind in which the government is required to show whether it acts from an "interest" more "compelling" than that "interest" of the individual in asserting a constitutional right. The Court thus assumes that it is constitutionally permissible for the government to have a more compelling interest than that of honoring constitutional rights. Willfulness appears also in the way in which a concern for our image as a people strong enough to exercise self-restraint is degraded as softness or sentimental foolishness. We recall Justice Rehnquist's tough talk about the discomfort of pretrial detainees in the *Wolfish* case, as if the discomfort of the detainees was the most disturbing thing about the body-cavity searches, even after visits from members of our American bar. Willful and resentful politicians yearn to curb the "social activism" of groups receiving federal contracts and grants, especially legal services lawyers, as if a self-respecting nation had something to lose by this and other institutionalized forms of self-examination, like a strong Civil Rights Commission, also on the defensive at this writing. Another sign of the times appears in the Court's current struggle over the admissibility at trial of illegally seized evidence. At the beginning of that struggle Chief Justice Burger derided as the theory of a "sporting contest" the view that excluding tainted evidence from trial was necessary for maintaining the government's integrity. The Chief Justice wanted the Court to adopt the different theory that the purpose of the exclusionary rule was to deter unlawful police conduct. This was his way of initiating movement toward a weaker rule, for one can argue that a strict policy of exclusion goes beyond what is necessary to deter unlawful police conduct.[9] Eventually the majority was to agree with him, and the rule was weakened.[10] Such are the prospects for honoring rights where the perspective of real lawgivers is lost to those who will not or cannot see beyond the checking and balancing of interests.

Is today's constitutionalism a constitutionalism of separated powers, the institutional principle that the system of checks and balances was designed to maintain? The answer to this question depends partly on the value that the nation attaches to the separation of powers per se. Much of the formal institutional separation is still there (for it has been practically impossible to dismantle), but it is doubtful that an effective separation of powers has much meaning in terms of the national image we want for ourselves. The usual explanation for our declining commitment to the separation of powers is that national survival depends on compromising the principle, especially in foreign affairs under modern conditions. But this theory is problematic even if we ignore the difficulties already discussed in what is meant by "national survival" in a constitutional context. There is, in addition, much to question in the assumption that we are in fact surviving our unwillingness to exercise the responsibilities and restraints of which the separation of powers is emblematic. The erosion of the separation of powers in foreign policy making is less a response to technical complexities and the uncertainties of modern conditions than the result of the needs of politicians in Congress to pass the buck in politically risky situations. The same can be said for many of the domestic abdications of congressional responsibility in this century, from the recovery policies of the Great Depression to recent efforts at economic recovery.[11] Of course, a Congress of buck passers is one of the results of the electorate's tendency to reward politicians who are responsive to its immediate wants, not its considered conceptions of constitutional duty. As *The Federalist* predicted, the electorate does not take its conceptions of constitutional duty seriously enough to restrain demands that conflict with those conceptions.[12] The decline of the separation of powers thus indicates a broader personal and public psychology of nonrestraint, which may not be conducive to "survival" at all. Without going further into the relationships between the nation's prospects for survival, its public psychology, and the separation of powers, it is evident that one can challenge the commonplace that national survival has necessitated a relaxation of our attachment to the separation of powers.

One might respond to all this by contending that, as a historical matter, there never really was an attachment to the separation of powers per se in this country, that it was always just a means to avoiding tyranny and lesser undesirable results, and that it was never a practice of the kind in which one could take pride or find intrinsic value. In support of this view one might observe the apologetic tone of the 51st *Federalist* when it says its proposal for a system of checks and balances reflects the fact that men are not angels and angels do not govern men. This may suggest that the separation of powers is something less than an end in itself. Nevertheless, there is more to the separation of powers than instrumental value despite the fact that instrumentalism is one of its characteristics, a property it shares in some measure with other constitutional provisions. We see another aspect to the separation of powers when we reflect on its link with what the 1st *Federalist* appeals to as our desire to show the world that "societies of men . . . are really capable . . . of establishing government from reflection and choice."[13] Along with the general theme of the separation of powers as a barrier to tyrannical government, the 51st *Federalist* stresses a more specific aim of the Constitution's version of the separation of powers: preventing Congress from usurping executive and judicial functions, something legislatures in democracies are said to have a tendency to do.[14] Madison outlines a system that will strengthen the executive and the judiciary at the expense of the legislature by giving the executive and the judiciary independent sources of power and dividing the legislature in such a way that the upper house will have a psychology and a set of duties that are not congruent with those of the lower house.[15] Later in The *Federalist*, when Madison and Hamilton turn to the kind of policy decisions one can expect from a government whose branches are divided in this way, they outline an institutional arrangement that makes the polity as a whole capable of repressing its raw, partisan demands in favor of options selected after a process of representative and sober deliberation.[16] It also seems that we are expected to take pride in being represented in this way—pride in having other nations see this system as representative of our national character.

Passages from the 63rd *Federalist* indicate several ways in which the public can benefit from processing raw political demands through a more respectable, more stable upper house linked almost as closely to the executive as it is to the lower house.

> A FIFTH desideratum illustrating the utility of a Senate, is the want of a due sense of national character in the House of Representatives. Without a select and stable member of the government, the esteem of foreign powers will not only be forfeited by an unenlightened and variable policy, proceeding from the causes already mentioned; but the national councils will not possess that sensibility to the opinion of the world, which is perhaps not less necessary in order to merit, than it is to obtain, its respect and confidence.
>
> An attention to the judgment of other nations is important to every government for two reasons: The one is, that independently of the merits of any particular plan or measure, it is desireable on various accounts, that it should appear to other nations as the offspring of a wise and honorable policy: The second is, that in doubtful cases, particularly where the national councils may be warped by some strong passion, or momentary interest, the presumed or known opinion of the impartial world, may be the best guide that can be followed. What has not America lost by her want of character with foreign nations? And how many errors and follies would she not have avoided, if the justice and propriety of her measures had in every instance been previously tried by the light in which they would probably appear to the unbiassed part of mankind?
>
> Yet however requisite a sense of national character may be, it is evident that it can never be sufficiently possessed by a numerous and changeable body. It can only be found in a number so small, that a sensible degree of the praise and blame of public measures may be the portion of each individual; or in an assembly so durably invested with public trust, that the pride and consequence of its members may be sensibly incorporated with the reputation and prosperity of the community.[17]

Evocative of still higher aspirations:

> To a people as little blinded by prejudice, or corrupted by flattery, as those whom I address, I shall not scruple to add, that such an institution may be sometimes necessary, as a def-

ence to the people against their own temporary errors and delusions. As the cool and deliberate sense of the community ought in all governments, and actually will in all free governments ultimately prevail over the views of its rulers; so there are particular moments in public affairs, when the people stimulated by some irregular passion, or some illicit advantage, or misled by the artful misrepresentations of interested men, may call for measures which they themselves will afterwards be the most ready to lament and condemn. In these critical moments, how salutary will be the interference of some temperate and respectable body of citizens, in order to check the misguided career, and to suspend the blow meditated by the people against themselves, until reason, justice and truth, can regain their authority over the public mind? What bitter anguish would not the people of Athens have often escaped, if their government had contained so provident a safeguard against the tyranny of their own passions? Popular liberty might then have escaped the indelible reproach of decreeing to the same citizens, the hemlock on one day, and statues on the next.[18]

Which view, then, should predominate with us: the separation of powers as means to preventing usurpations, or the separation of powers as something of an end in itself, the institutional embodiment of a national aspiration to rise above accident and force by governing ourselves by the claims of reason? The first understanding, isolated from the latter, has not always worked in practice and cannot work in theory as an ingredient of our real constitutional commitments. This conclusion finds support in my earlier argument that constitutional supremacy makes no sense unless we can understand the Constitution's ways as versions of practices that are ends in themselves. The second theory—the one that renders the separation of powers as something intrinsically praiseworthy—reflects what one might term the original position of the framers themselves, whereas the emphasis on dealing with encroaching power through checks and balances would be more salient to subsequent generations. As I noted in chapter 3, The *Federalist* does not expect subsequent generations to exhibit the virtues of the founding generation. In rejecting a reliance on public opinion for maintaining the separation of powers, Madison says in the 49th *Federalist* that the founding generation avoids the normal degree of factious division because of its proximity to the cohesive pressures of the Revolution and because of its "ardor" for showing the Old World its capacity to establish "new and opposite forms" of government. "The future situations in which we must expect to be usually placed," he says, "do not present any equivalent security against the danger which is apprehended."[19] So in explaining checks and balances to his generation he can present it as a "policy of supplying by opposite and rival interests, the defect of better motives."[20] He assumes by this statement that his generation is aware of what those better motives are and that it will test and accept his proposal for a new constitution at least partly in light of those better motives. Members of subsequent generations, it seems, will live by the Constitution with an eye to worse motives: their personal ambitions.

An error remains in Madison's thinking, however, for members of subsequent generations cannot see the separation of powers as part of the supreme law if their lack of better motives finds them following its provisions solely to further their personal ambitions. As a matter of constitutional logic, to accept the Constitution as supreme law, following its ways must be regarded as something of an end in itself. Constitutional supremacy is a reality in the mind of the fully conscious subject of the Constitution only at moments when its ways can be reaffirmed as the best current conception of the good society. This reaffirmation must be repeated over and again as one continually tests one's best conceptions of constitutional provisions and the good society. True, Madison is concerned with the average citizen, not with what I am calling the fully conscious citizen. Because Madison cannot hope for what he calls "a nation of philosphers," he says that "the most rational government will not find it a superfluous advantage to have the prejudices of the community on its side." Thus, it appears that "reverence for the laws" is to be achieved through the habits of obedience that ambitious people acquire over the years as they find obedience to the laws conducive to their interests.[21] For this proposal to work, however, those who are governed by interest, habit, or "reverence for the laws" would have to act as conscious persons act. But this is impossible unless "reverence for the laws" can be achieved through the recognition of constitutional supremacy, something that requires the act of constitutional reaffirmation. Unconscious persons cannot act in the decisive sense; they cannot perform the act of reaffirmation. Apart from allegedly more practical doubts about the success of checks and balances, genuine constitutional supremacy requires that something be done to restore the authentic perspective of the founding, the perspective of those who believe they have something to show the world about the possibility of government by reflection and choice. Admittedly, restoring the original perspective on a politically significant scale would require levels of public-spiritedness, leadership, and trust far beyond what seems likely any time soon in America. Nevertheless, these achievements are not impossible in a strict sense. Despite Madison's distracting reference, progress toward constitutional supremacy need not require a nation of philosophers, for it was not a nation of philosphers that established the Constitution, and that fact did not prevent Madison from assuming that the people he addressed could recognize and act upon a distinction between "ambition" and "better motives."

A final point about the separation of powers involves the idea of constitutional duty. We must not forget that the Constitution makes sense only in light of an ideal state of affairs that we are striving to achieve. Thus, while we can view rights negatively as exemptions from granted powers, a reasonably prosperous and secure community whose government and people honor rights is what we want to achieve. So the Constitution's ways are active and forward-looking as well as disciplined or restrained, as would be the case with any purposeful or focused effort. Just as the psychology of checks and balances has blinded us to the Constitution as an expression of national self-restraint, it has caused us to overlook the forward-looking aspect of constitutional government and the idea of constitutional duty. When the term *self-restraint* appears in constitutional discussion today, it usually denotes one or another form of abdication of responsibility. It rarely means overcoming those temptations and fears that obstruct officials' fulfilling their duty. An old idea has suffered as a consequence, the idea of government as a trust actively exercised in the people's behalf.

The idea of forward-looking, active, some say "positive," yet popular or democratic government was not an invention of the New Deal, even though events helped to make more people more aware of that idea after the Great Depression than before. In the 22nd *Federalist* Hamilton criticizes the Articles of Confederation by condemning equal voting for large and small states in Congress as undemocratic and the extraordinary majorities required for enacting legislation as a built-in guarantee of governmental impotence. "When the concurrence of a large number is required by the constitution to the doing of any national act, we are apt to rest satisfied that all is safe, because nothing is likely *to be done*," he said, "but we forget how much good may be prevented, and how much ill may be produced, by the power of hindering the doing what may be necessary, and of keeping affairs in the same unfavorable posture in which they may happen to stand at particular periods."[22] And in its defense of the proposed presidency, *The Federalist* argues forcefully for a strong, publicly accountable executive as the principal source of "energy in government," energy needed in both foreign and domestic affairs, in normal times and in emergencies, and energy that must be reconciled with democracy lest "the enlightened well wishers to this species of government" be forced to condemn democracy itself. These arguments express the governing thought of what is widely considered a twentieth-century view of government.[23]

The idea of constitutional duty in a forward-looking, popular government is found not only in the literature of the founding period and other parts of our public record and political thought, it is a conclusion of constitutional logic as well. One can state the argument briefly as follows: The government is established for the pursuit of certain ends; the prescribed arrangement of offices and powers is part of the supreme law, and therefore cannot be changed through inter-institutional abdications, abdications to the electorate, foreign powers, or entities of the government's own making; and power that cannot be abdicated must be exercised in behalf of the ends for which it was established. This means, at a minimum, that Congress cannot delegate its powers to administrators and others unless such delegations are good-faith means to choices among broader policy alternatives that Congress has already made or is committed to making after a specified period of administrative experimentation.[24] By the same argument, presidents are also obligated to exercise their legislative and executive powers in behalf of their best understanding of the ends of government.[25] Courts, too, should take every bona fide jurisdictional opportunity to decide legal questions—including constitutional questions—on the merits.[26] And government as a whole cannot abdicate its responsibility to strive for prosperity, security, the honoring of constitutional rights, and the other ends of government. As a general proposition this does not mean government has to be the proximate source of all that it is established to secure. Granted, for example, that full employment is an ingredient of national prosperity, the national government need not be everyone's employer. However, the notion of constitutional duty does mean that government is responsible and should take active responsibility if the ends envisioned by its powers are not achieved by individuals and groups independently of government. This responsibility cannot be delegated or abandoned consistently with constitutional logic. Thus, a constitutional government could not disclaim a duty to do what is needed to end widespread unemployment on the basis of some theory that the national government is not responsible for creating skilled workers or that "real jobs" are solely the creations of an unregulated or ungoverned market.

The idea of constitutional duty, like other constitutional norms, presupposes citizens who are attracted more to officials who exercise the powers of their offices "at the peril of . . . [the electorate's] displeasure" than to "sycophants," "parasites," and buck passers who do all that they can to make themselves popular without displeasing anyone.[27] But such citizens would possess precisely the kind of virtue that *The Federalist* says we cannot realistically hope for, and once again we confront Madison's observation that government would be unnecessary if men were angels. Without quarreling with Madison's statement of the problem, one can doubt the efficacy of his solution because, after almost two centuries, one can disagree that we are, in fact, conducting our affairs as the Constitution prescribes. Clearly, we have not been able to maintain an effective enumeration of powers, for the enumeration of powers is all but a dead letter. Nor is there any real commitment to the separation of powers, as we can see in our failure to appreciate its intrinsically praiseworthy nature and in such current constitutional controversies as those concerning the scope of executive prerogatives in foreign policy making, legislative vetoes of administrative decisions made all too often under original acts of congressional buck passing, and proposals to destroy judicial independence in certain cases involving the guarantees of equal protection and due process of law. As for constitutional rights themselves, all that we can see of them are certain shadows called "interests," which our courts freely compromise by balancing against other "interests." This is what becomes of "rights" whose enjoyment today seems to depend not so much on our personal and collective determination to raise ourselves to the level of what we have told the world we are, but on little more than indifference to one another's well-being and the character of the nation as a whole.[28] For a time the nation seemed to be moving toward a state of universal indifference by feeding a liberated desire to acquire ever larger amounts of private wealth, that desire appearing open to a relatively large number of creeds and tastes.[29] Such a society might have been viable in some primitive sense on a planet either of inexhaustible natural resources or of two kinds of creatures, one content to be in permanent service to the other, or some other place different from the one we occupy— one of "infinite worlds" sustained by robots and hallucinogens, perhaps. Some of us appear to feel that the life of unlimited acquisition and self-interest still has a long way to go, and that we can therefore continue to maintain the appearance of standing for what we say we stand for without really standing for anything in particular.[30] Time will tell, and soon enough. But I do not think anyone will contend today that Madison's solution to the problem of constitutional maintenance is as obviously the more realistic or workable solution it once appeared to be.[31] I contend, in any event, that whether Madison's theory ever has worked or will continue to work as intended, the Constitution makes no real sense from a checks and balances perspective.

The mere possession of executive and legislative powers and of the power of government generally has been used to claim authority for acts other than those expressly or implicitly authorized by the Constitution. Thus, Pritchett characterizes power over foreign affairs as "inherent power, which attaches automatically to the federal government as a sovereign entity, and derives from the Constitution only as the Constitution is the creator of that sovereign entity." This is a "constitutionally unlimited" power, he says, and therefore we may regard an absence of constitutional limit as a distinguishing feature of this "inherent" power.[32] Claims to this kind of power have occurred sporadically in our constitutional history. Some have classified Congress's power to meet emergencies as constitutionally unlimited; some have argued for the existence of a strong, or Lockean, prerogative in the president. I contend that such claims are inconsistent with the Constitution.

I noted in chapter 4 that commentators have been attracted to the notion of inherent powers because (1) they feel enumerated powers do not add up to all that is necessary to perform the acknowledged functions of the national government, and (2) emergency situations or the need for national self-preservation can force the government to exceed constitutional limitations. These two different arguments are often confounded; they should be distinguished, however, because a proper theory of the scope of granted powers will eliminate the first argument, leaving the second argument as the only defense of inherent powers. I argued in chapter 4 that Congress's explicit powers point to broad national ends, like national security and economic health, and that Congress can take legislative measures necessary and proper to pursue these ends.[33] We can assume in addition that the president is empowered to take a broad range of actions relative to these general constitutional objectives as chief executive and commander-in-chief and under his constitutional obligation faithfully to execute the laws. These propositions amount to a rather generous understanding of governmental power; yet, as permissive as this view might be, it is much easier to accept than the theory of inherent powers. If we accept a broad conception of the government's responsibilities we remove that justification for an extraconstitutional source of powers which says government must have power to perform its acknowledged functions. The doctrine of inherent powers then serves only as license to ignore the constitutional constraints found in the Bill of Rights, the separation of powers, and the idea of authorized national ends. This, in fact, is how the notion of inherent powers has been used in a number of governmental decisions and Supreme Court cases—some with infamous holdings—involving the unfair treatment of aliens, compulsory flag salutes, mass deprivations of the liberty and property of admittedly innocent Americans on racial grounds, denials of First Amendment rights of Communists, unauthorized and clandestine bombings of foreign lands, politically motivated burglaries, and other lawless acts.[34] The question, then, is not whether the government can pursue its authorized objectives but whether the Constitution can be conceived as authorizing the suspension of its provisions in emergencies or on grounds of national self-preservation.

I shall address this question through a comment on the best-known defense of such a power in constitutional history, Abraham Lincoln's explanation of his decision to suspend the writ of habeas corpus at the beginning of the Civil War.[35] On April 15, 1861, the day after the fall of Fort Sumter, Lincoln called Congress to a special session that was to commence not right away but two and a half months later, on July 4. In the interim, Lincoln lost no time taking steps that committed the nation to war. This he did, on his own, by ordering large increases in the size of the army and navy, a blockade of southern ports, the purchase of new ships, and other moves, including the suspension of the writ of habeas corpus wherever the army might encounter resistance to federal authority between the cities of Washington and Philadelphia. Lincoln issued this order despite the fact that explicit constitutional authorization to suspend the writ is found not in Article II, the executive article, but in section 9 of Article I, the legislative article. Lincoln also acted in the face of judicial precedent locating the power to suspend the writ in the legislature, not the executive. Lincoln's move was met by a forcefully worded attack from Chief Justice Taney in the performance of his circuit duties involving a petition for the writ by a John Merryman of Baltimore, whose arrest had been ordered by the commander of federal forces near that city.[36] After a brief period of doubt about whether Taney's order to release Merryman would be obeyed, the military authorities turned Merryman over to civilian authority. But Lincoln kept in force the general order to suspend the writ. In a special address to Congress on July 4, he tried to defend the steps he had taken against the rebellion.[37] This address contains the best known of our official attempts to justify the power of a constitutional officer to violate the Constitution. It is of special interest because of the paradox of couching an argument for violating the Constitution in an official statement. We shall see, however, that such an argument can be made by persons who no longer pretend to be acting as officials, and made in a responsible way.

In defending his suspension of the writ, Lincoln carefully avoided claiming that a power to violate the Constitution is necessary for the nation's preservation in emergencies—the power I am calling the *Lockean prerogative*. Instead, he tried to justify his action on constitutional grounds. But he also provided a rhetorically hypothetical defense of the Lockean prerogative for those who were not persuaded by his constitutional argument. One can extract three or four arguments from Lincoln's speech and subsequent events: (1) that circumstances had forced him to violate the constitutional provision vesting suspension of the writ in Congress in order not to violate his duty faithfully to execute the laws in rebellious areas; (2) that the framers' purposes would be served by permitting executive suspensions of the writ in emergencies that precluded legislative action; and (3) that the president could act in times of legislative silence in a manner consistent with legislative authority so long as he subsequently submitted his actions to the legislature. This last proposition flows as much from what Lincoln invited Congress to do as from what he asserted in his defense, having closed his remarks on the writ with a veiled request for some sort of congressional approval. Congress gave what was interpreted as retrospective approval in August of that year, but without authorizing future executive suspensions of the writ. Lincoln acted on his own again a year later. In September 1862, he authorized military arrests and courts-martial throughout the United States for those aiding the rebels, resisting the draft, or engaging in "any disloyal practice." It was not until March 1862 that Congress specifically authorized executive suspensions of the writ "during the present rebellion," thereby supplying a fourth defense, namely, that the executive could suspend the writ under valid delegations of congressional power.[38]

If Lincoln's speech is taken as claiming the Lockean prerogative, it risks the absurdity of saying, "An officer who shall be recognized by criteria set forth in this Constitution shall have power to act contrary to this Constitution." Such a power could be the prerogative of persons who are not officials, but *officials* cannot be understood to have such a power because we need rules they cannot lawfully change if we are to recognize those persons who lawfully claim the authority to act as officials. Thus, we have to know what rules constitute the presidency before anyone's claim to be the president can be tested. This makes it impossible for a president, as such, to violate the rules constituting the presidency. Someone claiming to be president cannot violate the rules constituting the presidency consistently with what he claims to be.[39] But this allusion to Hart's jurisprudence might suggest that a distinction between different kinds of rules, like the president's *powers* as opposed to the *structural rules* through which we elect and recognize presidents, could enable us to speak of the presidential prerogative because the person we could continue to recognize as president would have power to exceed his normal powers in catastrophic circumstances. After all, it would make sense to say that the president had sent the troops on his own, or closed Congress down, or removed the judges, and so on, because we could say that the person elected president did these things and that the person elected president is the president. A problem with this kind of solution as a *constitutional* solution, however, is that the supremacy clause does not differentiate among constitutional rules, and the reasons for exceeding presidential powers could be equally good for violating those structural rules by which we recognize the president, like those that provide for fixed terms of office, periodic elections, and so forth. Surely, the case for violating structural rules can be as strong as the case for exceeding powers, and it is perhaps somewhat puzzling in light of the government's regular disregard of limits on its powers that we have avoided suspending a national election for two centuries of intermittent crisis. Moreover, because an aspect of virtually every part of the body of the Constitution—including the rules by which we recognize those in authority—is that of means to the ends of the Preamble, we recognize presidents partly in light of expectations of what presidents are supposed to do. We cannot totally separate our recognition of constitutional officers from our beliefs about how they are supposed to act. It should be remembered that the supremacy clause is fully coherent only in light of a state of affairs in which officers do what their offices were established for and in ways that give the electorate cause to believe constitutional practices are constitutive of the good society. There is, therefore, a logical basis for contending that a *president* is someone who behaves more or less as we suppose a president ought to behave. This is reflected in the fact that everyone can easily imagine actions that no one would view as "presidential." The logic of the document thus precludes a sharp distinction between the authorized acts of institutions and the identity of the institutional actors as separable elements in our recognition of constitutional authority.[40]

This is not to argue that one who has achieved office should never violate the Constitution. As I have shown, the Constitution cannot be conceived as law without presupposing that circumstances can defeat its claim to supremacy or that we can justly reject its authority. Lincoln's first argument is best understood not as a claim of power for the presidency but as an explanation of why he, as a person strategically positioned, not strictly as president, chose to violate the law—better, why circumstances forced him to violate either one rule or another and why he made the choice he did. When officials have no choice but to offend one constitutional norm or another, they cannot choose to follow the ways of the Constitution. The person who occupies the presidency is not the only one who may face such circumstances; it could happen to anyone, and the argument that can justify the Lockean prerogative can, in appropriate circumstances, justify both revolution and milder forms of disobedience on the part of the president or anyone else. However, we need not understand events as forcing us to make choices between rules in conflict; some developments show merely that the Constitution presupposes more or less ideal circumstances. The conflict, in other words, need not be between the rules of the Constitution, it may be between the Constitution and events. The Constitution and the times do not always jibe. By characterizing conflict situations in this way it is possible for officials to continue to feel at least some obligation to follow the rules they are forced to breach, thus limiting violations of the rules to particular situations and seeking to restore that state of affairs in which the government can return to the rules.[41] Although Lincoln suggested this argument in his address to Congress, he nevertheless tried in a letter of April 4, 1864, to justify his conduct of the war by proposing that "measures, otherwise unconstitutional, might become lawful, by becoming indispensable to the preservation of the nation."[42] Holding fast to this last statement would lead one to affirm that any move could be constitutional eventually and that one could not assess the constitutionality of an act until after its ultimate success or failure had been determined.[43] As a follow-up, one could contend that since parchment barriers will inevitably give way to the necessities of the times anyway, and since the authority of the document will decline as necessity multiplies precedents of disobedience, we should preserve what we can of constitutional authority by construing the Constitution as needed to meet necessity.[44]

Of course, by pretending that the Constitution can be whatever necessity requires, one would erode the Constitution's authority by rendering it too shapeless and malleable to function as a standard for judging events.[45] In the minds of those who write and ratify constitutions, these documents are planning documents of sorts. As "supreme Law," the Constitution expresses a belief that the nation can plan for contingencies and that the plans can be more or less supreme. Not everyone agrees. Some commentators who profess to believe that contingencies control everything eventually conclude that planning or intentional action or, simply, *action* is an illusion. Of this group, those who somehow remain interested in constitutional questions will try to narrate versions of what people (judges mostly, for some reason) have said about the Constitution, or, instead of showing how one judicial doctrine came after another, they will try to look behind what people have said about the Constitution for the hidden psychological, biological, and other subrational forces believed to cause everyone to say what everyone says. (These forces do not control the scholarly observers themselves, however, for they act as if they can be moved by what they recognize as the truth or some qualified form thereof.) Other observers believe that though we cannot make adequate long-range plans, we can rise above contingencies in some ways, including the identification of ends whose value does not depend on contingencies. Because this last group will not believe that general legal prescriptions can cover contingencies, it will favor government by men and women who have a prudential feel or knack for maneuvering their way through contingencies, having acquired this special competence either from God, nature, education, or practical experience. But the relative merits of arguments in behalf of prudence and the rest is not at issue here. American constitutionalism makes less than practical good sense to those who believe in either the supremacy or the intractability of contingencies, or in the supremacy of history, divine providence, or prudence—and it is the Constitution whose meaning we explore here.

The Constitution is ill served by the myth of complete constitutional flexibility. We cannot perceive the Constitution as law in the absence of a disinclination to follow its provisions. The Constitution cannot be fully authoritative by its own test if it is believed that reasoned reaffirmation of its provisions is either meaningless or impossible. Reasoned reaffirmation is meaningless without the possibility of reasoned rejection. Without the latter possibility the need for reasoned defense disappears. To believe in advance that the Constitution can be anything it has to be is to eliminate the possibility of rejecting it. Disinclination to obey disappears at that point, and therewith the very context for recognizing the Constitution as law. This is why a plastic constitution cannot be a real constitution. Of course, repeated departures from the Constitution in the face of necessity should be regretted, but these instances do not prove that future events cannot be made to conform to the Constitution. Nor do departures from the Constitution create *constitutional* precedents for future departures. An Abraham Lincoln who would have been candid about the extraconstitutional nature of his actions would not have created precedents for future occupants of the presidency as such, for in his very candor he would have denied that his acts were authorized by the Constitution. Such a Lincoln might have provided a model for future Lincolns in comparable situations without having provided constitutional precedents for lesser individuals who happened to be president in less catastrophic circumstances.[46] In his debate with Douglas over Taney's opinion in *Dred Scott*, Lincoln correctly suggested that the Constitution has something to do with a state of affairs to be achieved. He was also correct to the extent that he admitted before Congress that circumstances can force departures from the Constitution. He erred later in suggesting that forced departures can be formulated as norms thereafter to be regarded as parts of the Constitution. If the power to suspend the writ belongs to Congress—a view Lincoln himself respected enough to grant hypothetically—nothing that events forced Lincoln to do could have altered this as a proposition of constitutional law.

Our interest in Lincoln's address lies in its hypothetical justification of a Lockean prerogative as a constitutional power of the presidency. Arguments against such a power in the presidency hold also for Congress and all other actors of the system, for the Constitution cannot be conceived as authorizing the disregard of its provisions by anyone, a proposition to which I shall return in a moment. Lincoln's second and third arguments do suggest an acceptable theory of constitutional prerogatives in the presidency, as long as these prerogatives are distinguished from the Lockean prerogative to violate the Constitution. Lincoln's second and third arguments claim a power to act in lieu of congressional action at times when Congress cannot act. As a historical matter Lincoln may have been disingenuous here in view of his decision to delay calling a special session of Congress for over two months after his first suspension of the writ in late April. Perhaps he sought to minimize Congress's opportunities to obstruct the national commitment he wanted to effect. Nevertheless, the claims Lincoln made in public are better evidence of his understanding of his constitutional obligations than purposes he kept to himself, and in those public claims he depicted his moves as actions taken in the presence of congressional silence.

Because silence can sometimes be construed as assent, Lincoln could have said that he acted as he thought necessary faithfully to execute the laws in the absence of contrary indications from Congress. Subsequent congressional disapproval could have forced Lincoln either to withdraw his order suspending the writ or to claim the Lockean prerogative. He might also have argued that Congress was evading its constitutional duty to enact measures necessary and proper for faithful presidential execution of the laws, for the necessary and proper clause empowers Congress to provide legislative instruments for executive as well as legislative power, and power in a constitutional regime implies duty, as we have seen. At any time prior to congressional action Lincoln was entitled to assume Congress intended to do its duty and that he was therefore acting in accordance with a defensible presumption of what Congress's response to the crisis would be. Thus, he told Congress he believed he had done nothing "beyond the constitutional competency of Congress" and that he trusted "then, as now, that Congress would ratify" his moves.[47] Had Congress failed to do what Lincoln thought consistent with its duty and his, he would have had justification for believing that the Constitution had ceased governing events and that there was no possibility of action consistent with the Constitution. Events might have overcome the Constitution in that case, and Lincoln or anyone else in a strategic position to do so could have been praised or blamed for succeeding or failing to establish a new order in place of the old order, which events had destroyed. Perhaps this is one way to understand what happened to the Constitution in the Civil War.

Now, I am contending that the Constitution cannot be understood to authorize its own violation, and therefore that the Lockean prerogative is not a constitutional prerogative even though extraconstitutional or unconstitutional action of one kind or another may have been and almost certainly will be welcomed sooner or later. The same argument applies to Congress and others, as well as to the executive; the Constitution can authorize *no one* to violate its provisions. But if this argument is correct, the wording of the power to suspend the writ of habeas corpus presents a problem. For to say that the privilege "shall not be suspended, unless when in Cases of Rebellion or Invasion the public Safety may require it" is to suggest that there is an affirmative authorization for Congress or one of its agents actively to suspend the privilege when the requisite conditions obtain.[48] This in turn would imply that Congress or one of its agents could weigh the factors bearing upon the public safety during rebellion or invasion and decide to close the courts to those persons who would claim that the government was failing to honor their constitutional rights. One might hold, as the Supreme Court has suggested, that such action in itself would not suspend the rights whose vindication is sought through the courts.[49] But, clearly, deciding to suspend the writ would suspend a large part of the means to honoring constitutional rights and deny the polity's obligation to honor constitutional rights at all costs. A power to suspend the honoring of constitutional rights would be an authorization to violate the Constitution, amounting as it would to a self-contradictory authorization to suspend rights that the logic of the Constitution as a whole requires us to honor regardless of the sacrifices.

There are ways to try to escape the conclusion that the power actively to suspend the writ is a constitutional contradiction. It may be said, for example, that the presence of this power in the Constitution need not amount to a denial that, constitutionally speaking, we destroy ourselves as a constitutional sovereignty when we cease honoring constitutional rights. It may merely recognize that we cannot always be what we say we are, as is to be expected when we define ourselves in terms of our aspirations. It may be argued further that the power to suspend the writ actually furthers our strivings to honor constitutional rights, since those strivings manifest our attraction to a place where reasons are given and exchanged when reasons are sought and since reasons cannot be understood as genuine where violence makes reflection and deliberation impossible. Of course, this argument would favor a very narrow view of the power to suspend the writ, limiting suspensions to places and times in which actual violence made any governmental operation other than military a physical impossibility. The Supreme Court has not consistently gone so far in limiting the power, but its thinking once tended in this direction. Thus, the Court's best-known opinion on the subject says:

> It follows, from what has been said on this subject, that there are occasions when martial rule can be properly applied. If, in foreign invasion or civil war, the courts are actually closed, and it is impossible to administer criminal justice according to law, *then*, on the theatre of active military operations, where war really prevails, there is a necessity to furnish a substitute for the civil authority, thus overthrown, to preserve the safety of the army and society; and as no power is left but the military, it is allowed to govern by martial rule until the laws can have their free course. As necessity creates the rule, so it limits its duration; for, if this government is continued *after* the courts are reinstated, it is a gross usurpation of power. Martial rule can never exist where the courts are open, and in the proper and unobstructed exercise of their jurisdiction. It is also confined to the locality of actual war.[50]

Thus, power to suspend the writ might be considered not as a power to do something in a deliberate way but as a mere capacity for reacting to something that has already happened to us. If we have a choice and elect to suspend the writ, we are not honoring constitutional rights at all costs. If the Constitution gives us power to suspend the honoring of constitutional rights, then the Constitution says that rights are not real exemptions from granted powers or that it is sometimes constitutional to enact conceptions of the ends of government that conflict with honoring constitutional rights. It might still be said that honoring constitutional rights is our highest aspiration, though not always our most urgent need. This would imply that on some occasions the Constitution does not require the honoring of constitutional rights until some time in the future when the sacrifices are of a kind we are willing to make. The Constitution would then lose that immediate obligational force that it must have if we are to look upon it as law. It is true that we must reaffirm the Constitution continually if we are to make sense of it as what it claims to be. Moreover, the Constitution presupposes possible rejection at the same time that it envisions reaffirmation. But though we need not reaffirm the Constitution in emergencies or, indeed, on any occasion, the Constitution still envisions its reaffirmation as law. Its supporters are obliged to create and maintain the conditions for its reaffirmation as law. Should they fail, the Constitution ceases to be what it says it is. It authorizes nothing at that point. Officials who claim extraconstitutional power concede that events have superseded the Constitution. Whether they are doing the right thing by some extraconstitutional standard, they deny the basis of their own authority. One must avoid a construction of the writ suspension provision that would admit this result.

For these reasons we might agree not to speak of "power to suspend the writ," but rather, the "writ suspension clause." If that clause is to make sense as part of the supreme law—and it does not have to in light of what the supremacy clause and the amending provisions presuppose about possible errors by the framers—we have to give it the narrowest interpretation. At the risk of disingenuousness, we would have to say as a general proposition of law that there is no real power to suspend the writ, there is only power "to furnish a substitute for the civil authority . . . overthrown" by events. Such actions on the part of the government would seek "to preserve the safety of the army and society," and it would be confined to places where it would be factually accurate to say that "no power is left but the military." Thus interpreted, the writ suspension clause would authorize little more than certain responses to large-scale and successful violence against the civil authorities. This would favor Lincoln's view that the clause is addressed as much to the executive as to the legislature, at least until the legislature has had time to review the government's immediate reaction, as opposed to the government's deliberate choice, which immediate reaction is all that the executive's action would represent. Courts that actually remained open, having not been closed down by hostilities around them, should order prisoners released in spite of legislative or executive pretexts that they in fact had been closed down, and regardless of the futility of judicial action in the face of such pretexts.

We turn now to the last group of institutional issues to be considered in this book, those surrounding the power of judicial review. The Constitution does not explicitly provide for the nearly monopolistic power we know today as judicial review, and no one has shown this monopoly to be a necessary implication of the Constitution. At best, John Marshall proved in *Marbury* v. *Madison* (1) that the Constitution should be the measure of ordinary governmental acts, and (2) that in performing their function of deciding cases judges are bound by the paramount law of the Constitution.[51] But this does not prove that the judiciary should be the sole agency to review the constitutionality of ordinary governmental acts, for there is no constitutional reason why all actors of the system should not be bound by their best understanding of the Constitution in the performance of their constitutional functions. The *Marbury* opinion itself does not call for a judicial monopoly of constitutional review in any clear way.[52] Presidents Jefferson, Jackson, and Lincoln felt that each department should construe that part of the document addressed to itself, and that judicial resolutions of particular cases should not be accepted as general political rules binding the other departments. Thus, Lincoln could campaign for a policy of active opposition to the rule announced in the *Dred Scott* decision without changing the effect of that decision on the parties in the case.[53] One cannot dismiss Lincoln's view altogether, for there is no denying as a general proposition that a president or a congress has a higher obligation to the Constitution than to the Supreme Court or to each other. As was argued in chapter 1, the Constitution cannot mean what the judges say it means in the sense that the judges must be infallible in constitutional interpretation. Moreover, one can question whether judicial decisions on constitutional questions should be final, even if we distinguish *finality* from *infallibility*. Hart criticizes the notion of judicial infallibility while contending nevertheless that a "supreme tribunal has the last word in saying what the law is and, when it has said it, the statement that the court was 'wrong' has no consequences within the system: no one's rights or duties are thereby altered."[54] He goes on to say that though the "decision may, of course be deprived of legal effect by legislation . . . the very fact that resort to this is necessary demonstrates the empty character, so far as the law is concerned, of the statement that the court's decision was wrong."[55] But surely one could wonder about the legal consequences of a wrong decision if enough people or the right people believed it clearly wrong and acted on that belief, as Jefferson did in remitting sentences under the Sedition Act of 1798 or as any executive might do by refusing to cooperate with a clearly unconstitutional judicial decision. The fate of the Sedition Act illustrates the point: Upheld by the lower federal courts at the time, it was condemned by the subsequent political opinion of the American people, and it was the latter "broad consensus" that the Supreme Court cited when it finally acknowledged the unconstitutionality of the act in 1965.[56]

The Constitution does not settle the question of who, if anyone, is to be the authoritative interpreter of its provisions. Admittedly, to be an effective prescription a law must prescribe either a single course of action or a compatible set of actions.[57] A rule cannot guide our actions if it tells us to do conflicting things; hence, the "one meaning" presupposed by those who want to find guidance in the Constitution.[58] But *one meaning* does not imply *one interpreter*. On the contrary, one interpreter seems consistent with many meanings or even no (special) meaning, as we see in the thought of those who regard the changing constitutional interpretations of the Supreme Court as essential for keeping the Constitution in step with the times. So the insistence on one interpreter may express a concern for some form of order, but it does not express a special concern for maintaining the Constitution as law. Relevant also to our understanding of the one-interpreter theory is the public and private psychology of nonrestraint that inadvertently supports the current judicial monopoly. For a long time now it has been the habit of citizens and officials to concentrate on their wants while delegating their constitutional consciences to their attorneys and attorneys general and through them to the courts. This attitude of leaving constitutional questions to the judges is altogether different from the active, reasoned self-restraint of what I have called the constitutional frame of mind—the attitude of those who actively aspire to reaffirm the Constitution's ways as their best conception of the good society. This frame of mind will predominate only in a constitutionally ideal state of affairs, as we have seen. The Constitution presupposes this attitude because no other attitude can fully comprehend or accept the Constitution as supreme law.[59] This constitutional frame of mind is poorly distributed and either cannot exist or cannot generally be known to exist where genuine reaffirmations of the Constitution are replaced by a widespread acquiescence in the impositions of some monopoly. Although we can agree with what others say about the Constitution, it is simply impossible for someone to *tell* us the meaning of *this* law; to understand it we have to understand it for ourselves. If judicial review as it is known and seems to be accepted today is necessary for "order," we cannot have a genuinely *constitutional* order in mind.

The one-interpreter thesis is incompatible with constitutional supremacy because constitutional supremacy implies independent constitutional criteria, and on the basis of these criteria one can always criticize any interpreter. We therefore ask the wrong question in trying to locate *the* power of constitutional review. No such monopoly can be found in the Constitution. Indeed, one can go so far as to say that such a monopoly cannot have been put in the Constitution in any manner consistent with supremacy for the law of the Constitution itself. Instead of a monopoly we find an obligation to act constitutionally that applies to all who exercise constitutional functions, not just to those who perform the judicial function. We should have seen the power of judicial review as an obligation of the courts to perform their function of deciding cases and controversies in a manner consistent with the supremacy of the Constitution over ordinary acts of government. This would not have been tantamount to a judicial monopoly because Congress has a similar obligation to the Constitution in the performance of its functions, as do the president, the states, and even ordinary citizens. In general, this obligation to follow the Constitution is a threefold obligation on everyone's part (1) to restrain one's demands or desires to act or exercise one's powers in ways that conflict with the ways of the Constitution, (2) to insist by exhortation, through example, and within the limits of one's official and personal powers that others do the same, *and* (3) to refuse to participate in actions that violate the Constitution. As the judiciary is obligated to refuse to apply an unconstitutional act of Congress—and Marshall could properly deduce that much from the principle of constitutional supremacy—there is no constitutional reason for a different obligation on the part of members of Congress, the president, and others who might be asked to cooperate with unconstitutional acts, including unconstitutional judicial acts.

This is an argument that can only be used to support restraint, exhortation, and refusals to cooperate with unconstitutional acts. It is not an argument for nullification, secession, bills of attainder, and other usurpations. An act may be right in some circumstances without being authorized or envisioned by the Constitution, as violent opposition to slavery would have been. Nevertheless, an obligation to refuse cooperation with unconstitutional acts can result in a very formidable power over unconstitutional practices. Consider how a constitutional judiciary would have responded to the fugitive slave acts of 1793 and 1850. These acts empowered private individuals to arrest alleged escaped slaves without warrants and bring them before federal judges and special commissioners for certificates authorizing their return to slave states. As interpreted by the judiciary, the acts gave the alleged slaves virtually no rights in the federal proceedings. They were refused a presumption of innocence, a jury, the right to testify in their own behalf—they were even refused impartial decision-makers, since the commissioners provided by the act of 1850 received a ten-dollar fee when they decided for the alleged master, as contrasted with a five-dollar fee when decision went the other way.[60] Congress enacted these measures under the fugitive slave clause of Article IV, section 2. This clause, in vague language, did direct the states to return persons who had actually escaped from slavery, but it did not expressly authorize the national government to assist in their return, and it did not have to be read as authorizing rendition proceedings that ignored procedural rights. With few exceptions, however, the courts cooperated with Congress's decision to assist the slave catchers.[61] Although it is not clear why the judges cooperated as they did, a good guess is that despite their antipathy to the policy, many of them felt powerless as judges to go beyond the political compromise embodied in the fugitive slave clause and other constitutional provisions and intrude into a controversy that increasingly threatened civil war.[62]

To illustrate the potential scope of a judicial refusal to cooperate with unconstitutional practices, let me apply the constitutional principles discussed so far and assume that the Supreme Court would have agreed with the following position: "Congress's fugitive slave policy is unconstitutional, root and branch. Congress has ignored procedural safeguards that must obtain in all federal proceedings involving liberty and property. More fundamentally, the fugitive slave clause authorizes no congressional legislation and cannot be construed to do so consistently with the Constitution's broader purposes. Nor does the clause or any other part of the Constitution force the federal courts to recognize a property right that they have to honor. The slave catchers are on their own." This position would have had the effect of dismantling the fugitive slave policy as something Congress could pursue through normal governmental machinery. It would have expressed an attitude of nonparticipation that the Court was to exhibit on a more limited scale a century later in *Shelley* v. *Kraemer*.[63]

This still might not have been enough for the Court fully to conform to constitutional principles, for it would have failed to reach the practice of slavery within individual states and among cooperating states. Independently of what a court as an institution might be able to do about it, judges with a constitutional attitude would have viewed the practice of slavery as inconsistent with the Constitution's broader purposes. They would have considered the fugitive slave clause and other parts of the Constitution that recognized slavery as constitutional contradictions. Taken together, these provisions constituted a mistake of the kind whose possibility is presupposed by the First Amendment, the amending procedures, and the Constitution's logical dependence on the process of reaffirmation. From a constitutional point of view, these provisions could not have embodied the real purposes of the framers as framers of the Constitution, for framers as framers cannot contradict themselves, and no one would consciously put a right to property in slaves on a list of American aspirations.[64] Whatever else they might have done, judges who fully understood the Constitution would have exhorted the nation to remove slavery as a manifest denial of the people's capacity to constitute a self-restraining and therefore truly sovereign authority.

One could have challenged the sufficiency even of this response, however, for it would not have opened the doors of the federal courts to those seeking declarations that the states were depriving persons of liberty and property without due process by providing the governmental framework for perpetuating slavery. If the Fifth Amendment had been held applicable to the states, as the Constitution required all along, and assuming a complete federal jurisdiction over federal questions (I shall defend that assumption momentarily), then the federal courts would have cooperated with slavery by not using their powers in ways that would have helped to dismantle slavery.

One could not have answered this argument with the contention that slavery was lawful, for nothing unconstitutional is lawful, and slavery was never really constitutional on any theory that would preserve the coherence of the Constitution as law. Slavery was there, but as a mistake, not as part of a coherent whole. A constitutional court could not have closed its doors to anyone on any theory predicated on the lawfulness of slavery.

The courts might have tried to close their doors on another kind of theory, one concerning the limits of the judicial function. They might have said that the amending provisions of Article V do imply the possibility of mistakes, but that they also assign the function of correcting mistakes to institutions other than courts. This theory of limits on the judicial power might have saved the courts from conceding lawfulness to slavery, but only if the judges had openly declared the unlawfulness of slavery at the same time that they were acknowledging their lack of power to base concrete holdings on that declaration. John Marshall showed the possibility of this kind of statement in *Marbury* v. *Madison* when he declared that Marbury's legal right had been violated at the same time that he found his court powerless to remedy that violation. But when courts say they cannot remedy continuing violations of constitutional rights they are actually conceding that the Constitution is not in control of events. The failures of the other branches or of the people make it impossible to perform the judicial function of vindicating the legal rights of litigants. If the judges do not try to remedy the violations they fall short of what judges are supposed to do. Yet if they breach institutional barriers in order to remedy the violations they exceed the limits of what judges are supposed to do. In such circumstances the judges cannot follow the Constitution because it is not really the effective law. With others in such situations, they are thrown back on whatever prudential devices they can get away with in an effort to restore conditions requisite to following the Constitution, if that is the end they seek. Exhortation is the least of such devices.

Now, many jurists and students of this subject believe that courts should not have a power to push constitutional principle to the point of explosion when events are simply ungovernable by constitutional principle. I have not denied this kind of thinking at any point in this book, though I take it as an argument grounded in extraconstitutional values—an argument that is appropriate when one has given up on the Constitution and rejected its claim to be supreme law for everyone, including judges. Nevertheless, there must be limits on what judges can do as judges. The courts have an obligation to refuse to apply unconstitutional laws because they have a duty to honor constitutional supremacy in the performance of their functions. But this does not mean that courts can perform executive and legislative functions or what their best understanding of the Constitution finds beyond the competence of a constitutional judiciary. The courts cannot constitutionally do any x simply because other entities will not do it or are not doing it constitutionally. Thus, questions persist about the use of the judiciary's equity powers to fashion highly detailed, long-range remedies covering many activities within a given system, and applicable to an indefinite number of people in such cases as those involving school desegregation, unconstitutional conditions in prisons and other state facilities, and unconstitutional personnel practices of public agencies. These broad-gauged judicial remedies often resemble rules of a kind that a legislative or administrative body would enact to coordinate a number of activities with an eye to some overall purpose. The judges who order these remedies often resemble administrative officials by retaining jurisdiction over the conditions the remedies are designed to remove or correct. This resemblance to legislative and administrative behavior has prompted recent critics of the federal judiciary to call for a narrowing of the range of activities that can be governed by a court's remedial powers.[65]

These critics of the modern judiciary may have a point. The courts can believe that Congress and the states have an obligation to stop a practice like racial discrimination in the public schools, and that an unconstitutional state of affairs exists should elected officials disagree or fail to remedy the unconstitutional condition for other reasons. But the mere fact of a legislature's failure to work toward a constitutional state of affairs does not empower a court to do the legislature's job. Sometimes courts might not be able to do much more than give legislatures lectures about their constitutional duties. Such lectures need not be ineffectual, as is evident from the eventual result of the lecture Marshall gave Jefferson in *Marbury* v. *Madison* about the nature of constitutional institutions. Opponents of a hortatory judiciary might reflect on this aspect of what happened in that case, as well as on Ely's point that we should not permit customary notions of the limits of the judicial function to override what he calls the Constitution's "institutional implications." Certainly, nothing in the Constitution prevents one branch from exhorting another; and exhortation would seem appropriate in light of what we have seen about the attitudes that must predominate in government and elsewhere in the society if constitutional institutions are to work. Essentially historical theories as to how most judges have in fact conducted themselves do not decide questions of how judges ought to behave. I have already shown that one cannot have a coherent preference for the status quo as such in any context that allows the need for government, and that argument should be enough to refute those who invoke what they call "tradition" in criticizing judges for departing from established practices. Criticism of judicial exhortation based on a preference for democracy is also flawed because it begs the important question whether democracies can institutionalize self-restraint in the form of constitutions that permit judges and others to remind all of their aspirations. The Constitution implicitly claims that "the People" are capable of this kind of supremacy, as I argued in showing that the Constitution must be understood as an expression of collective self-restraint.

Without trying to settle the question whether the modern expansion of the courts' equity powers amounts to a license for judicial legislation—beyond what I just suggested about prudence in unconstitutional situations—that question should be approached in a manner that is free both from the assumption that the Constitution ordains popular willfulness and from skepticism about the possibility of norms that transcend historical conceptions of general constitutional values. I can see how one might argue that section 5 of the Fourteenth Amendment imposes duties on Congress, not the courts. But this cannot mean that judges ought to confine themselves to legislative conceptions of general ideas like "due process" or "equal protection of the laws," or that judges have no power of their own to remedy violations of the Fourteenth Amendment. The Constitution clearly presupposes that even when Congress refuses to act, the states and their agencies can violate the Fourteenth Amendment. It is at least arguable that constitutional rights imply judicial remedies and that the nature and scope of the judicial remedies bear some relationship to the specific conditions to be remedied. One can hardly argue that the courts have no power just because Congress has power it can use to achieve a state of affairs in which no one would need judicial help. Such an argument would leave no independent power for the judiciary in any area. Moreover, those who really understand and accept constitutional supremacy know that power implies duty and therefore that the normative status of the ends envisioned by the Constitution does not depend on what legislative majorities are moved to do. Supporters of the Constitution would also be receptive to whatever institutional implications may reside in the general obligation to do everything possible to avoid violations of constitutional rights. Why, then, should we not give the courts the benefit of the doubt if that is what it takes for the polity effectively to honor certain rights? One wonders whether there is an answer to this question that is not rooted in a conception of the Constitution as an expression of popular willfulness. In any event, those who criticize broad-gauged judicial remedies rarely criticize failures of Congress and the states to do their duty, and legislative failure to correct unconstitutional conditions is certainly no less a denial of constitutional supremacy than unwarranted expansions of judicial power would be.

Unlike the courts, and the amending power aside, the states are assigned no constitutional function they can perform in ways that would suggest a power to nullify federal laws. While citizens may refuse to fight in unconstitutional wars and even whole communities may constitutionally refuse obedience to unconstitutional court orders, they can still believe that the undoing of the decisions in question is the lawful function of others. In the face of civil disobedience on constitutional grounds governmental officials would have to decide their own constitutional obligations. Anarchy might result, but sometimes anarchy is relative to one's criteria of lawful order, and there are many orderly situations well beyond the pale of constitutionality. A proposition's refutation does not always lie in its anarchic potential, for constitutional theory cannot exorcise the possibility of constitutional collapse. That constitutions cannot fail or that any one constitution is suitable for all circumstances are myths with no net value for the cause of constitutionalism, as I have contended. Short of refusals to obey unconstitutional commands, the states and the people can exercise their obligation of constitutional review by bringing constitutional criteria to bear on their own demands, their electoral decisions, and their functions under the amending provisions of Article V. As Madison suggested in explaining what the Virginia Resolutions had meant by a constitutional form of "interposition," the state governments are free to establish informal institutions for monitoring the actions of the national government and alerting the nation to departures from the Constitution.[66] One can imagine the impact on American public opinion had a majority or even a healthy minority of the states followed the Massachusetts legislature in 1970 when it adopted a resolution against the constitutionality of the Vietnam War.[67] An informal system of state legislative correspondence on constitutional questions could still acquire a great influence on the conduct of government in America. If they were not bothered by the irony of their action, the states could establish a central representative body to enhance the effectiveness of a system of interposition by formulating general propositions on constitutional questions for submission to the several states. As informal as state resolutions on constitutional issues would be, they could become the early stages of constitutional amendments, and the system of correspondence itself could become the mechanism for organizing state legislative petitions to Congress for convening constitutional conventions. Such a system of correspondence could take any of several forms without constitutional amendment or congressional clearance of any kind.

Congress's obligation of constitutional review also begins in restraint on its own actions. This proposition would not be of much interest were it not for the influence Congress might acquire in constitutional decision should Congress again come to take constitutional limitations seriously. Sense of Congress resolutions and other expressions of congressional opinion on general constitutional propositions might be influential in the community and with other governmental entities if Congress somehow could persuade the country that it had a genuine concern for problems of constitutional maintenance. The First Congress enjoyed this reputation; so have other congresses. Though one can disagree with the content of its decision, the Ninety-third Congress proved the institution still capable of self-restrained and principled constitutional interpretation by enacting the War Powers Resolution of 1973, an act that tried to specify the boundaries between the powers of Congress and those of the president to wage war. Of course, allowing a congressional power of constitutional review risks legitimizing a self-righteous willfulness that can destroy any possibility of achieving the self-critical frame of mind that must prevail if constitutional interpretation is to realize its aims. Pending in Congress at this writing are antibusing, antiabortion, school prayer, and other measures that are completely opposed to the attitudes and values of those who really accept the Constitution's supremacy. A significant part of current congressional opinion is working hard with elements in the executive branch to maintain public support for the Constitution—not through social and economic policies that strive for an equally protective state of affairs where all who can reason aright see their situations as something they could have chosen for themselves—but through the glorification of a widely corrupting and polarizing acquisitiveness subsidized by unequally protective laws and defended through jingoism, new restrictions on public access to what government is doing, new burdens on the freedoms of expression, petition, and litigation, and a heavier reliance on the coercive instruments of authority. Because constitutional commentary is obliged to be politically responsible, now may be a bad time to defend a pluralistic approach to constitutional maintenance. Nevertheless, I have given my reasons for believing that there is no constitutional gain in continuing to abdicate the nation's constitutional consciousness to a monopoly. If the values and attitudes outlined in the two preceding chapters cannot be strengthened and applied in our public and private lives through a pluralistic approach to constitutional issues, the nation's effort to constitute a true sovereign has failed.

This brings me to a general comment on the complex question whether Congress may exercise its powers in ways deliberately designed to reverse the broad political impact of unconstitutional judicial decisions. The answer in general must be yes—although there is a crucial distinction between Congress exercising *its* powers and Congress attempting to prevent the courts' exercise of their powers. Congress could not have the right to do the latter without creating a constitutional contradiction that would diminish the prescriptive quality of the Constitution as a whole. Let us consider three different problems: (1) whether Congress may attempt to influence judicial decisions by the manner in which it employs its powers over the Supreme Court's appellate jurisdiction, the jurisdiction of the lower federal courts, and the remedial powers of the courts; (2) whether Congress may use its powers to define constitutional rights to be applied by courts; and (3) whether Congress may refuse to follow or cooperate with judicial decisions that it believes are unconstitutional. Congress has the power for (3); not for (1) and (2).

In *The Federalist* Hamilton treats judicial independence as a principle of the "science of politics" comparable to the separation of powers and the representative legislature.[68] In the same work he declares an independent judiciary "peculiarly essential" in a constitution containing "certain specified exemptions to the legislative authority" similar to those later to be found in the Bill of Rights.

"Limitations of this kind can be preserved in practice no other way than through the medium of the courts of justice."[69] If we grant these propositions we have good reason to conclude that the Supreme Court erred in a series of nineteenth-century decisions whose effect was to make the jurisdiction of federal courts depend on affirmative congressional grants. Pritchett aptly calls the Court's unnecessary acquiescence in this practice a "judicial surrender."[70] In *Durousseau v. United States* (1810), the Supreme Court correctly stated as a general proposition of law that its appellate jurisdiction flows directly from the Constitution and that Congress is limited to making exceptions to that jurisdiction. However, the Court then reversed the effect of this proposition when it went on to say in the same opinion that by choosing to grant jurisdiction over some subjects, Congress had made "exceptions" of all that it had not granted.[71] This curious reasoning resulted in making affirmative acts of Congress the source of the Supreme Court's appellate jurisdiction. Later, in *Martin v. Hunter's Lessee* (1816), the Court gratuitously and erroneously said that though Congress had a duty to establish the lower federal courts it did not have to perform this duty, *and* that even if Congress did establish the lower federal courts it could decide not to vest them with the judicial power of the United States.[72] Had the Court construed the powers of Congress in terms of a complete federal jurisdiction already possessed by courts whose establishment was envisioned by the Constitution, and had the Court stressed the constitutional importance of an independent judiciary, the Court might have established a practice of scrutinizing the judiciary acts as necessary to prevent congressional attempts to limit the jurisdiction of the federal courts and take other measures designed to influence the outcome of litigation. Events would prove that one could not take Congress's respect for judicial independence for granted. Congress has attempted interference in judicial matters a number of times, with its greatest success coming in *Ex Parte McCardle* (1869),[73] where the Court reaffirmed *Durousseau* in an atmosphere of heavy political pressure from the Reconstruction Congress. Later, in *United States v. Klein* (1872), the Court recovered some of its integrity by invalidating a withdrawal of jurisdiction in which Congress was attempting to reverse judicial holdings regarding the implication of a presidential pardon for those seeking indemnification for property captured during the Civil War.[74] The courts had held that recipients of presidential pardons were not to be considered supporters of the rebellion; this decision entitled them to indemnification. The Reconstruction Congress opposed this decision and enacted a statute construing a pardon as proof that one had supported the rebellion and directing the courts to dismiss claims from the recipients of pardons for lack of jurisdiction. The Court held the new statute an unconstitutional attempt to employ the power over jurisdiction as a means to interfering in pending cases. The Court said such a move violated the separation of powers.

One can attempt to reconcile *McCardle* and *Klein*—or, more generally, Congress's power over federal jurisdiction with the idea of judicial independence—by distinguishing advance withdrawals of jurisdiction over specific classes of cases from withdrawals aimed at preventing further judicial applications of judicial doctrines that the courts have already announced. This is a distinction without substance, however, for advance withdrawals can be motivated by a desire to defeat the anticipated judgments of courts, as was the case with the withdrawal statute at issue in *McCardle*. In *Klein* the Court reasoned that Congress should not be permitted to reverse judicial decisions already made because such a power would defeat the value of an independent judiciary. Judicial independence would be compromised no less by the kind of withdrawal that occurred in *McCardle*. Certainly, everyone knew what motivated Congress in *McCardle*, and the Court gave the usual sign of its awareness of unconstitutional legislative motives when it said: "We are not at liberty to inquire into the motives of the legislature. We can only examine into its power under the Constitution; and the power to make exceptions to the appellate jurisdiction of this court is given by express words."[75] In light of my argument in chapter 4 about the consequences for constitutional government of the refusal to classify congressional actions in terms of Congress's purposes, the Court clearly erred in *McCardle*.[76] Instead of permitting Congress to get away with an act that the Court was not willing to describe in terms of the common knowledge of what Congress was doing, the Court should have declared that the Constitution's arrangement of offices and powers together with the value of judicial independence constituted exemptions from the powers granted Congress.[77] This would have reminded Congress to exercise its powers with an eye to a state of affairs in which judicial independence was honored as an institutional condition for honoring constitutional rights and as an ingredient of the separation of powers, a system that embodies the nation's constitutional desire to rise above the kind of anger and willfulness represented by the Reconstruction Congress. But the *McCardle* Court declined this opportunity for overruling *Durousseau* and confining Congress to good-faith attempts to improve the efficiency of the federal judiciary in ways that would preserve the right of individuals to take federal questions to federal courts and the right of the Supreme Court to be the supreme appellate court.

Admittedly, this resolution of the issue would have come close to reducing Congress's power over the Supreme Court's appellate jurisdiction to an aspect of the necessary and proper clause, thus rendering the exceptions clause superfluous.[78] But that is not a crucial objection to my position. To begin with, the exceptions clause would not be the Constitution's only superfluity. We can see this by recalling Hamilton's words about the supremacy clause and the necessary and proper clause themselves. "[I]t may be affirmed with perfect confidence, that the constitutional operation of the intended government would be precisely the same, if these clauses were entirely obliterated, as if they were repeated in every article."[79] Secondly, superfluity is not the kind of mistake that prevents law from guiding conduct; inconsistency is. It is clear that there is potential conflict between Congress's power to control federal jurisdiction and those provisions of the Constitution that seek to establish an independent judiciary, like the vesting provision of Article III, the provision for judicial tenure during good behavior, and the provision that forbids diminishing the salaries of federal judges while in office. The problem is how to interpret the Constitution in order to avoid this conflict. That requires a judgment as to which of two possible interpretations is consistent with our overall view of what the Constitution stands for. The basic alternatives are: (1) reducing Congress's powers over federal jurisdiction to aspects of the necessary and proper clause, or (2) allowing that Congress can manipulate federal jurisdiction at will. Senator Jesse Helms has given us a forthright statement of the case for the latter alternative: "In anticipation of judicial usurpations of power, the framers of our Constitution wisely gave Congress the authority, by a simple majority of both Houses, to check the Supreme Court by means of regulation of its appellate jurisdiction."[80] Our choice, then, is between judicial independence, or congressional supremacy over the performance of the judicial function; one of these notions must be rejected.

I have argued that Congress has a duty to use its powers in ways that might prevent the acceptance of unconstitutional judicial decisions as general rules governing the nation's political life. But that does not mean Congress can dictate the outcome of cases in the courts or tell the courts how they must interpret constitutional provisions in concrete cases. A congressional monopoly of constitutional interpretation would be at least as offensive to constitutional supremacy as a judicial monopoly—more so, given that closing the doors of the courts denies that we should institutionalize a practice of permitting minorities and what Madison called the "obnoxious individual" to remind the majority of its aspirations.[81] That one can respect the independence of courts while opposing the acceptance of their decisions as general political rules is indicated in Lincoln's account of his opposition to the *Dred Scott* decision:

> We oppose the Dred Scott decision in a certain way, upon which I ought perhaps to address you a few words. We do not propose that when Dred Scott has been decided to be a slave by the court, we, as a mob, will decide him to be free. We do not propose that, when any other one, or one thousand, shall be decided by that court to be slaves, we will in any violent way disturb the rights of property thus settled; but we nevertheless do oppose that decision as a political rule which shall be binding on the voter, to vote for nobody who thinks it's wrong, which shall be binding on the members of Congress or the President to favor no measure that does not actually concur with the principles of that decision. We do not propose to be bound by it as a political rule in that way, because we think it lays the foundation not merely of enlarging and spreading out what we consider an evil, but it lays the foundation for spreading that evil into the States themselves. We propose so resisting it as to have it reversed if we can, and a new judicial rule established upon this subject.[82]

I have have also argued that constitutional powers should be understood in terms of constitutional ends and a constitutionally ideal state of affairs. Few will try to locate in such a state of affairs a practice of congressional interference in judicial decision. All would agree that when the system is functioning as it should, Congress would respect the judiciary's independence. Senator Helms effectively acknowledges this when he classifies Congress's power to withdraw jurisdiction as an instrument for the correction of judicial usurpations. Assuming that there is something extraordinary about usurpation, judicial independence seems the norm, even for Senator Helms. He holds the power to withdraw jurisdiction a remedy for usurpations, perhaps akin to the impeachment provisions of Article I, section 3, and the amending provisions of Article V. Unlike these other remedies for extraordinary events like usurpations, however, Senator Helms's remedy of withdrawing jurisdiction does not require extraordinary majorities. The Constitution requires a two-thirds vote in the Senate for conviction in impeachments and a three-fourths concurrence among the states for amendments, and this pairing of extraordinary remedies with extraordinary majorities undermines the senator's conception of Congress's powers over federal jurisdiction as instruments for checking usurpations. Perhaps Senator Helms has a weaker sense of "usurpation" in mind. Can it be said that when judges fail to do their own work properly legislators can do it for them? If so, why can judges not do the work of legislators when the legislators fail? Many observers would say that this is precisely what accounts for the modern expansion of judicial power, and critics of the judiciary might argue from this that it is now Congress's turn to act on the same principle. But regardless of what its critics say about the judiciary's use of the equity power to correct unconstitutional conditions and about "judicial legislation" in general, the judiciary has not admitted that it is functioning improperly or that it is doing the work of legislatures. The critics can prove their charge against the judiciary only by showing that judges cannot and should not strive for their best understanding of constitutional powers, rights, and institutions— that is, that judges cannot and should not accept the *Constitution's* supremacy, as opposed to the supremacy of legislatures, public opinion, historical conceptions of constitutional norms, old judges, and other extraconstitutional authorities. This showing is not possible within a framework of constitutional supremacy. Unlike any claim the Court has ever made, Senator Helms is maintaining that Congress has a power through which it can do the admitted work of courts in constitutional cases. It is more plausible, however, that the Constitution equips no one but judges to do the work of courts, and it is clear that the special contribution of courts is essential to realizing the Constitution's aims.

In saying the judiciary does work no other branch can do, I assume that the Constitution provides for individual rights and vests courts with power they can use for protecting individual rights. But elaboration is necessary here because legislatures also make contributions to the protection of individual rights.[83] As a general matter of constitutional logic, a Congress that accepts constitutional supremacy will work to maintain the conditions of constitutional supremacy, and for Congress this entails exercising legislative powers in ways that combat unconstitutional conditions and maintain the widest possible public support for the premises of ratification.[84] Thus, each person has a right to a conscientious performance of the duties of legislators and other officials.[85] Each person, therefore, can be said to have a measure of such rights as personal security and the enjoyment of a general economic well-being, a measure that varies with resources and other contingencies and with what it takes to realize the higher values of the Bill of Rights, the Civil War Amendments, and other exemptions from granted powers.[86] Our general right to an exercise of governmental powers leads us to talk about specific rights to education, services to business and industry, the opportunity to make a living, consular services abroad, welfare assistance, internal improvements, and many other benefits.[87] The right to feasible levels of such benefits results from the nation's aspiration to a state of affairs in which all can reaffirm the Constitution as equally protective of everyone—that is, of persons with different needs, persons who have suffered and remain vulnerable to different degrees and kinds of injustice and misfortune. This state of affairs is also envisioned by the due process right of all to be governed only by policies that represent good-faith attempts to benefit everyone, not just those whom fortune has helped make relatively strong. Those with a constitutional attitude would eventually reach the same conclusion even if they were to begin with the modest proposal that the equal protection clause means no more than a right to equal opportunity. Most Americans would acknowledge such a right. Lincoln could say even to the people of his time that the "form and substance" of the government is one "whose leading object is to elevate the condition of men; to lift artificial weights from all shoulders; to clear the paths of laudable pursuit for all; to afford all an unfettered start and a fair chance in the race of life."[88] Yet, if the nation were genuinely committed to a "fair chance" alone, knowing what we do about the conditions that discourage personal development in a competitive society, our public and private agencies would do their best to provide a host of benefits for poor children from prenatal care to financial aid for college and professional school, with adequate nutrition, housing, recreation, and other benefits along the way. Nothing less could even pretend to reduce the undeserved competitive advantage enjoyed by the children of families who are not poor. In a constitutional state of affairs the relatively strong would not resent the provision of such benefits, partly because the government would have succeeded in making all classes equally aware that indolence, self-indulgence, and unfair advantage are wrong, and partly because the strong would not put wealth among their highest values or feel that they had a simple right to all that civil society had helped them acquire. Possessing a constitutional attitude, the relatively strong would repress willfulness, prejudice, and self-righteousness, generally striving to achieve a society of which they could be proud.

Courts can also contribute to an equally protective state of affairs. They can require government to extend a specific benefit equally, if at all, and they have exercised a broad-gauged power to correct unconstitutional conditions in certain state facilities. One wonders if there is good reason beyond the historical scope of the judicial function to prevent judges from ordering legislatures to provide new classes of benefits, as distinguished from fairer distributions of benefits already provided. One can show, after all, that the Constitution imposes an affirmative duty on the legislature to serve the good of all, and that the legislature fails in this duty when it neglects a persistent need, either by refusing to provide the benefit in question or by failing to persuade its proponents that it is not really a benefit or that its provision through government is not beneficial. Nevertheless, historical limits on the power of judges do constitute a barrier to trying to achieve the good society entirely through litigation. In looking for a reason behind these historical limits, there comes to mind Hamilton's famous observation that courts have "neither Force nor Will, but merely judgment."[89] The traditional division of legislative and judicial functions suggests that although courts are essential for clarifying and reminding the nation of its aspirations, legislatures eventually must want to live up to what the nation officially says it stands for. Because objects of aspiration must be desired to be known for what they are, and because the Constitution embodies the nation's aspirations, the nation cannot follow the Constitution unless it wants to. At some point the nation has to see and aspire to its better self. Courts can help lead, but they cannot really command obedience to the Constitution because it is impossible fully to understand conformity to the Constitution as a thing commanded. As I argued earlier in this chapter, a court cannot simply tell us the meaning of this Constitution; we have to see it for ourselves. Courts cannot achieve a constitutional state of affairs on their own.

Despite connections between legislative power and constitutional rights, however, the Constitution presupposes continuing conflicts between legislative and judicial conceptions of honoring constitutional rights and the conditions conducive thereto. The Constitution vests courts with power to hear individuals and minorities who invoke the sovereign people's most authoritative word in opposition to the actions of legislative majorities. This arrangement serves the interest of the majority as much as any other entity, assuming the majority wants to pursue constitutional policies only, as it implicitly says it does whenever its agent, the government, defends its position in a constitutional case. One of the reasons judicial independence is in the interest of a majority that accepts the Constitution's supremacy is that a constitutional majority appreciates the role of self-criticism and knows that the majority as such can be criticized only from the perspective of the individual and the minority. Fully conscious members of a constitutional majority would know that a self-willed and self-righteous attitude cannot comprehend the Constitution's supremacy. They would willingly institutionalize criticism of their conceptions of the Constitution from other perspectives.[90] With this attitude, they would hardly tolerate congressional interference with the constitutional duties of courts.

Congress does have ways of opposing unconstitutional judicial decisions without compromising judicial independence. Congress can issue remonstrances calling on the Court to change its opinions, as Lincoln did in opposition to the *Dred Scott* decision. Congress can refuse support to non-self-executing decisions, especially by withholding appropriations, as is often threatened with federal funds used to finance policies predicated on constitutional decisions of which Congress disapproves.[91] Congress can conduct inquiries into social conditions with the hope of persuading the courts that they had their facts wrong in deciding certain cases as they did.[92] Through moves like these Congress could oppose particular judicial decisions without denying that the courts have the power to persist in those decisions, it being possible to believe a court wrong while nevertheless retaining the power to correct itself. On the other hand, as with the actions of any other branch, we can imagine judicial pronouncements so far removed from recognizable constitutional conceptions as to destroy our perception of the established judiciary as part of what the Constitution envisions. As I argued in chapter 1, a court must be arguably right about the Constitution in order to be seen as a court established by or under the authority of the Constitution. If the courts—again, as with any other institution—should persist in decisions beyond the pale, we would eventually decide that we could not reaffirm the rules establishing the judiciary. We would believe at that point that the Constitution had ceased to be effective law and therefore that we were actually in a revolutionary situation. Only in such extreme circumstances would the Constitution be silent on the right of persons who had been elected to Congress, along with others, to seek to displace the authority or alter the structure of what is in fact the established judiciary. These individuals could either try to establish a new order or reestablish the old, but they would be employing extraconstitutional means in either case, the Constitution having ceased to exist as effective law, at least in their view. This, I submit, is the best one could say in behalf of constitutionally unauthorized moves like the ones Senator Helms contemplates against the federal judiciary.

Several cases in recent years have raised questions about the scope of Congress's power to enforce the Fourteenth Amendment without a prior finding by the judiciary that a state government has violated the amendment. The question is put most squarely in *Katzenbach* v. *Morgan* (1966).[93] In this case the Court upheld a section of the Voting Rights Act of 1965 that provided that states could not deny the right to vote to any person unable to read or write English who had com· pleted the sixth grade in Puerto Rico. The state of New York challenged the act with the argument that the courts had not held its English literacy requirement a violation of the equal protection clause and that Congress could not act under the enforcement provision of the Fourteenth Amendment unless the judiciary had reached a prior decision that there was a state violation of the amendment for federal authorities to remedy. In other words, New York was proceeding on the theory that Congress possessed no power to pursue its own view of what it would take for the nation to live up to the equal protection clause. The Court did not agree, however, and it upheld the act without determining whether, in its judgment, the state's English literacy requirement violated the equal protection clause. For the majority, Justice William Brennan treated the act as the Court would have treated an exercise of the commerce power or any other substantive power. He said that section 5 of the Fourteenth Amendment "is a positive grant of legislative power authorizing Congress to exercise its discretion in determining whether and what legislation is needed to secure the guarantees of the 14th Amendment."[94] He then said that there was no doubt that the action could be viewed "as a measure to secure for the Puerto Rican community residing in New York nondiscriminatory treatment by government—both in the imposition of voting qualifications and the provision or administration of governmental services, such as public schools, public housing, and law enforcement. [The act] may be readily seen as 'plainly adapted' to furthering these aims of the Equal Protection Clause."[95] He went on to say that it was up to Congress "to assess and weigh the various conflicting considerations" on how to exercise its power under section 5. The Court would confine itself to asking whether the congressional action had a rational basis, as "plainly" it did in this case.[96] Having answered what he considered a question of constitutional power, Justice Brennan then turned to a question of individual or minority rights: Did the act discriminate against those non-English-speaking groups other than Puerto Ricans to whom it did not grant relief? No, said Justice Brennan. This was an act expanding the right to vote, not contracting it, and, said Justice Brennan in accordance with long-standing judicial doctrine, Congress could move toward the goals of the equal protection clause one step at a time without discriminating against those who were not benefited right away. Thus, he concluded, "[we] have no occasion to determine in this case" whether Congress would have reasons sufficiently weighty to justify "a voting-qualification law that denied the franchise to persons educated in non-American-flag [i.e., non–Puerto Rican] schools."[97]

Following the lead of the dissent in *Morgan* by Justice John Marshall Harlan,[98] some observers wonder whether *Morgan* provides an opening through which Congress can enact laws that order changes in the Court's conceptions of Fourteenth Amendment rights. One can wonder, for example, whether *Morgan* leaves Congress free to decide that despite the holding of *Brown* v. *Board of Education* (1954)[99] an equally protective state of affairs in the public schools entails no more than the equalization of tangible facilities, as under the old separate-but-equal doctrine. Or one can wonder whether Congress has the power to decide that the states are depriving "persons" of "life" without due process of law by failing to prosecute those who elect to have or who perform abortions? Or, to take a section of the recently proposed Family Protection Act, one can wonder whether Congress can reverse judicial judgments by a statutory declaration that the right of groups of children to pray in public classrooms is a federally protected right of free religious exercise?[100] In light of my argument against a judicial monopoly in constitutional interpretation, I see no constitutional reason why Congress should have to await or settle for judicial definitions of congressional powers. I see no reason why Congress lacks the competence to form conceptions of its Fourteenth Amendment powers any less than its Article I powers. If Congress can form opinions of national security and other ends that it believes consistent with First Amendment and other rights, Congress is free to form opinions of what constitutes an equally protective state of affairs for Fourteenth Amendment purposes as well as states of affairs protective of other constitutional rights incorporated by the Fourteenth Amendment. Congress makes decisions tantamount to conceptualizing constitutional rights whenever it passes laws that are known to offend particular conceptions of those rights, and the courts have acknowledged Congress's power to form such conceptions by refusing to provide advisory opinions or act in other ways in advance of cases and controversies properly brought before judges.[101] Indeed, members of Congress violate their oaths when supporting legislative proposals without full attention to constitutional limitations of all kinds: rights, powers, and institutional norms.

As Congress should reach its independent understanding of the Constitution when performing its duties, however, so should the courts—for the respect of neither branch for the other takes precedence over that of each for the Constitution. The Court is as obligated not to follow congressional mistakes as Congress is obligated to withhold cooperation from the Court's mistakes. If Congress can express its opinion on abortion, school prayer, and the rest, that does not mean Congress can decide these questions for the courts. *Morgan* asks whether Congress is empowered to reach an independent understanding of the Constitution in exercising legislative powers; the answer is yes. But *Morgan* cannot be read as deferring to Congress with respect to questions the Court had to answer in performing its duties to the litigants. In fact, *Morgan* decides on the merits that (1) the act serves a responsible version of the common good, and (2) the act does not violate anyone's right to equal protection of the laws.[102] I need not inquire here whether the Court answered these questions correctly. That the Court raised and answered them at all is enough to show that the Court can recognize an independent power of constitutional interpretation in Congress without abdicating constitutional obligations of its own.

I emphasize, in conclusion, that in performing its duties the judiciary has no constitutional warrant for deferring to any other branch. As the term appears in current discussion, maxims of *judicial self-restraint* flow sometimes from attempts to locate the boundaries between the judiciary and other "equal and coordinate branches." Thus, the Supreme Court decided at an early point in the nation's history that it is empowered only to decide "cases and controversies" and that this power excludes judicial findings of the law in the form of advisory opinions sought by those who prefer to consult courts rather than their own best understanding of the Constitution or who would avoid the need to litigate.[103] Sometimes, however, a different kind of argument is advanced for judicial self-restraint: judges are exhorted to restrain themselves out of deference to other, more democratic branches or because of a multifaceted skepticism over the ability of judges to find and apply the law in opposition to their partisan preferences. In other words, judges can be exhorted to restrain themselves by those who feel that something is wrong with the judiciary and with the claims judges typically make about the ways in which laws, precedents, and other norms guide their decisions in concrete cases.

One can appreciate the self-doubts of judges who urge judicial self-restraint from questions about their capacities to be good judges. I have argued in this book that the Constitution claims supremacy only for itself and that it is illogical to vest final authority for constitutional interpretation in anyone whose interpretations are supposed to be governed by the Constitution. Judges, too, are subjects of the law. As subjects of the law they must understand themselves to be capable of violating the law. Conscious subjects must have misgivings about the conformity of their conceptions of the law to the law itself. Self-criticism, self-doubt, and a resulting distrust of precedent are therefore parts of a fully developed constitutional attitude, and this may incline one to accept a maxim of judicial deference to the constitutional conceptions of the other branches. On the other hand, judges take an oath that they will try to be good judges; and, clearly, whatever doubts they have about themselves as subjects of the Constitution, they have no reason for believing that others are more committed to maintaining the Constitution than they are. If a consciousness of their status as subjects brings skepticism about their own abilities, judges should be at least equally skeptical about the constitutionalism of others, since all are equally subjects of the Constitution as law. It is therefore difficult to see how constitutional judges can follow anything less than their best conceptions of what the Constitution requires—in defiance of the other branches of government and public opinion, if need be.

Advocates of judicial self-restraint might argue further that all versions of general constitutional ideas are equal—that there can be no reason for judges to prefer their best conceptions of such ideas as equal protection of the laws and procedural fairness. But this argument could prove only that judges have no reason *not* to prefer their own conceptions. If all conceptions of general normative ideas are equal, why not prefer one's own conception? The usual response, of course, is that it would be undemocratic for judges to prefer their own conceptions, judges being less responsive to electoral majorities than are other officials.[104] One could criticize this argument for judicial self-restraint by noting that it relies on an extraconstitutional sense of "democracy" that elevates popular willfulness over popular self-restraint. But I need not repeat that criticism here, for it is obvious that those who adjudge the judiciary undemocratic employ one of several competing conceptions of a general normative idea, *democracy*. Now, reason either can support their conception of democracy or it cannot. If reason cannot support their preference for their understanding of what democracy requires, then there is no reason why others cannot adopt a different conception of democracy. If they should respond that reason does support one conception of democracy over others, they contradict their initial proposition about the equality of different conceptions of general normative ideas. Either way, they fail to show why judicial review must be viewed as undemocratic.

As fully conscious subjects of the law, constitutional judges deciding constitutional cases must recognize their disinclination to follow the law's guidance, and they should try to overcome that disinclination. They cannot justify self-righteous or self-willed refusals to challenge their conceptions. Theirs must be a continuing effort to find the best understanding of constitutional norms. It makes no sense for judges to understand their duty in this way if they are persuaded that sooner or later they will confront alternative decisions distinguishable only by their raw preferences. Although some thinkers try to argue otherwise, it is difficult to see how one can believe *both* that judicial decision must be bottomed in impenetrable personal preference *and* that judges have a continuing duty to submit their conceptions to dialectical processes.[105] A judge who believes that it is possible to find and apply the law, even if only through progressively better understandings of the law, has a duty to be active in that pursuit.[106] We have seen, moreover, that a judge who is convinced judicial decisions must be bottomed in personal preference has no reason not to pursue those preferences either willfully or as prudential consideration permits.[107] No real constitutional defense seems available for judicial self-restraint in either case.

Notes

CHAPTER 1

1. Thurgood Marshall, "Remarks of Thurgood Marshall, Second Circuit Judicial Conference," Buck Hill Falls, Pa., May 1979.

2. 441 U.S. 153 (1979).

3. 441 U.S. 520 (1979).

4. Ibid., at 542.

5. Ibid., at 578. Before Justice Rehnquist's time, Justice Felix Frankfurter also opposed judicially liberal or generous readings of the due process clause and other Fourteenth Amendment guarantees. However, in Rochin v. California, 342 U.S. 165 (1952), Frankfurter held that, independently of more specific constitutional guarantees, the due process clause prohibited police conduct shocking to the civilized conscience. Marshall's use of Frankfurter's words suggests the limits of judicial conservatism.

6. See Walter F. Murphy, *Elements of Judicial Strategy* (Chicago: University of Chicago Press, 1964), pp. 24–26, 104–6, 121–22; see also J. W. Peltason, *Fifty-eight Lonely Men* (New York: Harcourt, Brace, World, 1961), pp. 82–92, 115–22, 132–34.

7. 441 U.S. at 562.

8. For an overview of the debate, see Paul Brest, "The Fundamental Rights Controversy: The Essential Contradictions of Normative Constitutional Scholarship," *Yale Law Journal* 90 (1981):1063–1105.

9. See ibid., pp. 1065–66; John Hart Ely, *Democracy and Distrust* (Cambridge, Mass.: Harvard University Press, 1980), pp. 7–8, 101–4.

10. Ely, *Democracy and Distrust*, p. 11.

11. I would include the following works in this category: Ronald A. Dworkin, *Taking Rights Seriously* (Cambridge, Mass.: Harvard University Press, 1977), pp. 106–

10, 130–49; idem, " 'Natural' Law Revisited," *University of Florida Law Review* 34 (1982):165; Walter F. Murphy, "The Art of Constitutional Interpretation: A Preliminary Showing," in *Essays on the Constitution of the United States*, ed. M. Judd Harmon (Port Washington, N.Y.: Kennikat Press, 1978), 130; David A. J. Richards, *The Moral Criticism of Law* (Encino, Calif.: Dickenson, 1977); and, with qualifications, Michael J. Perry, "Noninterpretive Review in Human Rights Cases: A Functional Justification," *New York University Law Review* 56 (1981):278.

12. This may appear to be an unfair description of the view that constitutional interpretation should be governed by the framers' conceptions of the general ideas embodied in constitutional provisions. But if the framers' intentions lie in their historical conceptions—right or wrong and as opposed to better conceptions—then, relative to better conceptions, the framers intended to impose their mere likes and dislikes. Works advocating a focus on historical conceptions include: Raoul Berger, *Government by Judiciary* (Cambridge, Mass.: Harvard University Press, 1977), pp. 363–72; William H. Rehnquist, "The Notion of a Living Constitution," *Texas Law Review* 54 (1976):693.

13. Cf. Philip Bobbitt, "Constitutional Fate," *Texas Law Review* 58 (1980):734–41.

14. This is the thrust of the following: Brest, "The Fundamental Rights Controversy," pp. 1105–9; Richard D. Parker, "The Past of Constitutional Theory—And Its Future," *Ohio State Law Journal* 42 (1981):257–59; Mark Tushnet, "Darkness on the Edge of Town: The Contributions of John Hart Ely to Constitutional Theory," *Yale Law Journal* 89 (1980):1037.

CHAPTER 2

1. See Wilfrid E. Rumble, *American Legal Realism: Skepticism, Reform, and the Judicial Process* (Ithaca, N.Y.: Cornell University Press, 1968); Theodore M. Benditt, *Law as Rule and Principle* (Stanford: Stanford University Press, 1978), chaps. 1, 2.

2. See, e.g., Thurman Arnold, "Professor Hart's Theology," *Harvard Law Review* 73 (1960):1298.

3. H.L.A. Hart, The *Concept of Law* (Oxford: Clarendon Press, 1961), p. 135.

4. Ibid., p. 133.

5. Charles P. Curtis, "The Role of the Constitutional Text," in *Supreme Court and Supreme Law*, ed. Edmond Cahn (Bloomington: Indiana University Press, 1954), pp. 64–70.

6. Richard E. Flathman, *Political Obligation* (New York: Atheneum, 1972), pp. 156–67.

7. Curtis, "Role of the Constitutional Text," pp. 64–66.

8. 4 Wheat. 316 (1819).

9. Curtis, "Role of the Constitutional Text," p. 64.

10. Robert K. Faulkner, *The Jurisprudence of John Marshall* (Princeton: Princeton University Press, 1968), pp. 65–79, 200–223.

11. John Hart Ely, "Constitutional Interpretivism: Its Allure and Impossibility," *Indiana Law Journal* 53 (1978):399–448.

12. Ibid., p. 445.

13. Ibid., p. 402 n. 12.

14. John Hart Ely, *Democracy and Distrust* (Cambridge, Mass.: Harvard University Press, 1980), pp. 12–13, 87–89. Ely claimed in his 1978 article that interpretivism is impossible; he promised a theory that would reconcile noninterpretivist or extracon-

stitutional decision with democracy. The book abandons the claim and the promise of the article, largely through a shift in terminology. The article described interpretivism as one or another form of the view that the Constitution can guide or provide the "starting points" for judicial decision. Ely said this is impossible because of the existence of the three open-ended clauses. But in chap. 4 of the book, Ely finds the solution to the open-ended clauses in what he calls the Constitution's "broader themes"— i.e., the Constitution's commitment to democratic processes, which keep the channels of political change open to changing majorities and which prevent the exclusion of minorities from equal respect and concern. This, of course, is a form of the view that the Constitution can guide decision, as Ely acknowledges in saying that he is "tempted to claim that the mode of review developed here is the ultimate interpretivism" (pp. 87–88). So a broad form of interpretivism is possible after all, and Ely now criticizes only a narrow, or "clause-bound interpretivism," which he defines as "[t]he suggestion . . . that the various provisions of the Constitution are approached essentially as self-contained units and interpreted on the basis of their language, with whatever interpretive help the legislative history can provide, without significant injection of content from outside the provision" (pp. 12–13). Yet the article clearly criticized both narrow and broad forms of the view that the Constitution can guide judicial decision. See Ely, "Constitutional Interpretivism," pp. 399–401.

15. I criticize this approach below; see text at chap. 3, nn. 14–17.

16. See Paul Brest, "The Fundamental Rights Controversy: The Essential Contradictions of Normative Constitutional Scholarship," *Yale Law Journal* 90 (1981): 1089, 1092.

17. Ely, "Constitutional Interpretivism," pp. 399–400.

18. Raoul Berger, *Government by Judiciary* (Cambridge, Mass.: Harvard University Press, 1977), p. 9.

19. Ely, "Constitutional Interpretivism," pp. 399–400.

20. Ibid., pp. 403, 421–23.

21. Ibid., pp. 426–45.

22. Ibid., p. 445.

23. Ibid., pp. 408–11, 445–48.

24. Ibid., p. 448.

25. See Raoul Berger, "Ely's 'Theory of Judicial Review,'" *Ohio State Law Journal* 42 (1982):123.

26. Ely, "Constitutional Interpretivism," pp. 434, 438.

27. Ibid., p. 436, citing Alexander M. Bickel, "The Original Understanding and the Segregation Decision," *Harvard Law Review* 69 (1955):59.

28. Ely, "Constitutional Interpretivism," p. 400.

29. Ibid., pp. 408–11, 414.

30. See Jacob E. Cooke, ed., *The Federalist* (Middletown, Conn.: Wesleyan University Press, 1961), pp. 146–51.

31. Ely, "Constitutional Interpretivism," p. 442.

32. Jonathan Eliot, ed., *The Debates in the Several State Conventions on the Adoption of the Federal Constitution*, 2d ed., 4 vols. (Washington, D.C., 1854), 3:44.

33. Ely, "Constitutional Interpretivism," p. 418.

34. Ibid.

35. Ibid., pp. 427–28.

36. See Trimble v. Gordon, 430 U.S. 762, 776–78 (1977) (Rehnquist, J., dissenting).

37. See Duncan v. Louisiana, 391 U.S. 145, 162–71 (1968) (Black, J., concurring).

38. See Griswold v. Connecticut,, 381 U.S. 479, 486–99 (1965) (Goldberg, J., concurring).

39. See n. 14.

40. Ely, "Constitutional Interpretivism," p. 420. See also Board of Regents v. Roth, 408 U.S. 564 (1972), and Perry v. Sindermann, 408 U.S. 509 (1972).

41. Ely, "Constitutional Interpretivism," pp. 420-21.

42. See John Hart Ely, "Foreword: On Discovering Fundamental Values," *Harvard Law Review* 92 (1978):5.

43. For a recent, unsuccessful attempt to deny that legal and moral disagreements presuppose right answers, see Neil MacCormick, *Legal Reasoning and Legal Theory* (Oxford: Clarendon Press, 1978). MacCormick acknowledges the force of the argument that when two people "genuinely disagree . . . there must be a right answer in principle, even if it is not in practice possible for anyone to be certain which of them is right" (pp. 246-47). But he contends that this argument applies only to disagreements about matters of fact, not about practical disagreements of the kind one finds in legal and moral debate (pp. 247-48). This response suggests that practical disagreements are not real disagreements for MacCormick, and in fact he defends his distinction between practical and factual disagreements with a hypothetical example involving a purely aesthetic disagreement between two people over the purchase of watercolor paintings (pp. 247-48). He does "stress" that the use of his "picture-buying analogy" as an argument "is not dependent on any particularly strong asserted similarity between aesthetic standards and legal standards" (p. 248). But this disclaimer only underscores the fact that his hypothetical example is one of an aesthetic dispute. It was Mac-Cormick's example to offer, and he offers no other. He simply observes a distinction between factual disagreement and moral disagreement and arbitrarily treats the former as the only genuine type of disagreement.

The weakness of MacCormick's view, of course, is that it fails to account for the presuppositions of persons engaged in what they regard as serious political, legal, or moral debate. For insofar as they seriously debate, they assume a distinction between better arguments and worse arguments, and they assume that, somehow, minds can be changed through what they would call a process of reason. Parts of his book show that MacCormick is quite aware of these presuppositions and their implications for legal and moral theory. He rejects "total irrationalism," or the view that "talk of justice is no more than an expression of emotions, equivalent to banging on the table" (p. 265). He also holds that "[h]uman beings are not organisms set in motion by mere reaction to stimuli in the environment, . . . that human beings act *for reasons* when they act at all, and that no 'explanation' of human behavior which omits reference to the subjective reasons for which it is performed can be a full or adequate one" (p. 6, his emphasis). Failing to maintain a consistent perspective, however, he also suggests that, at bottom, our preference for a life of giving and exchanging reasons is to "be explained" with reference to "social and familial background" or, perhaps, "a biological nature . . . to favor rationality" or even one's personal "revulsion from the prospect of a life without reasoned discourse" (p. 268). He says that "even in the case of reason, it is not *reason* which is expressed if we set value on rationality" (p. 269, his emphasis). He claims also that "[w]e have a choice to be rational or not" (p. 269). But, surely, from the perspective of those who believe they "act *for reasons* when they act at all," we do express our rationality when we value rationality. From the same perspective, if choosing to do something is an act, then choice is always accompanied by reasons, and it would not be strictly true that someone who appeared to do so was actually choosing to live an irrational life—such a person would have reasons to the extent that he was choosing something, and he would therefore be rational to some extent. Of course, we could still talk of persons with "method in their madness" or choosing to "play dumb." We could also assess someone's choice as "irrational" in the sense of a bad choice. We could talk of someone's "going mad," as opposed to "choosing madness," with no possibility of knowing whether he had chosen madness, since knowing that would require knowledge of the reason requisite for calling an event a choice, and the testimony that would establish the existence of such a reason would disprove the existence of madness. We could talk of someone's having chosen something that subsequently made him go mad, but that is different from choosing madness or having the power to choose to be mad.

44. Ely, "Constitutional Interpretivism," pp. 420–21.

45. Ibid., p. 423.

46. Ibid., p. 422.

47. See Note, "Fourteenth Amendment: Due Process for Prisoners in Commitment Proceedings," *Journal of Criminal Law and Criminology* 71 (1980):592.

48. Ibid., p. 446. See also Ely, "Fundamental Values," pp. 27–32.

49. Berger, *Government by Judiciary*, pp. 17–18, 87–90.

50. Ely, "Fundamental Values," pp. 31–32.

51. Ibid., pp. 39–43.

52. Ely, "Constitutional Interpretivism," p. 446. See also Ely, "Fundamental Values," pp. 22–23.

53. See, e.g., Berger, *Government by Judiciary*, p. 87.

54. Ely, "Constitutional Interpretivism," pp. 409–10.

55. See ibid., p. 405 n. 22; cf. Ely, "Fundamental Values," pp. 41–42.

56. Roy P. Basler, ed., *Abraham Lincoln: Speeches and Writings* (New York: Grosset & Dunlap, 1962), pp. 352–65.

57. Ibid., p. 360–61.

58. See Ronald A. Dworkin, "The Law of the Slave Catchers," *Times Literary Supplement*, December 5, 1975, p. 1437; Herbert J. Storing, "Slavery and the Moral Foundations of the American Republic," in *The Moral Foundations of the American Republic*, 2d ed., ed. Robert H. Horwitz (Charlottesville: University Press of Virginia, 1979), pp. 214–33.

59. Bernard Bailyn, *The Ideological Origins of the American Revolution* (Cambridge, Mass.: Harvard University Press, Belknap Press, 1967), p. 20.

CHAPTER 3

1. Raoul Berger, *Government by Judiciary* (Cambridge, Mass.: Harvard University Press, 1977), p. 10.

2. John Hart Ely, "Constitutional Interpretivism: Its Allure and Impossibility," *Indiana Law Journal* 53 (1978): 410–14.

3. James Madison, *The Virginia Report of 1799–1800 together with the Virginia Resolutions of 1798* (New York: Da Capo Press, 1970), pp. 190–202.

4. See Gerald Gunther, *Cases and Materials on Constitutional Law*, 10th ed. (Mineola, N.Y.: Foundation Press, 1980), pp. 96–99. See also McCulloch v. Maryland, 4 Wheat. 316 (1819).

5. Jacob E. Cooke, ed., *The Federalist* (Middletown, Conn.: Wesleyan University Press, 1961), p. 6.

6. Ibid., pp. 258–67.

7. See text at chap. 1, nn. 7–10.

8. Richard E. Flathman, *Political Obligation* (New York: Atheneum, 1972), pp. 156–58.

9. H.L.A. Hart, *The Concept of Law* (Oxford: Clarendon Press, 1961), p. 6.

10. C. Herman Pritchett, *The American Constitution*, 2d ed. (New York: McGraw-Hill, 1968), pp. 72–73.

11. Cooke, *The Federalist*, p. 349.

12. See Walter F. Murphy, "An Ordering of Constitutional Values," *Southern California Law Review* 53 (1980):754–57.

13. Edward S. Corwin, *The Constitution and What It Means Today* (Princeton: Princeton University Press, 1946), p. 141.

14. The best statement of this position is John Hart Ely, *Democracy and Distrust* (Cambridge, Mass.: Harvard University Press, 1980), chap. 4.

15. Ibid., pp. 88–101.

16. Cooke, *The Federalist*, pp. 159–60.

17. Of course, this shows we cannot even hypothesize a set of procedures neutral toward all conceivable wants. A universally neutral set of procedures could not satisfy the demand for procedures that exclude some outcomes. This is one reason why genuinely neutral procedures are inconceivable. Another is our inability to imagine a procedure that satisfies the demand to get something for nothing, the demand to do away with the need for procedure itself.

18. Cooke, *The Federalist*, p. 260.

19. Ibid., pp. 51, 57, 88–89, 327, 331.

20. Ibid., p. 57.

21. Ibid., p. 3.

22. Jefferson to Samuel Kercheval, July 12, 1816, in Paul L. Ford, ed., *The Works of Thomas Jefferson*, 12 vols. (New York: G. P. Putnam's Sons, 1904–5), 12:12–13.

23. Cf. George Anastaplo, *The Constitutionalist: Notes on the First Amendment* (Dallas: Southern Methodist University Press, 1971), pp. 102–6.

24. See Hart, *The Concept of Law*, pp. 89–93.

25. Cooke, *The Federalist*, p. 204.

26. Ibid., p. 340.

27. Ibid.

28. See Flathman, *Political Obligation*, pp. 48–49.

29. Cooke, The *Federalist*, p. 204. Hamilton was speaking of the necessary and proper clause as well as the supremacy clause.

30. Ibid., p. 207.

31. Ibid., pp. 259–60.

32. Ibid., pp. 258–59.

33. Laurence Tribe, "The Puzzling Persistence of Process-Based Constitutional Theories," *Yale Law Journal* 89 (1980):1070–71.

34. Cf. Ronald A. Dworkin, *Taking Rights Seriously* (Cambridge, Mass.: Harvard University Press, 1977), pp. 106–7, 132, 137.

35. See ibid., pp. 279–83.

36. Cf. Flathman, *Political Obligation*, pp. 58–62, 69–77, 87–111.

37. Cf. text at chap. 4, nn. 73–74.

38. See text at chap. 5, nn. 25–28.

CHAPTER 4

1. See, e.g., Jacob E. Cooke, ed., *The Federalist* (Middletown, Conn.: Wesleyan University Press, 1961), pp. 203–6, 339, 356–57, 379–80.

2. A recent paper illustrates the dilemma facing today's defenders of federalism. A. E. Dick Howard calls on the Court to be more "sensitive to federalism as a value of constitutional dimension." But he acknowledges that the states are often unresponsive to national needs and that they often seek "repressive or discriminatory ends."

He concedes that "federalism may have to yield to . . . the Bill of Rights or a considered judgment by Congress about a legitimate national interest." This leaves us wondering whether the states have any real rights beyond the maintenance of their basic institutions and the few state powers expressly mentioned in the Constitution. In the end, Howard suggests only that Congress be required carefully to weigh the values in conflict before it decides to "displace the most integral decisions of local government"—which, he implicitly concedes, Congress has the power to do. See A. E. Dick Howard, "Judicial Federalism: The States and the Supreme Court," paper presented at Federalism Conference, Institute for Contemporary Studies, Washington, D.C., September 8–9, 1981, pp. 23–26.

3. S. 1378, in U.S. Congress, Senate, *Congressional Record*, 97th Cong., 1st sess., 1981, pp. 6329–36.

4. Ibid., p. 6329, sec. 2 (4).

5. Ibid., p. 6335, sec. 302(a), (1–3).

6. Ibid., pp. 6329–30, sec. 104(a-c).

7. Ibid., pp. 6330, sec. 105.

8. Ibid., pp. 6327–28.

9. Ibid., p. 6344.

10. Ibid.

11. Ibid., p. 6329, secs. 102(a), 440A.

12. Ibid., p. 6330, sec. 108.

13. Ibid., p. 6334, sec. 440B(1).

14. Ibid., sec. 440B(3).

15. Ibid., sec. 440B(4).

16. Ibid., sec. 440C.

17. Ibid., p. 6327.

18. Ibid., p. 6334, sec. 440C(c)(1)-(2).

19. See Gary L. McDowell, *Equity and the Constitution: The Supreme Court, Equitable Relief, and Public Policy* (Chicago: University of Chicago Press, 1982), chaps. 6–7.

20. C. Herman Pritchett, *The American Constitution*, 2d ed. (New York: McGraw-Hill, 1978), pp. 72–73.

21. See Cooke, *The Federalist*, no. 10. See also Robert K. Faulkner, *The Jurisprudence of John Marshall* (Princeton: Princeton University Press, 1968), chap. 1; Benjamin Barber, "The Compromised Republic: Public Purposelessness in America," in *The Moral Foundations of the American Republic*, ed. Robert H. Horwitz, 2d ed. (Charlottesville: University Press of Virginia, 1979), pp. 19–38.

22. See Herbert J. Storing, "The Constitution and the Bill of Rights," in *Essays on the Constitution of the United States*, ed. M. Judd Harmon (Port Washington, N.Y.: Kennikat Press, 1978), pp. 32–48.

23. The process of incorporation is usually considered to have begun in Gitlow v. New York, 268 U.S. 652 (1925).

24. United States v. Darby, 312 U.S. 100, 124 (1941).

25. Walter Berns, "The Meaning of the Tenth Amendment," in *A Nation of States,* ed. Robert A. Goldwin, (Chicago: Rand McNally, 1963), pp. 130–32.

26. Pritchett, *The American Constitution*, pp. 10–15.

27. Cooke, *The Federalist*, p. 92.

28. Ibid., p. 146.

29. Ibid., pp. 147–48.

30. Ibid., p. 269.

31. For typical criticisms of mere office seekers, see Cooke, *The Federalist*, pp. 4, 425, 482.

32. Ibid., p. 6.

33. Ibid., pp. 308–9.

34. See text at chap. 3, nn. 14–17, 23–24.

35. See Cooke, *The Federalist*, nos. 41, 63.

36. Ibid., nos. 29, 41.

37. Ibid., nos. 42, 43.

38. Ibid., no. 43.

39. Ibid., no. 42, pp. 285–86.

40. Ibid., no. 42, pp. 281–82.

41. See text at chap. 5, nn. 14–18.

42. See text at chap. 3, nn. 68–74; text at chap. 5, nn. 14–27; text at chap. 6, nn. 83–88.

43. See text at chap. 5, nn. 81–86.

44. See text at chap. 3, nn. 34–37.

45. See text at chap. 5, nn. 4–6; text at chap. 6, nn. 12–18.

46. See text at chap. 5, nn. 5–6.

47. 4 Wheat. 316, 400 (1819).

48. National League of Cities v. Usery, 426 U.S. 833 (1976). See Karen H. Flax, " In the Wake of *National League of Cities* v. *Usery*: A Derelict Makes Waves," *South Carolina Law Review* 34 (1983):649–86.

49. Gerald Gunther, *John Marshall's Defense of* McCulloch v. Maryland (Stanford: Stanford University Press, 1969), pp. 3–4.

50. 4 Wheat. 316, 401–2 (1819).

51. Ibid., at 402.

52. Ibid., at 402–5.

53. Ibid., at 405–7.

54. Ibid., at 407–8.

55. See Pritchett, *The American Constitution*, pp. 353–56; Louis Henkin, *Foreign Affairs and the Constitution* (Mineola, N.Y.: Foundation Press, 1972), pp. 15–19.

56. 4 Wheat. 316, 421 (1819).

57. See text at chap. 3, n. 24.

58. 4 Wheat. 316, 413 (1819).

59. Ibid., at 413–15.

60. Ibid., at 415–16.

61. Cooke, *The Federalist*, pp. 204–5.

62. Gunther, *John Marshall's Defense*, pp. 64–77.

63. See Georg Henrik von Wright, *Norm and Action* (London: Routledge & Kegan Paul, 1963), pp. 35–38.

64. 4 Wheat. 316, 423 (1819).

65. See Champion v. Ames, 188 U.S. 321 (1903); Hoke v. United States, 277 U.S. 308 (1913); United States v. Dellinger, 472 F.2d 340 (7th Cir. 1972), *cert. denied*, 410 U.S. 970 (1973); Heart of Atlanta Motel v. United States, 379 U.S. 241 (1964).

66. See *Ex parte* Jackson, 96 U.S. 727 (1878). See also 70 Stat. 699 (1956).

67. See United States v. Sanchez, 340 U.S. 42 (1950); United States v. Kahriger, 345 U.S. 22 (1953).

68. Individual views of Senator Winston L. Prouty, U.S. Congress, Senate, Committee on Commerce, 88th Cong., 2d sess., *Report on S. 1732*, pp. 1–11 (1964).

69. Civil Rights Cases, 109 U.S. 3 (1883).

70. Ibid., at 17.

71. 334 U.S. 1 (1948).

72. 365 U.S. 715 (1961).

73. Peterson v. Greenville, 373 U.S. 244 (1963); Lombard v. Louisiana, 373 U.S. 267 (1963).

74. See text at chap. 5, nn. 52–53, 82–84.

75. 379 U.S. 241, 257 (1964).

76. See the questions put to Attorney General Robert F. Kennedy by Senator J. Strom Thurmond during the hearings on the bill. U.S. Congress, Senate, Committee on Commerce, *Hearings before the Senate Committee on Commerce on S. 1732*, 88th Cong., 1st sess., parts 1 and 2, cited in Gerald Gunther, Cases and Materials on Constitutional Law, 10th ed. (Mineola, N.Y.: Foundation Press, 1980), pp. 200–201.

77. See Pritchett, *The American Constitution*, pp. 252–58.

78. 9 Wheat. 1 (1824).

79. Ibid., at 9–10.

80. Cooke, *The Federalist*, pp. 579–80.

81. Thus, John Marshall said in Gibbons v. Ogden, 9 Wheat. 1, 189–90 (1824): "Commerce, undoubtedly, is traffic, but it is something more: it is intercourse between nations, and parts of nations, in all its branches."

82. See Hoke v. United States, 227 U.S. 308 (1913); *Ex parte* Jackson, 96 U.S. 727 (1878); Wickard v. Filburn, 317 U.S. 111 (1942).

83. Congress, however, could not avoid responsibility for the state of the nation's economy. See text at chap. 6, nn. 22–26.

84. Sotirios A. Barber, " *National League of Cities* v. *Usery*: New Meaning for the Tenth Amendment?," in *1976 Supreme Court Review*, ed. Philip B. Kurland (Chicago: University of Chicago Press, 1977), pp. 169–73.

85. Ibid., pp. 169–73.

86. See chap. 5, n. 28.

87. United States v. Darby Lumber Co., 312 U.S. 100, 115 (1941).

88. United States v. O'Brien 391 U.S. 367 (1968). See Dean Alfange, "Free Speech and Symbolic Conduct: The Draft-Card Burning Case," in *1968 Supreme Court Review*, ed. Philip B. Kurland (Chicago: University of Chicago Press, 1969), pp. 27–38.

89. See Max Weber, *The Theory of Social and Economic Organization*, ed. Talcott Parsons (Glencoe, Ill.: Free Press, 1964), pp. 90–100.

CHAPTER 5

1. Jacob E. Cooke, ed., *The Federalist* (Middletown, Conn.: Wesleyan University Press, 1961), pp. 579–80.

2. Ibid.

3. For a different view, see Walter Berns, *For Capital Punishment* (New York: Basic Books, 1979), pp. 145–48. In a recent opinion Justice Stevens reminded federal judges that their mission in death penalty cases "is to adjudicate federal questions," not to vindicate "certain States' interest in carrying out the death penalty." Coleman v. Balkcom, 451 U.S. 949, 950 (1981).

4. See, e.g., Cooke, *The Federalist*, pp. 524–79.

5. These words are taken from Justice Robert H. Jackson's dissent in Terminiello v. Chicago, 337 U.S. 1, 37 (1949). Justice Jackson, however, was not a consistent adherent to the suicide-pact argument. See his dissent in Korematsu v. United States, 323 U.S. 214, 245–46 (1944).

6. See, e.g., text at chap. 2, nn. 41–59.

7. Cooke, *The Federalist*, pp. 259–60.

8. H.L.A. Hart, *The Concept of Law* (Oxford: Clarendon Press, 1961), pp. 125–26.

9. Ronald A. Dworkin, *Taking Rights Seriously* (Cambridge, Mass.: Harvard University Press, 1977), p. 134.

10. See, e.g., Dartmouth College v. Woodward, 4 Wheat. 518 (1819); Hurtado v. California, 110 U.S. 516 (1884).

11. See text at chap. 6, nn. 55–59.

12. Cooke, *The Federalist*, p. 349.

13. Cf. Plato *The Republic* 337d-382c.

14. See generally Gerald Gunther, *Cases and Materials on Constitutional Law*, 10th ed. (Mineola, N.Y.: Foundation Press, 1980), chaps. 8, 9.

15. An expansive reading of the words "life, liberty and property" is defended by John Hart Ely, *Democracy and Distrust* (Cambridge, Mass.: Harvard University Press, 1980), pp. 18–20, 192 n. 28. Surely, it is only through an expansive reading that one can avoid the implication Ely finds in Board of Regents v. Roth, 408 U.S. 564 (1972): that government can sometimes hurt people without due process. It is also clear that no one could aspire to or defend a government that allows itself a sphere of arbitrary action. For this reason, one must agree with this part of Ely's reading of the due process clause and his implicit criticism of *Roth* as an incoherent decision. However, I disagree with Ely's contention that *Roth* is understandable, if indefensible, as a reaction by the Court to its own decision in Roe v. Wade, 410 U.S. 113 (1973). Ely attacks *Roe* because he says substantive due process is a contradiction in terms; *Roth*, he says, is an attempt to rein in the license for substantive judicial judgments unleashed by *Roe*. But if Ely were really serious about eliminating substantive judgments, he would have no basis for his attack on *Roth*. If Ely were the thoroughgoing legal positivist he sometimes says he is, he would not be able to reach a judgment different from the government's as to when someone had been "hurt." He would therefore have to abandon his criticism of the Burger Court's suggestion that government can hurt people without due process.

16. See, e.g., Lochner v. New York, 198 U.S. 45, 75–76 (1905) (Holmes, J., dissenting); Galvan v. Press, 347 U.S. 522, 530–32 (1954); Calder v. Bull, 3 Dallas 385, 398–99 (1798) (Iredell, J., concurring).

17. Lochner v. New York, 198 U.S. 45, 56–65 (1905).

18. See, e.g., Ely, *Democracy and Distrust*, pp. 56–60.

19. See Rochin v. California, 342 U.S. 165, 169 (1952).

20. See, e.g., Adamson v. California, 332 U.S. 46, 71–72 (1947) (Black, J., dissenting).

21. See, e.g., Palko v. Connecticut, 302 U.S. 319, 322–28 (1937).

22. Ely, *Democracy and Distrust*, pp. 18–19, 22–30, 152–54.

23. Ibid., pp. 152–79. Ely derives this thesis from what he calls the Constitution's broader themes. The equal protection clause and the Ninth Amendment are the textual bases for judicial intervention in behalf of legislative policies that are "representative" in a substantive sense. For a similar criticism of Ely, see Laurence Tribe, "The Puzzling Persistence of Process-Based Constitutional Theories," *Yale Law Journal* 89 (1980): 1063–80.

24. Griswold v. Connecticut, 381 U.S. 479 (1965), Roe v. Wade, 410 U.S. 113 (1973); Pierce v. Society of Sisters, 268 U.S. 510 (1925); Myer v. Nebraska, 262 U.S. 390 (1923).

25. Day-Brite Lighting v. Missouri, 342 U.S. 421 (1952); Paul v. Davis, 424 U.S. 693 (1976); Bishop v. Wood, 426 U.S. 341 (1976); Doe v. Commonwealth's Attorney, 425 U.S. 901 (1976).

26. See text at chap. 6, nn. 21–26, 84–89.

27. See text at chap. 2, nn. 3–10, 41–44.

28. See generally Gunther, *Constitutional Law*, pp. 503–44.

29. See, e.g., Letter to the Editor of the *New York Times*, July 14, 1981, Richard L. Lesher, president, Chamber of Commerce of the United States.

30. See New Orleans v. Dukes, 427 U.S. 297, 303–4 (1976).

31. See Thomas S. Shrock, "The Liberal Court, the Conservative Court, and Constitutional Jurisprudence," in *Left, Right and Center*, ed. Robert A. Goldwin (Chicago: Rand McNally, 1965), pp. 87–120.

32. Williamson v. Lee Optical Co., 348 U.S. 483 (1955).

33. Consider Leo Strauss, *Natural Right and History* (Chicago: University of Chicago Press, 1953), pp. 86–89, 123–26.

34. C. Herman Pritchett, *The American Constitution*, 2d ed. (New York: McGraw-Hill, 1968), p. 681.

35. Williamson v. Lee Optical Co., 348 U.S. 483, 487–88 (1955).

36. Justice Douglas said the legislature "might have concluded," among other things, that eyeglass wearers need to see medical experts frequently. He conceded that some provisions of the law were inconsistent with this putative aim. But the inconsistency did not move him to drop his imputation of purpose. Instead, he said that laws do not have to be fully consistent with their aims to be constitutional. He added that the people should use the polls, not the courts, to correct legislative abuses. Ibid., at 478–88.

37. See Board of Regents v. Roth, 408 U.S. 564, 579–87 (1972) (Douglas, J., dissenting); Arnett v. Kennedy, 416 U.S. 134, 210–11 (1973) (Marshall, J., dissenting); Bishop v. Wood, 426 U.S. 341, 353–54 (1976) (Brennan, J., dissenting); Pruneyard Shopping Center v. Robins, 447 U.S. 74, 93–94 (1980) (Marshall, J., concurring). See also, Ronald A. Dworkin, "Dissent on Douglas," *New York Review of Books*, February 19, 1981, pp. 3–6.

38. Roe v. Wade, 410 U.S. 113 (1973).

39. Ibid., at 159–62.

40. Ibid., at 162–63.

41. Ibid., at 163–64.

42. For a typically disingenuous denial of the religious intent see Harris v. McRae, 448 U.S. 297, 319–20 (1980).

43. See text following chap. 4, n. 73.

44. Jefferson to Roger C. Whiteman, June 24, 1826, in Paul L. Ford, ed., *The Works of Thomas Jefferson*, 12 vols. (New York: G. P. Putnam's Sons, 1904–5), 12:477. Jefferson died on the day of the celebration, July 4, 1826.

45. See Plato *The Republic* 382a-c, 413c-414e, 415a-d, 459c-d, 484a-486e, 490a-495b, 500b-c, 502d-503b, 537c-539e.

46. Some treat repressive morality as a means to the nation's security and good order, and on this basis they call for a relaxation of the Supreme Court's policy of separating church and state. I see two problems with this view. First, those who take religion and religious morality seriously do not consider them mere means to secular ends, and those who consider them mere means cannot really support them in a manner acceptable to true believers without misrepresenting the nature of their support. Second, as I have argued, true believers cannot really be good citizens of *this* regime because they cannot really reaffirm the Constitution's supremacy. I will not deny that misrepresentations of all sorts are a practical necessity of political life, for I have not forgotten Madison's statement that even the most enlightened government needs the prejudices of the community on its side. I am saying only that fully conscious subjects of the Constitution cannot truthfully defend repressive moralism and that, therefore, the latter has no place in an explication of constitutional ideals or aspirations. Cf.

Walter Berns, *The First Amendment and the Future of American Democracy* (New York: Basic Books, 1976), chap. 1.

47. See Plato *The Republic* 519c-e, 592a-b.

48. See ibid., 596a-e, 557b-558a.

49. See David Hume, *A Treatise of Human Nature*, bk. II, sec. III.

50. This does not mean that religious groups should remain silent on public issues. It means only that they should accept what are understood to be secular criteria for judging their proposals for governmental action. Consider the following by Archbishop John Roach of Minneapolis to the National Conference of Catholic Bishops, as reported in the *New York Times*, November 18, 1981:

> A focal point in the debate about religion and politics has been the role played by Moral Majority. Some have argued that Moral Majority's role is an example of why religion and politics should be kept absolutely separate, and religious organizations should be silent on political questions. I reject this contention while defending the right of Moral Majority or any religious organization to address the public issues of the day.
>
> The right of religious organizations, of varying views, to speak must be defended by all who understand the meaning of religious liberty and the social role of religion. But religious organizations should be subjected to the same standards of rational, rigorous presentation of their views as any other participant in the public debate.
>
> These same standards of discourse are the ones by which our position should be judged.

51. This formulation is taken from Laurent B. Frantz, "Is the First Amendment Law? A Reply to Professor Mendelson," *California Law Review* 51 (1963):750–53.

52. Compare Marsh v. Alabama, 326 U.S. 501, 506–09 (1946). The Court's recent refusal to extend the public-function argument of *Marsh* has not eliminated the general idea from the Court's thinking. See Hudgens v. National Labor Relations Board, 424 U.S. 507, 513, 520 (1976).

53. See Lemon v. Kurtzman, 403 U.S. 602, 619–22 (1971). See also Committee for Public Education and Religious Liberty v. Regan, 100 S. Ct. 840, 846 (1980).

54. Ely, "Constitutional Interpretivism," pp. 424–28.

55. Dworkin, *Taking Rights Seriously*, pp. 132–37.

56. See text at chap. 2, nn. 53–55.

57. Flathman, *Political Obligation*, pp. 36–40.

58. John Hart Ely, "Constitutional Interpretivisim: Its Allure and Impossibility," *Indiana Law Journal* 53 (1978): 418.

59. See Harris v. McRae, 448 U.S. 297, 334–37 (Brennan, J., dissenting).

60. See generally Leonard W. Levy, *Legacy of Suppression* (Cambridge, Mass.: Harvard University Press, Belknap Press, 1960).

61. We cannot assume that every provision of the Bill of Rights deserves to be there. As we have seen, the Constitution itself assumes that some of its provisions can be mistakes. Thus, it is difficult for us to imagine ourselves aspiring to be a nation armed with "Saturday-night specials" and other paraphernalia of fear, depravation, and aggression. This may account for the desuetude of the Second Amendment as a source of personal rights. On the other hand, even supporters of gun control can appreciate the connection between the Second Amendment and the First Amendment. As Justice Story said, "The right of the citizens to keep and bear arms, has justly been considered as the palladium of the liberties of a republic; since it offers a strong moral check against the usurpation and arbitrary power of rulers; and will generally, even if these are successful in the first instance, enable the people to resist and triumph

over them." Joseph Story, *Commentaries on the Constitution of the United States*, 2d ed. (Boston: Little, Brown, 1851), chap. 44, sec. 1897. My thinking inclines toward Justice Story's position at present, though I am not unmindful about what I have said about the doubtful status of such inclinations.

62. See A Book Named John Cleland's Memoirs of a Woman of Pleasure v. Attorney General, 383 U.S. 413, 419 (1966).

63. See Curtis Publishing Co. v. Butts, 388 U.S. 130, 155 (1967).

64. See Cohen v. California, 403 U.S. 15, 20 (1971); National Socialist Party v. Skokie, 432 U.S. 43 (1977).

65. See Tinker v. Des Moines School District, 393 U.S. 503, 508–9 (1969); Brown v. Glines 444 U.S. 348, 361 (1980) (Brennan, J., dissenting).

66. See United States v. Nixon, 418 U.S. 683, 706–7 (1974); Freedman v. Maryland, 380 U.S. 51, 58–59 (1965).

67. Joseph Tussman, *Government and the Mind* (New York: Oxford University Press, 1977), p. 171.

68. Ely, "Constitutional Interpretivism," pp. 445–56.

69. Laurent B. Frantz, "The First Amendment in the Balance," *Yale Law Journal* 71 (1962):1434–35.

70. Wallace Mendelson, "On the Meaning of the First Amendment: Absolutes in the Balance," *California Law Review* 50 (1962):824–25.

71. See generally Gunther, *Constitutional Law*, chap. 8.

72. Barron v. Baltimore, 7 Pet. 243 (1833).

73. Jefferson to James Madison, December 20, 1787, *Works*, pp. 371–72.

74. See Schneider v. Irvington, 308 U.S. 147, 162 (1939).

75. See text at chap. 4, n. 60.

76. Walter Berns, "The Meaning of the Tenth Amendment," in *A Nation of States*, ed. Robert A. Goldwin (Chicago: Rand McNally, 1963), pp. 141–43.

77. Ibid., pp. 130–32, 145–48.

78. James Madison, *Letters and Other Writings of James Madison*, 4 vols. (New York: R. Worthington, 1884), 4:145–48.

79. For discussions of pluralist approaches to constitutional review, see George Anastaplo, *The Constitutionalist: Notes on the First Amendment* (Dallas: Southern Methodist University Press, 1971), p. 431 n. 9; Sanford Levinson, " 'The Constitution' in American Civil Religion," in *1979 Supreme Court Review*, ed. Philip B. Kurland (Chicago: University of Chicago Press, 1979), pp. 123–51.

80. However, the Court did not evince what I have described as a constitutional attitude when it watered down the Sixth Amendment right to trial by jury in Williams v. Florida, 329 U.S. 78 (1970), and Apodaca v. Oregon, 406 U.S. 404 (1972). Since that time, the Burger Court has effectively weakened constitutional guarantees to defendants in state criminal proceedings under the Fourth and Fifth Amendments, as well as the constitutional rights of state prisoners under the Eighth Amendment. See also chap. 5, n. 26.

81. See Frantz, "The First Amendment in the Balance," p. 1446 n. 91; see also Ely, *Democracy and Distrust*, pp. 14–30.

82. Cooke, *The Federalist*, p. 580.

83. It is not an easy assumption to disclaim, as one can see from contradictions in Neil MacCormick's criticism of what he sees as Ronald Dworkin's theory of judicial decision. Upon charging Dworkin with "ultra-rationalism," or the belief that reason can "wholly determine what we ought to do," MacCormick expresses his admiration for Hume and says that whether we "pursue rationality" or "strive for consistency and coherence . . . are open questions for us in matters both of practice and of speculation." But MacCormick also feels that we could press a thoroughgoing emotivist

or irrationalist to admit that he does have "some kind of irresistible propensity to set his thoughts in order and try to make sense of the world." And he says that "human beings act *for reasons* [his emphasis] when they act at all, and no 'explanation' of human behavior which omits reference to the subjective reasons for which it is performed can be a full or adequate one." Neil MacCormick, *Legal Reasoning and Legal Theory* (Oxford: Clarendon Press, 1978), pp. 6, 265, 268–69. See also chap. 2, n. 43.

84. As I have suggested, regimes that elevate race, religion, the status quo, or any other consideration above truth are merely pretending to a genuine submission of claims. These regimes do not try to live up to what they themselves implicitly acknowledge they ought to be.

85. Ely, *Democracy and Distrust*, pp. 101–4.

86. See Sotirios A. Barber, "*National League of Cities* v. *Usery*: New Meaning for the Tenth Amendment?," in *1976 Supreme Court Review*, ed. Philip B. Kurland (Chicago: University of Chicago Press, 1977), p. 168 n. 36.

87. The principal obstacle to this conclusion would be the states' right argument I rejected in chap. 4. See also text at chap. 6, nn. 83–88.

CHAPTER 6

1. Jacob E. Cooke, ed., *The Federalist* (Middletown, Conn.: Wesleyan University Press, 1961), pp. 580–81. In the asterisked note Hamilton responds more bluntly to the concern that the taxing power could be used to abridge freedom of the press. At one point he states, "We know that newspapers are taxed in Great-Britain, and yet it is notorious that the press no-where enjoys greater liberty than in that country. And if duties of any kind may be laid without a violation of that liberty, it is evident that the extent must depend on legislative discretion, regulated by public opinion; so that after all, general declarations respecting the liberty of the press will give it no greater security than it will have without them."

2. Ibid., pp. 532–33.

3. Ibid., pp. 538–45.

4. Ibid., p. 349.

5. Ibid., p. 353.

6. Ibid., p. 352.

7. Consider Madison's view that "the most common and durable source of factions has been the various and unequal distribution of property," not "[a] zeal for different opinions concerning religion, concerning government, and many other points, as well of speculation as of practice." Ibid., pp. 58–59.

8. See Sotirios A. Barber, "The Supreme Court and Congress's Responsibility in Foreign Affairs," in *Taking the Constitution Seriously: Essays on the Constitution and Constitutional Law*, ed. Gary L. McDowell (Dubuque, Iowa: Kendall/Hunt, 1981), pp. 231–44.

9. Bivens v. Six Unknown Named Agents, 403 U.S. 388, 413–16 (1971) (Burger, C. J., dissenting).

10. United States v. Calandra, 414 U.S. 388 (1974).

11. Sotirios A. Barber, *The Constitution and the Delegation of Congressional Power* (Chicago: University of Chicago Press, 1975), chap. 3; Theodore J. Lowi, *The End of Liberalism*, 2d ed. (New York: W. W. Norton, 1979), chap. 5.

12. Cooke, *The Federalist*, pp. 341–43.

13. Ibid., p. 3.

14. See M.J.C. Vile, *Constitutionalism and the Separation of Powers* (Oxford: Clarendon Press, 1967), pp. 153–54, 157–58.

15. Cooke, *The Federalist*, pp. 348–50.

16. See, e.g., ibid., pp. 422–25, 481–84.

17. Ibid., pp. 422–23.

18. Ibid., p. 425.

19. Ibid., pp. 340–41.

20. Ibid., p. 349.

21. Ibid., p. 340.

22. Ibid., p. 141.

23. Ibid., pp. 471–72.

24. S. Barber, *Delegation of Congressional Power*, chap. 2.

25. Ibid., pp. 38–41.

26. See Cohens v. Virginia, 6 Wheat. 264, 404 (1821). A different and, in terms of this analysis, unconstitutional attitude toward judicial duty is manifest in several recent Supreme Court decisions that force many would-be federal plaintiffs to submit to state courts their charges that state officials have violated their federal constitutional rights. Although this series of decisions was initiated under the leadership of Justice Black, who sought to prevent federal intervention in pending state criminal proceedings, Younger v. Harris, 401 U.S. 37 (1971), the doctrine of "*Younger* abstention" is now being extended to a growing variety of civil proceedings as a niggardly view of constitutional rights fuels an expanding notion of what constitutes respect for state courts. This effort is being led by Justice Rehnquist, and it is accompanied with overtones of the pre–Civil War theme that the primary responsibility for protecting civil rights belongs to the state courts. For an overview and an apt criticism of this development, see Juidice v. Vail, 430 U.S. 327, 341–47 (1977) (Brennan, J., dissenting); see also Moore v. Sims, 442 U.S. 415 (1979) (Stevens, J., dissenting).

27. See Cooke, *The Federalist*, pp. 424, 482–83.

28. This indifference is the basis of the "liberalism" that Ronald Dworkin has described; see his "Liberalism," in *Public and Private Morality*, ed. Stuart Hampshire (Cambridge: Cambridge University Press, 1978), pp. 113–43. See especially pp. 142–43, where Dworkin asserts that "liberals, as such, are indifferent as to whether people choose . . . to behave as liberals are supposed to prefer." Dworkin argues that if it were not for this indifference, liberalism would be self-contradictory. But I am arguing that liberals can, indeed must, favor liberalism as a way of life while tolerating some measure of illiberalism, at least insofar as one can find a form of liberalism that is consistent with constitutional supremacy.

29. Robert K. Faulkner, *The Jurisprudence of John Marshall* (Princeton: Princeton University Press, 1968), pp. 22, 33–38.

30. See Martin Diamond, "Ethics and Politics: The American Way," in *The Moral Foundations of the American Republic*, ed. Robert H. Horwitz, 2d ed. (Charlottesville: University Press of Virginia, 1979), pp. 39–74.

31. Benjamin Barber, "The Compromised Republic: Public Purposelessness in America," in Horwitz, *Moral Foundations*, pp. 19–38.

32. C. Herman Pritchett, *The American Constitution*, 2d ed. (New York: McGraw-Hill, 1968), p. 235.

33. See text at chap. 4, nn. 30–34, 52–56.

34. See Galvan v. Press, 347 U.S. 522 (1954); Minersville School Dist. v. Gobitis, 310 U.S. 586 (1940); Korematsu v. United States, 323 U.S. 214 (1944); Dennis v. United States, 341 U.S. 494 (1951); U.S. Congress, Senate, Committee on Foreign Relations, Testimony by William H. Rehnquist, 91st Cong., 2nd sess., *Documents Relating to the War Powers of Congress, the President's Authority as Commander in*

Chief, and the War in Indochina, p. 181 (1970); David Frost interview with Richard M. Nixon, *New York Times*, May 21, 1977.

35. See generally Arthur E. Sutherland, *Constitutionalism in America* (New York: Blaisdell, 1965), pp. 400–422.

36. *Ex parte* Merryman, 17 Fed. Cases 144, 152–53 (1861). Quoted in ibid., pp. 406–8.

37. Of his actions Lincoln said:

These measures, whether strictly legal or not, were ventured upon, under what appeared to be a popular demand, and a public necessity; trusting, then as now, that Congress would readily ratify them. It is believed that nothing has been done beyond the constitutional competency of Congress.

Soon after the first call for militia, it was considered a duty to authorize the Commanding General, in proper cases, according to his discretion, to suspend the privilege of the writ of habeas corpus; or, in other words, to arrest, and detain, without resort to the ordinary processes and forms of law, such individuals as he might deem dangerous to the public safety. This authority has purposely been exercised but very sparingly. Nevertheless, the legality and propriety of what has been done under it, are questioned; and the attention of the country has been called to the proposition that one who is sworn to "take care that the laws be faithfully executed," should not himself violate them. Of course some consideration was given to the questions of power, and propriety, before this matter was acted upon. The whole of the laws which were required to be faithfully executed, were being resisted, and failing of execution, in nearly one-third of the States. Must they be allowed to finally fail of execution, even had it been perfectly clear, that by the use of the means necessary to their execution, some single law, made in such extreme tenderness of the citizen's liberty, that practically, it relieves more of the guilty, than of the innocent, should, to a very limited extent, be violated? To state the question more directly, are all the laws, *but one*, to go unexecuted, and the government itself go to pieces, lest that one be violated? Even in such a case, would not the official oath be broken, if the government should be overthrown, when it was believed that disregarding the single law, would tend to preserve it? But it was not believed that this question was presented. It was not believed that any law was violated. The provision of the Constitution that "The privilege of the writ of habeas corpus, shall not be suspended unless when, in cases of rebellion or invasion, the public safety may require it," is equivalent to a provision—is a provision—that such privilege may be suspended when, in cases of rebellion, or invasion, the public safety *does* require it. It was decided that we have a case of rebellion, and that the public safety does require the qualified suspension of the privilege of the writ which was authorized to be made. Now it is insisted that Congress, and not the Executive, is vested with this power. But the Constitution itself, is silent as to which, or who, is to exercise the power; and as the provision was plainly made for a dangerous emergency, it cannot be believed the framers of the instrument intended, that in every case, the danger should run its course, until Congress could be called together; the very assembling of which might be prevented, as was intended in this case, by the rebellion.

No more extended argument is now offered; as an opinion, at some length, will probably be presented by the Attorney General. Whether there shall be any legislation upon the subject, and if any, what, is submitted entirely to the better judgment of Congress.

James D. Richardson, ed., *Messages and Papers of the Presidents*, 10 vols. (Washington, D.C.: Government Printing Office, 1896–), 6:24–25.

38. 12 Stat. at Large 755. A section of this act placed substantial qualifications upon the president's power to suspend the writ. It required military authorities to submit lists of persons held as prisoners to the circuit and district courts that remained open. Persons not subsequently indicted were to be discharged from military custody. In *Ex parte* Milligan, 4 Wall. 2 (1866), the Supreme Court relied upon this provision to discharge Lambdin Milligan from custody after he had been sentenced to be hanged by a military commission acting under the presidential proclamation of September 24, 1862. The effect of this decision was to declare that proclamation unconstitutional insofar as it applied to areas where the civil authorities had not been closed down by the war. This decision implicitly recognized the power of Congress to modify executive suspensions of the writ.

39. Cf. George Winterton, "The Concept of Extraconstitutional Executive Power in Domestic Affairs," *Hastings Constitutional Law Quarterly* 7 (1979): 7 n. 42.

40. Cf. Lon L. Fuller, *The Morality of Law*, 2d ed. (New Haven: Yale University Press, 1969), pp. 137–41; Neil MacCormick, *Legal Reasoning and Legal Theory* (Oxford: Clarendon Press, 1978), pp. 139–41.

41. See Winterton, "Extraconstitutional Executive Power," pp. 11–12, 42–46.

42. John G. Nicolay and John Hay, eds., *The Complete Works of Abraham Lincoln*, 12 vols. (New York: Century, 1894), 10:66. To be contrasted with this statement is the remark that Corwin attributed to Lincoln in the following passage:

> The true nature of the presidential prerogative in war time was comprehended by Lincoln perfectly, who, when he was confronted with the argument that some of his measures were likely to constitute precedents injurious to liberty, answered the objection in his characteristic strain: "Nor," said he, "am I able to appreciate the danger apprehended that the American people will, by means of military arrests during the rebellion lose the right of public discussion, the liberty of speech and the press, the laws of evidence, trial by jury, and habeas corpus, throughout the indefinite peaceful future which I trust lies before them, any more than I am able to believe that a man could contract so strong an appetite for emetics during a temporary illness as to persist in feeding upon them during the remainder of his healthful life."

Edward S. Corwin, *Presidential Power and the Constitution*, ed. Richard Loss (Ithaca, N.Y.: Cornell University Press, 1976), pp. 23–24.

43. Cf. H.L.A. Hart, *The Concept of Law* (Oxford: Clarendon Press, 1961), p. 149.

44. Joseph M. Bessette and Jeffrey Tulis, "The Constitution, Politics, and the Presidency," in *The Presidency and the Constitution*, Joseph M. Bessette and Jeffrey Tulis, eds. (Baton Rouge: Louisiana State University Press, 1980), pp. 16–26; Cooke, *The Federalist*, p. 160.

45. Arthur M. Schlesinger, Jr., *The Imperial Presidency* (Boston: Houghton Mifflin, 1973), pp. 321–24.

46. See David Frost interview with Richard M. Nixon, *New York Times*, May 21, 1977.

47. See n. 37.

48. This was Lincoln's position. See n. 37.

49. *Ex parte* Milligan, 4 Wall. 2, 126 (1866).

50. Ibid., at 127.

51. 1 Cranch 137, 176–180 (1803).

52. For an overview of the broad and narrow interpretations of *Marbury*, see Gerald Gunther, *Cases and Materials on Constitutional Law*, 10th ed. (Mineola, N.Y.: Foundation Press, 1980), pp. 30–35.

53. The positions of several presidents on the exclusiveness of judicial review are reproduced in ibid., pp. 26–30.

54. Hart, *The Concept of Law*, p. 138. See also Ronald A. Dworkin, *Taking Rights Seriously* (Cambridge, Mass.: Harvard University Press, 1977), p. 186.

55. Hart, *The Concept of Law*, p. 138.

56. New York Times Co. v. Sullivan, 376 U.S. 254, 273–76 (1963).

57. Fuller, *Morality of Law*, pp. 63–70; Francis Leiber, *Legal and Political Hermeneutics* (St. Louis: F. H. Thomas, 1880), pp. 74–76; Cooke, *The Federalist*, pp. 259–60.

58. Cf. Dworkin, *Taking Rights Seriously*, pp. 106–7, 132–37, 289–90.

59. See text at chap. 3, nn. 32–36.

60. Robert M. Cover, *Justice Accused* (New Haven: Yale University Press, 1975), pp. 162–75.

61. Ibid., chaps. 10, 11.

62. Dworkin, "The Law of the Slave-Catchers," *Times Literary Supplement*, December 5, 1975, p. 1437.

63. See text at chap. 4, nn. 72–73.

64. Cf. Herbert J. Storing, "Slavery and the Moral Foundations of the American Republic," in Horwitz, *Moral Foundations*, pp. 225–27.

65. See Gary L. McDowell, *Equity and the Constitution: The Supreme Court, Equitable Relief, and Public Policy* (Chicago: University of Chicago Press, 1982), pp. 8–11, 43–44, 102–04, 129–35.

66. James Madison, *Letters and Other Writings of James Madison*, 4 vols. (New York: R. Worthington, 1884), 4:409–15.

67. Massachusetts v. Laird, 400 U.S. 886 (1970).

68. Cooke, *The Federalist*, p. 51.

69. Ibid., pp. 524–28.

70. Pritchett, *The American Constitution*, p. 96. See also Raoul Berger, *Congress v. the Supreme Court* (Cambridge, Mass.: Harvard University Press, 1969).

71. 6 Cranch 307 (1810).

72. 1 Wheat. 304 (1816).

73. 7 Wall. 506 (1869).

74. 13 Wall. 128, 147–48 (1872).

75. 7 Wall. 506, 514 (1869).

76. See text at chap. 4, nn. 84–89.

77. See S. Barber, *Delegation of Congressional Power*, pp. 15–16.

78. Cf. the 1953 proposal for a constitutional amendment that would assure the Supreme Court's appellate jurisdiction in all constitutional cases. Gunther, *Constitutional Law*, p. 55.

79. Cooke, *The Federalist*, p. 204.

80. Quoted in Gunther, *Constitutional Law*, p. 57.

81. Cooke, *The Federalist*, p. 61.

82. John G. Nicolay and John Hay, eds. *Complete Works of Abraham Lincoln*, 12 vols. (New York: Francis D. Tandy, 1905), 4:329–30.

83. Cf. text at chap. 5, nn. 4–5.

84. See text at chap. 3, nn. 35–38; text at chap. 4, nn. 25–43; text at chap. 5, nn. 25–29, 83–85; text at chap. 6, nn. 22–26.

85. See S. Barber, *Delegation of Congressional Power*, pp. 38–41. See also John Hart Ely, *Democracy and Distrust* (Cambridge, Mass.: Harvard University Press, 1980), pp. 131–34.

86. See text at chap. 5, nn. 1–5.

87. Problems of the judiciary's role aside, this kind of thinking is not alien to the Supreme Court's understanding of legislative duty. Although it treats welfare benefits as statutory entitlements, the Court has suggested that legislatures have a duty to provide such benefits. With only one of the Justices suggesting disagreement with the leading points therein, a passage from a 1969 decision reads:

> From its founding the Nation's basic commitment has been to foster the dignity and well-being of all persons within its borders. We have come to recognize that forces not within the control of the poor contribute to their poverty. This perception, against the background of our traditions, has significantly influenced the development of the contemporary public assistance system. Welfare, by meeting the basic demands of subsistence, can help bring within the reach of the poor the same opportunities that are available to others to participate meaningfully in the life of the community. At the same time, welfare guards against the societal malaise that may flow from a widespread sense of unjustified frustration and insecurity. *Public assistance, then, is not mere charity, but a means to "promote the general Welfare, and secure the Blessings of Liberty to ourselves and our Posterity."*

Goldberg v. Kelley, 397 U.S. 254, 264 (emphasis supplied). See also Walter F. Murphy, "An Ordering of Constitutional Values," *Southern California Law Review* 53 (1980): 724, 731–34, 740–46.

88. Roy P. Basler, ed., *Abraham Lincoln: Speeches and Writings* (New York: Grosset & Dunlap, 1962), p. 607.

89. Cooke, *The Federalist*, p. 523.

90. Cf. Ely, *Democracy and Distrust,* pp. 73–88.

91. State and federal refusal to fund abortions makes sense only from the perspective of those who deny a constitutional right to have an abortion. In upholding such refusals, the Court has permitted the legislatures to single out for a denial of public services a class of persons identified solely by their decision to exercise a constitutional right. From the perspective of those who maintain that the judiciary has a monopoly of constitutional interpretation it was irrational for the Court to permit such discriminatory funding. See Harris v. McCrae, 448 U.S. 297, 334 (1980) (Brennan, J., dissenting).

92. A recent Senate subcommittee "inquiry" into the question of when life begins is a rather patently bad-faith instance of what I have in mind. The subcommittee would have improved its constitutional position had it envisioned remonstrance instead of legislation aimed at substituting legislative judgment for judicial judgment in the performance of judicial duty.

93. 384 U.S. 641 (1966).

94. Ibid., at 651.

95. Ibid., at 652.

96. Ibid., at 653.

97. Ibid., at 657–58.

98. Ibid., at 667–68.

99. 347 U.S. 483 (1954).

100. S. 1378 in U.S. Congress, Senate, *Congressional Record*, 97th Cong., 1st sess., 1981, pp. 6335–36. The fate of this provision may be contained in the Court's subsequent refusal to review a lower court's denial that the First Amendment protects

high school students from conducting voluntary communal prayer meetings on school premises before classes. Brandon v. Board of Education of Guilderland, 102 S. Ct. 970 (1981).

101. See generally Gunther, *Constitutional Law*, pp. 1607-14.

102. 384 U.S. 641, 653-58 (1966).

103. Pritchett, *The American Constitution*, p. 52.

104. One can easily challenge the common assumption that judges do not speak for the majority. Surely, this would depend in part on what the majority wants to express—in particular, whether it is expressing its raw demands for prosperity and the like or its best conception of constitutional aspirations. There is every reason to believe that the majority itself accepts a distinction between raw demands and constitutional norms and that it supports the abstract proposition that the former should give way to the latter in cases of conflict. Granted, arguendo, that legislatures register popular demands, there is no reason to believe either that those demands always constitute the majority's best conception of constitutional norms or that judicial opinions contrary to popular demands are equally contrary to the majority's best conception of constitutional norms. One can consider in this connection the fate of this century's court-packing and court-stripping proposals. The view that judicial review is an antimajoritarian institution thus begs important questions. Cf. text at chap. 3, nn. 22–23.

105. See, e.g., MacCormick, *Legal Reasoning*, pp. 253–55, 267–72.

106. Dworkin, *Taking Rights Seriously*, pp. 137–49.

107. See Alexander M. Bickel, *The Least Dangerous Branch* (Indianapolis: Bobbs-Merrill, 1962), pp. 81–84; John P. Roche, "Judicial Self-Restraint," *American Political Science Review* 49 (1955) 762–72.

Index

Abortion, right to, 133–40, 144–47
Amending power, 43, 49
Arms, right to bear, 148, 165, 232 n.61
Aspirations, constitutional: and constitutional rights, 107–9, 115, 141, 156–57, 159, 167–68, 182; derivation of, 54–55; historical facts as inadequate evidence of, 33–34, 146; and interpretation of the Constitution, 34–37; and reaffirmation of the Constitution, 60–62, 114; and separation of powers, 178–81, 210; and states' rights, 155–59, 169–70
Attitude, constitutional: and constitutional duties, feasibility of, 164–68; and constitutional rights, 113, 141–42, 147, 213; and constitutional supremacy, 59–61, 198, 214; as contrasted with willfulness, 174–77, 205–6; inculcation of, 159–65; inculcation of, and maintenance of constitutional government, 172; and judicial review, 197–98; and judicial self-restraint, 219–20; and welfare rights, 213

Balancing, of constitutional rights, 108, 141, 176
Barron v. *Baltimore*, 154
Bell v. *Wolfish*, 2–4, 6

Berger, Raoul, 20, 32–33, 39–40, 146, 222 n.12
Berns, Walter, 157–58
Bickel, Alexander M., 23
Bill of Rights: argument against adoption of, 106, 159, 171–72; nationalization of, 124, 154–59
Black, Hugo L., 21
Board of Regents v. *Roth*, 27, 29
Brennan, William J., Jr., 215–16
Burger, Warren E., 176–77
Burger Court, 133, 233 n.80

Censorship, 150–54
Checks and balances, 172–74, 182, 184–85
Civil Rights Act of 1883, 91–92, 94
Civil Rights Act of 1964, 91, 93–95, 100–101
Commerce clause, scope of, 95–99
Conflicts, between constitutional rights, 164–68
Constitution: instrumental aspect of, 40–42, 45, 59–61, 61–62; obligational aspect of, 40, 42–45
Constitutionalism, willfulness in present-day understanding of, 175–76. *See also* Attitude, constitutional; Self-restraint

241

The Johns Hopkins University Press
ON WHAT THE CONSTITUTION MEANS

This book was composed in Times Roman text and Palatino display type by EPS Group, Inc., from a design by Susan P. Fillion. It was printed on S. D. Warren's 50-lb. Sebago Eggshell Cream paper and bound in Kivar 5 by the Maple Press Company.

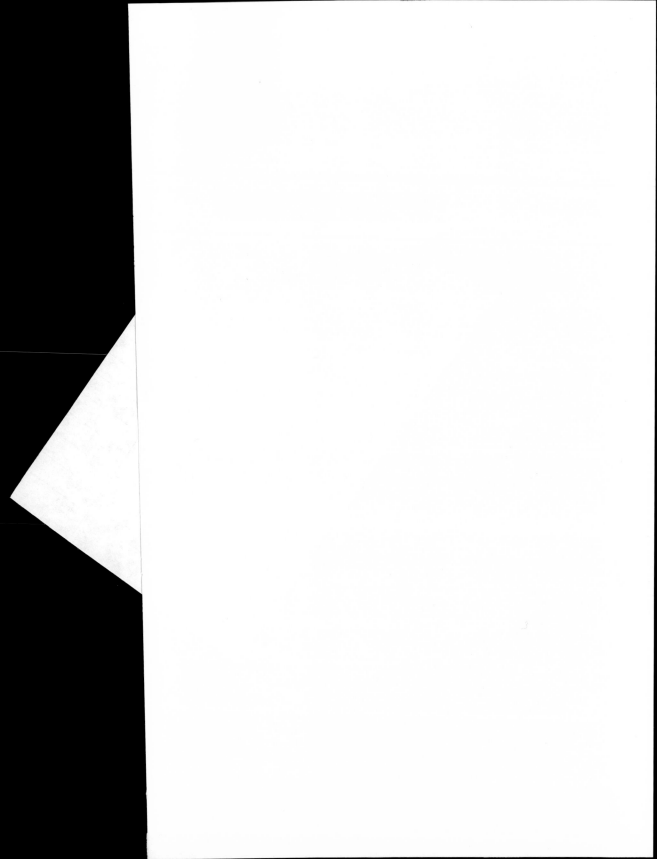

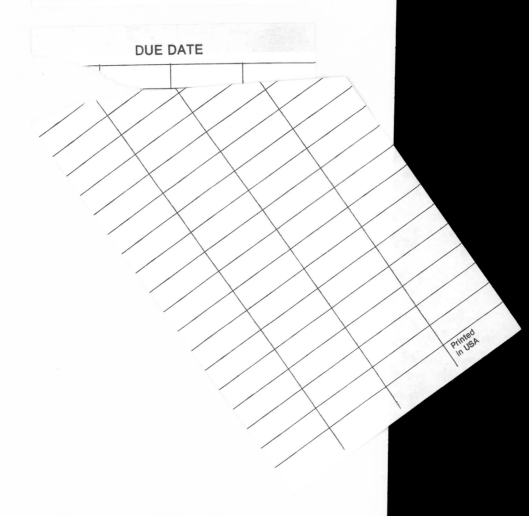

DUE DATE

Printed
In USA